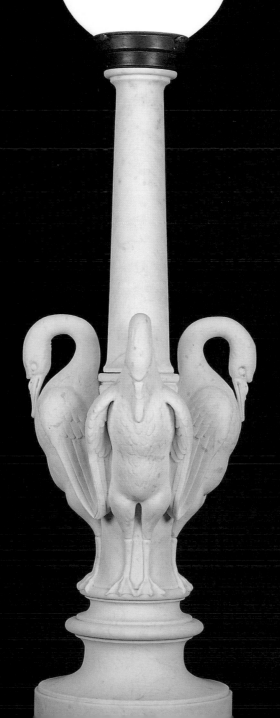

HEARST CASTLE

HEARST

CASTLE

The Biography of a Country House

Victoria Kastner

Principal photography by

Victoria Garagliano

Foreword by

George Plimpton

Harry N. Abrams, Inc.,

Publishers

DEDICATED TO
THE CREATIVE SPIRIT OF
WILLIAM RANDOLPH HEARST
AND JULIA MORGAN

Editor: Elisa Urbanelli
Designer: Robert McKee

Library of Congress Cataloging-in-Publication Data
Kastner, Victoria.
Hearst Castle : biography of a country house /
Victoria Kastner ; principal
photography by Victoria Garagliano ;
foreword by George Plimpton.
p. cm.
Includes bibliographical references and index.
ISBN 0–8109–3415–9 (hardcover)
1. Hearst Castle (Calif.) 2. Castles—
California—San Simeon. 3. Hearst, William
Randolph, 1863–1951—Homes and haunts—
California—San Simeon. 4. Morgan, Julia,
1872–1957—Contributions in domestic
architecture. 5. Hearst, William Randolph,
1863–1951—Art collections—California—San
Simeon. 6. San Simeon (Calif.)—Buildings,
structures, etc. I. Garagliano, Victoria. II. Title.

NA7615.H43 K37 2000
728.8'09794'78—dc21   00–21506

Printed and bound in Japan
10 9 8 7 6 5

Harry N. Abrams, Inc.
100 Fifth Avenue
New York, N.Y. 10011
www.abramsbooks.com

ENDPAPERS: *The Neptune Pool at night glows
with its original lighting, designed in 1934.*

PAGE 1: *This graceful marble swan lamp standard
was designed for the estate by Julia Morgan's
chief architectural draftsman, Thaddeus Joy.*

PAGE 2: *A cast-stone ornamental head on the
south tower of Casa Grande, with the
Pacific Ocean in the background.*

THIS SPREAD: *Light dapples the Neptune
Terrace, shaded by a group of California Bay
trees, native to the hilltop. Beneath the
trees is Ernst Seger's Ganymede.*

PAGE 6: *The Sitting Room of the Doge's
Suite, a guest suite on the mezzanine
level of Casa Grande.*

CONTENTS

PREFACE

I have, just now, returned to my office in the old communications headquarters on the hilltop, after a brief walk through the Castle's grounds, surveying the gardens and sculpture on this gorgeous January morning. For over thirty years, as a member of Hearst Castle's staff, I have had the privilege of enjoying the history and elegance of William Randolph Hearst's San Simeon estate.

How better to showcase this gem of a historic house museum than to share it with others in such a magnificent medium as this book provides? A national treasure, seen by over thirty million people during the last forty-two years, Hearst Castle is one of the very few private country houses left intact, its collections in place, available for the public to experience. This volume presents to us a world-renowned and remarkably diverse art collection and shows us the result of a decades-long creative collaboration between two dynamic individuals, William Randolph Hearst and architect Julia Morgan.

In early 1996, I first met with Hearst Castle staff to explore options for publications about the Castle. Victoria Kastner, long-time Hearst Castle scholar, presented me with a proposal for a book on part of the estate's art collection. But we became convinced that because the collection is so enormous and varied, to select just one aspect of the art would not do justice to all the artifacts, the structures, and the gardens at San Simeon. So, from that eventful day evolved *Hearst Castle: The Biography of a Country House*.

This book has been a long time coming. Since the Castle was donated to the State of California by the Hearst Corporation in 1957, many attempts have been made to describe the character and ambience of La Cuesta Encantada, William Randolph Hearst's Enchanted Hill. But no one, until now, has been able to evoke the subject so successfully. Author Victoria Kastner has captured the essence of Hearst Castle in words, and photographer Victoria Garagliano, in pictures.

Before, we who are the stewards of this hilltop site could only hope to convey the enchantment of the Castle to those who visited San Simeon in person. Now it is possible to savor the true flavor of Hearst Castle through the pages of this book. It makes us all very proud to have had even a small part in this endeavor.

HOYT FIELDS, CHIEF CURATOR
HEARST SAN SIMEON STATE HISTORICAL MONUMENT

WILLIAM RANDOLPH HEARST and his guests dine in the Refectory. This formal setting was the site of informal, western-style hospitality.

FOREWORD

I always had it in my mind in a kind of reverie that in 1943, perhaps in late August when the fogbanks drift in on the Pacific coast, a Japanese submarine surfaced two or three miles out and lobbed a couple of shells toward San Simeon that burst back in the hills and startled the yaks, the gnus, the giraffes, the zebras, and one or two ostriches into temporary flight. I don't know where I came by this. The rationale for bombarding San Simeon rather than a military facility or a township seems odd—perhaps what the Japanese had in mind, I reasoned, was that the desecration of a major symbol of American capitalism, a gesture of contempt, might boost home morale.

I must have been carried away by the mental picture of giraffes stampeding across the California hills. It turns out that no such attack ever occurred. I had it wrong. But then not completely. Hearst himself worried that a Japanese submarine would surface off San Simeon (a tanker had been sunk up the coast) and do just that . . . in retribution for the fifty years he had railed in his publishing empire against the Japanese—the yellow peril. On one occasion, at some dynamite blasting during the landscaping of the grounds, Hearst got it into his head that the Castle was indeed being shelled, and in a panic sent servants down to check what was going on. The possibility of such an attack was actually one of the reasons (the main one was the financial chaos of his holdings) that he closed down the Castle during the war and spent most of his time far inland at Wyntoon, his estate amongst the pines on the swift-moving waters of the McCloud River in northern California.

A lot else other than the apparition of a submarine comes to mind (thank goodness!) when I think about San Simeon. I have been there twice—taken the tours, read the guides, the appropriate books. After both visits, the overall impression I was left with was the looming presence of W. R. Hearst himself. After all, San Simeon is (or was) a private residence—no public rooms as at Versailles or Sans Souci. In the days when Hearst was in residence the only glimpse the public could get of the Castle was through a coin-in-the-slot telescope from the coastside village five miles away.

Of course, the vague wish comes to mind that one had been around in those grand times, a personal friend of "The Chief" as he was known, and thus invited for a weekend to what the family referred to as the "Ranch." What a guest list he invited! And how eagerly the mighty wished to be on it. At night the floodlights were turned on so that arriving guests would see the ghostly spectacle from miles away—a fairytale turreted castle like those that rise out of a blue mist in a Maxfield Parrish illustration.

I would have been shown around San Simeon, what novelist J. P. Marquand in a clever reference spoke of as the home of a man with an "edifice complex." Indeed, consider the excesses—that one year, on Easter Sunday, at least so legend has it, the guests awoke to find the castle surrounded by Easter lilies in bloom . . . planted during the night by a battalion of gardeners working under floodlights.

True, there were house rules that I might have found irksome. Only one cocktail was allowed before dinner; since the cocktail hour started at six and dinner was announced at nine, one can imagine the problems involved in nursing a single drink for three hours. Servants were on occasion fired for smuggling liquor to supply anguished guests. As for the guests themselves, those who strayed too far in matters of decorum would find that their bags had been packed and set out on the front courtyard—stark evidence that their stay at San Simeon was over.

I like to think I would have behaved, at least long enough to sit at dinner with forty other guests at the long table of the Refectory. In its medieval splendor it was a nice touch that down the length of the table the condiments—the Worcestershire sauces, the Heinz ketchup—were still in their original bottles . . . apparently reminding Hearst of the simple pre-castle days when picnics were held on the grounds. But still, how baronial it all must have seemed. Irene Castle wrote that at dinner in the Refectory she felt as if she should be chewing on big legs of mutton and throwing the bones over her shoulder to the dogs.

I would like to have gone on the long rides and hikes. Hearst was a yodeler and practiced it in the gaunt hills behind the castle, turning the heads of the yaks, the ibex, the gazelles. He was a famously generous man, and I suppose if one had a particular yen for an ibex, it would have been provided to take home. He had fifty dachshunds in the dog kennels, and these were the usual gifts if one professed to be a dog-lover. Animals! Mice were everywhere in the castle. Hearst's feelings weren't sympathetic toward rats (they were done away with) but the mice were another matter. They were trapped in nonlethal traps and the next morning the staff's first duty was to let them loose on the grounds. One of the mice, a constant visitor despite nightly incarceration, Hearst recognized and nicknamed Mortimer. He felt so strongly about the mice that when his dachshund Helena went after one and killed it in front of the evening gathering in the Assembly Room, he criticized neither the dog nor the mouse for being in the wrong place at the wrong time but the startled guests for not taking the appropriate action ("How could you stand by and let that happen?").

Hearst's enthusiasm for animals at San Simeon is wonderfully suggested in one of his letters to Julia Morgan, his architect. He asks: "How about a maze in connection with the zoo. I think getting lost in the maze and coming unexpectedly upon lions, tigers, pumas, panthers, wildcats, monkeys, macaws and cockatoos, etc. etc. would be a thrill for even the most blasé." I'll say. One observer, driving at night, said there were so many animals out on the hills that their eyes, lit up by the headlights, made him think of the "lights of a distant city."

It amused me to learn, though, that some of the animals weren't as complacent as Hearst might have wished. He was once sued for $40,000 by an employee at San Simeon working at the back of a truck who had an ostrich come up behind him, knock him down, and trample on him—an indignity during which the employee sustained a hernia, concussion, and shock, and vowed that he had never been the same since.

Victoria Kastner's fascinating and illuminating pages that follow concentrate mostly on the building of San Simeon itself. It would please house-owners who remember the quirky problems involved in building their own homes to know that Hearst suffered the same sort of thing if on a grander scale. Apparently, the enormous fireplaces of San Simeon smoked unbearably. "We have the unsatisfying alternative of freezing to death without a fire or smothering to death from smoke," he wrote Julia Morgan. If it wasn't one problem it was another. After a wicked storm he wrote, "The wind flows in through the cracks and crevices until the rugs flap on the floors . . . let us have COMFORT and HEALTH before so much art. The art won't do us any good if we are all dead of pneumonia."

An odd comment coming from Hearst. Whatever his concern about health matters, the art kept coming. He was once described as a "gigantic and voracious magpie." Imagine Julia Morgan's dismay at this infestation of acquisitions coming into San Simeon by the carload. She wrote, "I don't see myself where we are ever going to use half suitably, but I find that the idea is to try things out and if they are not satisfactory, discard them for the next thing that comes that promises better."

So much space was devoted to art and artifacts that such plebeian requirements as closet space were at a premium. The writer and illustrator Ludwig Bemelmans describes hanging his clothes on wire coat hangers suspended from a chandelier in his bedroom. "And the rest I put on the floor."

But finally it was done, whatever its lack of conveniences—one of the marvels of the American West if not the Western world. "Grand exuberance," Victoria Kastner says of San Simeon—an identification brought wonderfully to life in the pages that follow.

GEORGE PLIMPTON

INTRODUCTION *We know them through fiction not fact:*

William Randolph Hearst and Marion Davies have been fixed in our minds by two scenes

in *Citizen Kane*—Hearst depicted as a dying Charles Foster Kane, gasping the word "Rosebud," Davies as Susan Alexander Kane alone in a dark, cavernous room, jigsaw puzzle pieces scattered around her. Their beloved hilltop home, La Cuesta Encantada ("The Enchanted Hill"), has been cast as Xanadu, a forbidding, deserted pile, filled with meaningless junk. That these scenes were played by actors on a sound stage, that Hearst did not die until 1951 (a decade after the film appeared), that Orson Welles had never been to San Simeon—and had almost certainly not met Hearst or Davies—makes no difference. Welles and Hearst both knew the power of a visual image and thought nothing of bending the facts to get a better story. There could be no greater irony than for a press lord like Hearst to be remembered by a media event that played exactly by his own rules.

These images in *Citizen Kane* are compelling as metaphor but offer little else. They were conjured up by Welles, his collaborator John Houseman, and the screenplay's coauthor Herman Mankiewicz, a writer who had been Hearst's guest at San Simeon but whose excessive drinking had probably prevented him from receiving further invitations. With the simplicity of all metaphor, these scenes give us a pared-down glimpse

that works only because it does not introduce facts or nuances that would weaken the story. Yet historians, critics, and the general public have been largely content to rely on the lore of a two-hour film for their insights into Hearst and San Simeon.

In the scholarly world "Hearst Castle"—the name most commonly used for the estate since the thirties, though Hearst himself is recorded as using it only once, and his architect Julia Morgan and Marion Davies never—has been occasionally scoffed at and most frequently ignored. There are no widely distributed books available on La Cuesta Encantada—generally called "San Simeon" by both Hearst and Morgan, though that is technically the name of the bay and the small coastal hamlet below the estate, rather than the name of the hilltop structures themselves. The sole biography of Marion Davies was written in 1972, and it is only recently that scholars have begun to reevaluate Hearst, fifty years after his death. The shadow of *Citizen Kane* has darkened the Castle, obscuring an exuberant home whose construction engendered one of the longest and most creative dialogues between an architect and a client in the history of American architecture.

Hearst's encompassing tastes have also offended scholars. His mixture of high art and low, decorative arts and fine arts, celebrated objects and minor ones, could have only one interpretation, the critics felt: here was

13

someone who could not tell good art from bad, who occasionally, just from the sheer amount he accumulated, stumbled onto a worthy piece but who generally bought indiscriminately and without knowledge. Little thought has been given to the possibility that Hearst's buying methods were by his choice rather than the side effect of money and ignorance. His *omnium-gatherum* approach to art collecting echoed the methods of many collectors from the Renaissance through the eighteenth century, whose highly personal holdings celebrated a wide range of natural and manmade wonders, rather than the more selective, dealer-influenced range of nineteenth- and twentieth-century American art collectors. Critics have further inaccurately assumed that Hearst's art collection was all purchased abroad in a grand pillage of Europe. After World War I, however, import duties on European art entering America were reduced just at the time when estate taxes abroad rose, an opportune situation for American collectors that was further enhanced by postwar Europe's need for cash to rebuild. Hearst bought the vast majority of his collection at auction sales and art galleries in New York City, acquiring relatively few of San Simeon's pieces on his travels abroad.

Another factor that has encouraged misconceptions about San Simeon and its collections is the great success of the art museum. Actually, the modern American art museum—born not as a palace or a royal collection, as were most of the greatest European examples, but as a public repository for collections of art—is a concept so entrenched in our culture that we may not remember how relatively recent the institution is. The first two

American art museums—the Museum of Fine Arts, Boston, and the Metropolitan Museum of Art in New York—claim birth dates of only 1870, and these dates are generous, since they record the formation of committees to create these museums, not the actual construction of buildings or the purchase and display of collections. Art museums as we know them, with carefully selected objects displayed in neutral surroundings, are the new phenomenon: houses like Hearst's, with a richly layered presentation of objects, are the far older reality. To wonder, "Why not take the good things out of this jumble and put them in a museum?" is to misunder-

The first woman architect of prominence in America, Morgan

stand completely the relationship between the building and its objects.

In the last twenty years Hearst's architect Julia Morgan has risen from obscurity to prominence, thanks largely to the pioneering efforts of the late Sara Holmes Boutelle, who worked for fourteen years researching a biography of her recalcitrant subject. Boutelle gave only one chapter to the complex topic of San Simeon, and while her treatment is very illuminating, it is by nature of its length a cursory examination. Morgan died unheralded, having destroyed many of her papers when she closed her architectural office in the early 1950s. Piecing together records was a challenge. It is significant that the largest group of documents that Morgan saved concerned San Simeon. But the books in Morgan's library—on which she and Hearst relied for inspiration for the motifs that give San Simeon its character and the art collection a proper setting—were sold by her family after her death. Dispersing this architectural library cast to the winds the numerous historical references San Simeon contains, encouraging the idea that the place was a hodgepodge of things put together haphazardly and with little aesthetic conception.

Ironically, the sheer number of specific records that survive concerning San Simeon has probably also discouraged thoughtful examination. There are nearly ten thousand architectural drawings—from tissue-paper

scribbles to structural specifications to watercolor presentation drawings to full-size details of eighteen-foot-high ornaments on the Main Building's facade. Hearst's handwritten notes on many of the drawings attest to his great involvement in every aspect of the design and construction. The trove of documents that exists between William Randolph Hearst and Julia Morgan and their associates numbers over four thousand items. The heart of the material is the nearly one thousand letters and telegrams between Hearst and Morgan themselves, providing a revealing portrait of the authors as well as an incomparable construction record. This vast correspondence—concerning matters both mundane and high-flown—has never before been extensively quoted in print. There are also hundreds of oral-history interviews, conducted by farsighted researchers at the Castle and elsewhere, which captured the social history of the place before the loss of the participants.

Examining all this material and weaving a story from the wealth of specific detail has been challenging, partly because of the length of the building process: from 1919 through 1947. It is remarkable for a construction project to last twenty-eight years. In this, San Simeon is very different from other American country houses, almost all of which were built in the usual fashion: a brief period of building, in which the architect was involved, followed by a long period of use, in which the architect played no part. At La Cuesta Encantada the profile is closer to that of Thomas Jefferson's Monticello, where the owner built his country estate for four decades, creating it as he was using it, further refining it and adding onto it, to the bewilderment of those around him. Though Hearst was not Jefferson, he had some of the same passions. The Castle was his primary creative expression and he could not stop adding to it, not only because completing it would mean that his beloved building process would cease, but because his relationship to the site and his role as creator would cease as well. The myth that Hearst could not stand to hear the word *death* spoken has no basis; what he did have was a fear of stopping and of the stagnation it would bring. Life for Hearst was action, and nothing seems to have given him a greater sense of vitality than the act of building.

The current interest in Morgan has been in part influenced by feminism, and it is indeed her remarkable achievement to be the first woman architect of prominence in America, and the very first woman to study at the premier Paris school, the Ecole des Beaux-Arts, which trained nearly all of America's influential architects from 1875 through 1910. Seeing Morgan chiefly as

died unheralded, having destroyed many of her papers.

JULIA MORGAN
ARCHITECT
MERCHANTS EXCHANGE
SAN FRANCISCO

113

March 10, 1926.

Mr. William Randolph Hearst,
New York American,
New York, N.Y.

Dear Mr. Hearst:

The antique bookcase has very crude working doors, drawers, shelving, etc., which give it a certain "ensemble" character. We can, as telegraphed, either make the new work in all respects a copy, or can merely copy the design, reasonably "antiqued" on the exterior, and make modern drawers on guides, tight fitting doors, true shelving, etc. The reason I telegraphed was that the carver had sufficient material on hand to begin assemblying and I suddenly realized looking at the fine old case, that one would feel a lack of genuineness in the compromise -- especially if we use the original cases. The original fronts could be removed and used on new backs. The material is all very much wormed.

Yours very truly,

Juli Morgan.

JM-deM

I think moderately antiqued is the proper plan

MORGAN QUERIES HEARST *about the bookcases in Casa Grande's Library, wondering if the emphasis should be on their antiquity or their usefulness. Hearst chose the latter in most cases. In their adaptation of antiques, effect was secondary to utility.*

OPPOSITE: JULIA MORGAN *poses with Marianne, the baby elephant in Hearst's zoo, c. 1929. Even in such an informal pursuit, Morgan retains her dignity.*

the architect of La Cuesta Encantada would be to misrepresent her achievements, since she designed more than seven hundred buildings in her career, several hundred of them during the time San Simeon was under construction. Seeing her as a victim of Hearst's tyranny is also tempting. It is easy to do considering that he was so self-indulgent and she was by nature so self-denying. But this too demeans Morgan, implying that she was not strong enough to make her own decision to work for a client who was perpetually in debt and whose ideas always outpaced his resources, vast as they were. Morgan chose to work for Hearst and received satisfaction from doing so—the pleasure of close contact with antique objects, the challenge of building such an enormous structure sited amidst one of the world's loveliest settings, and the genuine camaraderie of two platonic friends whose passion for art, architecture, and work in all its forms exceeded the appetites of those around them.

San Simeon may be the most flamboyant example of an American country house, but countless others were built in the first three decades of the century. Art critic Fiske Kimball mentioned many dwellings large and small that qualified as American country houses in his October 1919 article for *The Architectural Record*, written at the precise time William Randolph Hearst and Julia Morgan began their plans for San Simeon. Kimball concluded: "Yet the common characteristic of all is clear enough—a site free of the arid blocks and circumscribed 'lots' of the city, where one may enjoy the informality of nature out-of-doors." The largest and most stately country house in America is George Washington Vanderbilt's Biltmore near Asheville, North Carolina, inspired by the country houses of the French Renaissance and completed in 1896 by architect Richard

Morris Hunt. The most self-consciously created country house in America—designed to showcase the architectural styles of four centuries, from the Renaissance through the Rococo—is James Deering's Villa Vizcaya in Coral Gables, Florida, completed in 1917 by architect F. Burrall Hoffman and designer Paul Chalfin. These two great country houses and many others that survive—such as Olana in Hudson, New York, and Ca' d'Zan in Sarasota, Florida—all provide examples of an expansive approach to architecture, entertainment, and landscape. Great numbers of these houses did not weather the changing tastes of modernism and the increasing tax and maintenance costs of the post–World War II era. San Simeon's isolation on the West Coast, and the clouding of its reputation, both by Hearst's political controversies and by *Citizen Kane*, have encouraged the misconception that Hearst Castle is a West Coast anomaly rather than a representative example of the American country-house tradition.

Looking closely at this house puts much of America's life in the twentieth century under examination as well. We have seen our bid for international cultural domination at the century's start subside into a weary hegemony as the century closes. We have consigned much of our lives to the media, influenced by a system of fame and sensation that Hearst had a large role in creating. We have watched women rise to near equality with men, and are looking here at an early manifestation of great responsibility being given to a unique and remarkable woman architect. We have relaxed our social systems, and now regard the dissolution of a marriage—whether by legal means or merely circumstantial ones—in a far different light from that in which Hearst's marital separation was

viewed in the 1920s. We have rejected social rules of money and birth to substitute new ones of money and celebrity, something Hearst understood well. We have celebrated the virtues of genuine craftsmanship: there are few buildings remaining in America in which craftsmen have figured as largely as they do at Hearst Castle. We have rediscovered the importance of objects—not just fine art and paintings in particular, but elements of

architecture, the decorative arts, and the history of technology—all categories Hearst valued in his collections. And we have watched architectural modernism rise and fall, replaced by a mixture of historical references that parallels San Simeon's lively period revival style. To examine La Cuesta Encantada is to see reflected many facets of America's twentieth century in the life of one country house.

PROLOGUE

William Randolph Hearst wrote in 1930 of his beloved estate at San Simeon, then in its heyday: "Now, I am going to board a train and go down to my ranch and find my little hide-away on my little hilltop at San Simeon, and look down on the blue sea, and up at the blue sky, and bask in the glorious sunshine of the greatest State of the greatest nation in the whole world."[1] It may be hard to think of four Mediterranean-style buildings containing 165 rooms surrounded by two classically inspired swimming pools and acres of gardens, this ensemble set on a hill sixteen hundred feet above sea level with three-hundred-sixty-degree views of the ocean and mountains, as a "little hide-away." But for Hearst there was no site more filled with meaning, no place where he felt more at home, than the hills above San Simeon Bay. On the California coast midway between San Francisco and Los Angeles, "the ranch"—as he often called it—combined for Hearst both pastoral beauty and happy childhood associations. It embodied the essences of two of his favorite settings, the rugged scenery of the West and the natural and architectural beauty of the southern Mediterranean countryside.

CASA GRANDE, from the south side of the Esplanade. Its blended facade—made up of antique fragments and copies of historic elements— may lack unity of scale, but it compensates with its lively animation.

*GEORGE HEARST in the late 1880s,
when he was a U.S. Senator from
California. He died in office in 1891.*

*PHOEBE APPERSON HEARST at
twenty, holding young William Randolph
Hearst, in 1863.*

William Randolph Hearst learned his love of the unspoiled landscapes of California from his father, George Hearst, who declared in 1890, while he was serving a term as California's senator in Washington: "As to the future of the State of California, I think that it is the best and most congenial country that I ever saw. . . ."[2] George Hearst was born on September 3, 1820, in Franklin County, Missouri, the son of a prosperous farmer.[3] George did not think much of farming, writing that it "was such a slow way to make money. You could make a living at it and that was about all." He had observed lead mining in Missouri and prided himself on learning methods there that he later applied to his western mining ventures.[4] While George resisted the first news of the gold strikes in California, he left his widowed mother and sister on May 12, 1850, and joined a series of wagon trains across the country, hoping to finish the journey before winter. After surviving a bout with cholera, he made it to the state, where he looked unsuccessfully for gold for the next decade. It was actually in silver that George Hearst first made his fortune, when in 1859 he bought a one-sixth interest in the Ophir Mine, part of the Comstock Lode, an investment that yielded nearly $100,000 for him and his partners. In the spring of 1860, when he was thirty-nine, he received

word that his sister had died and his mother was seriously ill. He returned to Franklin County to visit his mother, whose health never improved. She died on April 1, 1861.

While in Missouri, George was attracted to the eighteen-year-old Phebe (as she spelled her name for many years) Elizabeth Apperson, who had been a schoolgirl when he left the area ten years before. She had grown into an accomplished schoolteacher who spoke French and demonstrated both an intellect and a cultural sophistication rare for her country setting. They agreed to wed, signing a prenuptial agreement on June 14, 1862, which ensured that Phoebe received fifty shares of George's interest in the Gould and Curry silver mine, and marrying the next day. The couple crossed the Isthmus of Panama and sailed to San Francisco, where their only child, William Randolph Hearst, was born on April 29, 1863.[5]

San Francisco in the 1860s was a wild-spirited town, flush with mining money, where very few proper women like Phoebe were in evidence. George recalled: "The first five years in California a woman was a curiosity."[6] George was often away at the mines and it was left to Phoebe to raise young Willie. She was an indulgent parent, evident in her frequent letters to his former nurse-

THE PIEDRAS BLANCAS *Lighthouse, completed in 1875, warned coastal vessels of the rocky shore north of San Simeon Bay.*

GEORGE HEARST *built this one-thousand-foot-long wharf, used for shipping lumber, farm produce, and mining equipment, at San Simeon in 1878.*

maid, Eliza Pike, for instance, describing Willie at age three: "He is very well and grows finely, has not been sick this winter at all. . . . He has improved [in his studies] very much. Knows several of his letters and is getting to be a very good boy sometimes. He was very much put out when Papa came home because he could not sleep with me. I talked to him and told him when his Papa went away again, he could sleep with me. He said, Well, he wished he would go."[7] Phoebe's time was devoted to acquiring culture for herself and her son, and to beginning the habit of philanthropy that later in her life put her in the ranks of America's greatest charitable givers, particularly to educational causes. George's mining fortunes were up and down for the next decade, but his successful purchases of the Ontario silver mine in Utah in 1872, the Homestake gold mine in South Dakota in 1877, and the Anaconda copper mine in Montana in 1880 all brought great and enduring wealth.[8]

He had also begun to invest in both horses and real estate soon after Willie's birth. In 1865 he purchased some thirty thousand acres of land near San Simeon from the Rancho Piedra Blanca, a Mexican land grant.[9] A severe drought in 1863–64 had rendered the land temporarily worthless for cattle. At this time there was a shore whaling operation on San Simeon Point, where

twenty-two families were soon living, and also a mining boom in the nearby hills, where cinnabar, or quicksilver, was mined, an essential component in processing silver.[10] George also bought up portions of the forty-eight-hundred-acre adjoining Rancho San Simeon and eventually about three thousand acres of the thirteen-thousand-acre Rancho Santa Rosa, both of which had been on lands under the jurisdiction of Mission San Miguel Archangel, thirty miles to the east, until the missions were secularized by the Mexican government in the early 1830s.[11] Hearst was interested in San Simeon Bay, already used for shipping by the coastal vessels from San Francisco. Until the railroad came through the city of San Luis Obispo, forty miles to the south, in 1894, San Simeon was a central shipping port. In 1868 Hearst first applied for a permit to construct a wharf on the bay. He built a second wharf in 1878—one thousand feet long, with a warehouse onshore for storing materials. It handled many shipments, including those to and from the mercury mines in the area. His purchases did not go unnoticed or unprotested: Hearst employed agents to buy up the land on his behalf, and there were many lawsuits and protests of his claim.[12] He also constructed a Victorian redwood ranch house inland from San Simeon Bay in the 1870s, which provided a base of operations

23

THE BEACH near San Simeon Point. The name San Simeon was first recorded in 1819, probably given by the padres of nearby Mission San Miguel Archangel. St. Simeon Stylites was a fifth-century Christian ascetic who lived atop a pillar for nearly forty years.

Almost completely wiped out by their lack of immunity to Western infectious diseases—smallpox, syphilis, and also many minor maladies—by the time the twenty-one missions that dotted California were secularized, the Chumash and their culture remain in part a mystery.[15]

We are certain they were sophisticated hunter-gatherers who had daily religious rituals and a complex social structure. In addition to foraging the plants in their localities, the Chumash regularly burned grassland and chaparral areas in order to increase the productivity of the plant communities, thus practicing a form of agriculture. Judging from archaeological evidence, they lived on the banks of the smaller streams and the sea bluffs above the coastal shelf. They ate shellfish, particularly the rock-dwelling top shell, mussel, and chiton, prepared both raw and cooked, as well as fish and mammals, including rodents and deer.[16]

for the dairy and horse farms and gave the Hearsts a place to stay when they journeyed from San Francisco to San Simeon in Willie's boyhood.[13]

The land George Hearst purchased had been occupied for nine thousand years, or about three hundred generations, by the Native Americans known as the Chumash, a loosely grouped number of tribes who ranged from south of Santa Barbara to slightly north of San Simeon. These Native Americans were the first California tribe to have contact with Europeans. Described by the Spanish explorers on their expedition through the region in 1769 as "well built and of a good disposition, very agile and alert and ingenious to a degree," they were initially friendly toward the Spanish.[14]

The land the Chumash occupied at San Simeon is at the base of the Santa Lucia mountain range, a region of gently sloping marine terrace between the shoreline and the steep peaks to the east that rise to elevations of twenty-five- to thirty-four-hundred feet. Geologically formed 140 to 150 million years ago, in the late Jurassic to early Cretaceous period, the land at San Simeon is a mixture of sedimentary and metamorphic rocks. Both earthquakes and landslides are common in this region,

"THE HILLTOP," a Hearst family camp site from the nineteenth century, became the building site of La Cuesta Encantada from 1919 through 1947. It is seen here from the location in San Simeon Bay where the family disembarked from the coastal steamer.

in fog, creating a magical atmosphere at the top of the hill. This was likely the inspiration for William Randolph Hearst's christening his estate in 1924 with the formal name La Cuesta Encantada, "The Enchanted Hill."

A beautiful tree common to the region is the coastal live oak, an evergreen whose twisted, gnarled limbs provide a welcome shady canopy throughout the brushy hillsides. The Chumash relied on its acorns as a dietary staple and its sturdy wood provided both charcoal and tools for later settlers.[19] William Randolph Hearst insisted that these venerable trees, some of them hundreds of years old, were never to be cut down, and several were moved out of the way of proposed building sites during San Simeon's construction. English naturalist Joseph Smeaton Chase rode horseback in 1911 up the coast of the entire state and described San Simeon's abundant landscape:

> The coast now curved to the pretty bay of San Simeon, fringed with islets of rock round which the sea coiled in dazzling whiteness of spray. Along the cliff large sea-asters grew thickly, with lavender lupines, yellow tarweed, and eschscholtzias of that splendid deep orange

made up of grasslands in which scattered boulders of different shapes and sizes stick up out of the soil. Water is not abundant. The climate is classified as Mediterranean, meaning cool wet winters and hot dry summers, with most of the rainfall occurring in the winter months.[17] The summer weather pattern is characterized by low clouds that hang over the coast and penetrate into the seaward canyons in the late evening and early morning, persisting until the growing sunlight evaporates them. This maritime influence ensures that the coastline areas remain cool, while the high mountain tops, where ridges prevent the fog from spreading, stay hot and dry.[18] The hills above San Simeon, at sixteen hundred feet, are therefore often sunny while the surrounding lower landscape is swathed

THE HILLS east of the Castle are twice its elevation, though from the coastline it appears that the Castle is built on the highest prominence. The easternmost ridge contains mountain springs that provided the water for the entire project.

THE COASTAL LIVE OAK, Quercus agrifolia, *an evergreen known for its dramatic asymmetry and rugged resistance to drought and periodic fires, is characteristic in the chaparral landscape of the central coast of California.*

that suggests the Arabian nights, or the court of Ahasuerus; like sunshine filtered through silken curtains of crimson and gold. Inland, gray farms lay in bends and hollows of the mountains; wind-shorn oaks and laurels filled the narrower cañons; and whenever the road swung in to round the head of one of these, I found myself suddenly in a different world, among wild roses, ferns, blackberries, and phenomenal thickets of coarse flowering weeds.[20]

George Hearst continued to buy land in the San Simeon area until his death in 1891, after which Phoebe made additional purchases. Their son maintained the tradition, until by the time construction began in 1919 his ranch extended over fourteen miles of coastline and approximately sixty thousand acres. Hearst continued to acquire land to the east through the 1920s, his holdings ultimately reaching two hundred fifty thousand acres. Rather than developing the land into a population center, all three of the Hearsts preferred to keep it largely as their private preserve. Early in his childhood, William Randolph Hearst roamed the ranch with his father, traveling up to a hilltop site high above the coastal fog, hiking the hills, and glorying in the views. He joked that

the climb was so steep that in his younger years he had to hold onto the horse's tail.[21]

Hearst grew up rambunctious and very aware of his status as a westerner and the son of a mining pioneer. He was a bright child raised by two determined parents who did not recognize limits, for themselves or for him. He was sent to St. Paul's School in New Hampshire, then on to Harvard, where George said of his son's education: "I do not think . . . that he worked very hard there, because he was too fond of fun."[22] The older Hearst had entered politics, which William followed avidly from college while playing the role of a rich man's son, staging lavish parties for his friends. Will had a healthy and self-deprecating sense of humor that ingratiated him to many. He did not think much of the eastern scenery when compared with the West, writing to Phoebe:

I have had the "molly grubs" for the last week or so. I am beginning to get awfully tired of this place, and I long to get out West somewhere where I can stretch myself without coming in contact with the narrow walls with which the prejudice of the beaneaters has surrounded us.

HEARST (left) in a play at Harvard. He once wrote Phoebe that he had been given "permission to cut [rehearsals] as much as I please, just so I know my part on the evening of the performance. I wish the faculty would adopt the same measures as regards recitations."

I long to get out in the woods and breathe the fresh mountain air and listen to the moaning of the pines. It makes me almost crazy with homesickness when I think of it and I hate their weak, pretty New England scenery with its gently rolling hills, its pea green foliage, its vistas, tame enough to begin with but totally disfigured by houses and barns which could not be told apart save for the respective inhabitants.

I hate it as I do a weak pretty face without force or character. I long to see our own woods, the jagged rocks and towering mountains, the majestic pines, the grand impressive scenery of the "far West."

I shall never live anywhere but in California. I like to be away for a while only to appreciate it the more when I return.[23]

William's longing to return to the West showed in his studies, which he did not take seriously. In fact, after several perilously close calls, Will left Harvard in his junior year, never completing his degree. While Phoebe was severely disappointed, he did not seem upset himself. A cheerful Philistine, Hearst often declared in his later years: "It takes a good mind to resist education."[24]

He had been the business editor of the Harvard *Lampoon*, and unlike his wealthy predecessors, he had done more than just pour his own money into its operation. He sold advertising and put it on a solid economic basis, becoming very interested in journalism in the process.[25] He wanted to run a newspaper, specifically the *San Francisco Examiner*, which his father had purchased in 1880 in order to have a Democratic voice to assist his successful bid for the U.S. Senate.[26] George recalled: "After I had lost about a quarter of a million by the paper, my boy Will came out of school, and said he wanted to try his hand at the paper. I thought it was the very worst thing he could do; and told him so, adding that I could not make it pay. He said, however, that the reason that the paper did not pay was, because it was not the best paper in the country. He said that if he had it he would make it the best paper, and that then it would pay."[27] George and Phoebe gave the twenty-four-year-old William the *Examiner* in 1887, and almost immediately he transformed it, modeling its heavy use of illustration and sensationalism on Joseph Pulitzer's popular *New York World*. George Hearst declared in 1890: "My son, Will, is one of the hardest workers I ever

saw, and he certainly has made the paper a decided success. . . . I believe it is now worth upwards of a million [dollars]."[28] At the *Examiner*, Hearst honed his journalistic style to a mix of news, entertainment, and propaganda, which he not only exported east to his other newspapers but which broadly influenced mass communication as a whole in the twentieth century.[29]

George Hearst died in 1891, leaving his twenty-million-dollar fortune entirely to Phoebe and commending Will to her care, "having full confidence that she will make suitable provisions for him."[30] This meant that

IN HER LATER YEARS, *Phoebe Apperson Hearst became California's greatest philanthropist, fascinated with art, archaeology, and education. Her benefactions to the Parents and Teachers Association, Sempervirens Fund, Traveler's Aid Society, and the Young Women's Christian Association, as well as her unceasing generosity to the University of California, left a legacy still at work.*

until Phoebe's death in 1919, Will was often in the embarrassing position of having to go to his mother for funds. It was a frequent necessity, since improvidence about money both for the newspapers and for his private expenses was a lifelong, defining trait. As a kind of inheritance, Phoebe gave him $180,000 in 1895 to buy

THE VIEW of San Simeon Bay as seen from the Castle. Hearst called the entire estate "the ranch" at San Simeon, referring to the vast expanse of coastal acreage that had been a family ranch since his boyhood, as well as to the hilltop buildings themselves.

the East Coast newspaper he had long coveted, the *New York Morning Journal* (which he later named the *New York Journal-American*), making him at thirty-two the youngest newspaper owner in that city.[31] Hearst concocted a whirlwind campaign of publicity stunts, muckraking, and sensational news—even egging the nation into declaring war against Spain with the *Journal's* fiery and often imaginative accounts of Spanish treachery after the sinking of the USS *Maine* in 1898 (then considered sabotage, but now generally regarded as an accident).[32] The circulation battle Hearst waged with Pulitzer's *World* included a bidding war for the services of Richard Outcault, who drew the "Yellow Kid," a mischievous cartoon character. For a while there were competing "Yellow Kids" in the two rival newspapers, which prompted the coining of the term "yellow journalism."[33]

Hearst's next twenty years were spent in quest of public office and increased circulation, as he expanded his newspaper empire and began buying magazines such as *Motor* and *Good Housekeeping*. He ran unsuccessful

campaigns for governor of New York and mayor of New York City, but succeeded in serving two terms as a United States congressman from New York. His presidential aspirations, pursued in the first and second decades of the century, failed miserably, though he was the chairman of the Association of Democratic Clubs for many years.

Hearst married twenty-one-year-old New York stage dancer Millicent Veronica Willson in 1903, on the eve of his fortieth birthday. Their first son, George, was born in 1904. Then followed William Jr. in 1908, John in 1909, and twins Randolph and David (who changed his name from the christened Elbert) in 1915. Hearst was indulgent of his scapegrace sons, writing with irony to Phoebe around 1913:

> The children are well and William is entirely over his train sickness. The old man whom John shot in the eye is not recovering as quickly. He is a cranky, unreasonable old man and complained about John's innocent amusements. He can't see a joke—in fact he can't see anything just now.

John explained to the old man that he hadn't meant to hit him in the eye. He was aiming at his nose. The old man is still cranky however and looks worried every time John shoots. Some people don't understand children.[34]

Having a family and waging an exhausting run of campaigns, both journalistic and political, not only took up Hearst's time but also made him long for the simpler life he had known in childhood on the San Simeon ranch. In 1917 he wrote to Phoebe, then living on her five-hundred-acre estate in Pleasanton, while he, Millicent, and the boys all camped at San Simeon:

> I am sorry that you would not try this hilltop with us just once. I am not sure that you would like things as rough as we have it here, but I think you might, and if you like it at all you would like it a lot. It is perfect in its way. Of course, we do not try to make it too refined, because that would take away some of the charm of camp life, but if you wanted it more refined, you could easily have it so. . . . It is great stuff, and I really feel that New York is like one big office building and that you do not really get out to breathe good air and get good sunshine until you get at least west of the Mississippi river.[35]

Sometimes it was a more rugged experience than Hearst's wife, Millicent, really liked. Many years later her daughter-in-law, Austine Hearst, related the story that Millicent had once taken a horseback ride with W. R. all the way from Monterey down to San Simeon,

> sleeping along the way wherever they could find shelter. Mexican guides led them on the mountain trails. One night [Millicent] remembered sleeping in a cave. "It was full of bones and had a funny smell. An old codger we ran into later on the trail laughed at us. Told us it was a well-known mountain lion den!
>
> "The couple we started out with turned back after two days, but I stuck it out. . . . That was not the only time W. R. ever lied to me," she winked. "He had told me it was a short ride!"[36]

Hearst wrote to Phoebe again in 1917, in the midst of the family's San Simeon vacation:

> If you could see your son and your grandsons today on the ranch you would be highly entertained and pleased too. . . .
>
> We have been up to the Sancho Pojo and rode from there up the coast for ten or twelve miles. We went last night up to Pat Garrity's and camped. This morning the two youngest [aged two at the time of this letter] woke us all up at half past four.
>
> We had breakfast and then came down to the Arroyo La Cruz and went in swimming in a big pool, first the children, then the girls and finally the men. . . .
>
> We are back in our regular camp at the top of the hill now, tired and sleepy on account of those kids. I love this ranch. It is wonderful. I love the sea and I love the mountains and the hollows in the hills and the shady places in the creeks and the fine old oaks and even the hot brushy hillsides—full of quail—and the canyons full of deer. It's a wonderful place. I would rather spend a month here than any place in the world. And as a sanitarium! Mother it has Nauheim, Carlsbad, Vichy, Wiesbaden, French Lick, Saratoga and every other so-called health resort beaten a nautical mile.
>
> I don't feel as if I had ever been sick and I don't want to leave here at all and go back to work and worries.[37]

It was only two years after writing this affectionate tribute to San Simeon that William Randolph Hearst became the sole owner of his beloved ranch, when Phoebe Hearst died of influenza in the spring of 1919. Hearst had contemplated building on the hilltop site while Phoebe was still alive. Now that he had inherited the property, his dreams for the place could be realized on a grander scale.

CHAPTER ONE

Early Visions

Walter Steilberg remembered that it all started simply enough. San Francisco architect Julia Morgan was working late in her office at the Merchants Exchange Building when Steilberg, a trusted employee and close friend of Morgan's who later served as the first project engi-neer at San Simeon, couldn't help hearing William Randolph Hearst's voice through an open door.

For such a large man, it seemed to me his pitch was very high, so it carried. I heard him say to Miss Morgan, "I would like to build something up on the hill at San Simeon. I get tired of going up there and camping in tents. I'm getting a little old for that. I'd like to get something that would be more comfortable. The other day I was in Los Angeles, prowling around second-hand bookstores, as I often do, and I came upon this stack of books called Bungalow Books. Among them I saw one which has a picture—this isn't what I want, but it gives you an idea of my thought about the thing, keeping it sim-ple—of a Jappo-Swisso bunga-low." He laughed at that, and so did she.

In the years that followed Steilberg laughed too, whenever he saw the lavish Mediterranean Revival estate at San Simeon, and said to himself, "Well, there's the Jappo-Swisso bungalow."[1]

The bungalow was a natural ini-tial choice for William Randolph Hearst's country house in 1919, considering its popularity in the state at the time.[2] Influenced in design by such diverse building types as West Indian planters' shacks, New England cottages, and Japanese wooden houses, the California bungalow's low-pitched roofs, native materi-als, and simple floor plans were perfect for the outdoor life in the West. The earliest surviving studies for struc-tures at San Simeon in the vast body of Julia Morgan's drawings do indeed show modest single-story bungalows looking much like those being built throughout southern California at the time. The "moral and modest" bungalow style was not on the San Simeon drawing board for long, however. Steilberg recalled, "I don't think it was a month before we were going on the grand scale."[3] It was the only scale in which William Randolph Hearst seemed comfortable.

Hearst's architectural eye was well developed by 1919. From 1907, his New York residence had been the Clarendon Apartments at 137 Riverside Drive, which Hearst eventually enlarged to five floors and thirty rooms, so irritating the owners that he settled the matter by buying the building in 1913.[4] His powerful urge to build had even caused friction between Hearst and his mother, Phoebe, dating from 1894 when he had hired the architect A. C. Schweinfurth to build him a residence on land Phoebe owned in Pleasanton, California, a pastoral landscape of rolling hills east of San Francisco Bay. Phoebe, displeased to find her son building on her land without her permission, responded decisively: she appropriated the Mission Revival mansion for herself in 1897, naming it Hacienda del Pozo de Verona, "House of the Wellhead of Verona," after an antique wellhead her son had purchased for her while traveling abroad.[5] Phoebe expanded the house's amenities with

MORGAN NOTED *that the hilltop construction on the steep slopes required "endless steps and terraces." These graceful steps are located on the ocean side of House A.*

Schweinfurth as the presiding architect, then hired Julia Morgan for an extensive remodeling, from 1903 through 1910.[6] William Randolph Hearst and Morgan probably met at the Hacienda, or while she was working on the Hearst architectural commission for the University of California at Berkeley. Under John Galen Howard, Morgan participated in designing the Hearst Memorial Mining Building, donated by Phoebe Hearst in memory of her husband, George Hearst, and constructed in 1901–7; and the Greek Theater, donated by William Randolph Hearst and built in 1903.[7]

By the time of Hearst's after-hours visit in 1919, Morgan was forty-seven and at the peak of her career, having practiced in California since 1902.[8] She had designed the concrete campanile at Mills College in Oakland in 1903, which survived the 1906 San Francisco earthquake without damage; supervised the reconstruction of San Francisco's Fairmont Hotel on Nob Hill in 1906–7 after the earthquake; and achieved a reputation as a perceptive designer of schools, homes, and churches. Known for carefully considering the use of each building and the character of each client, Morgan had demonstrated her ability to work sensitively in a great number of architectural styles, from the woodsy naturalism of her 1913–37 Asilomar Conference Grounds in Pacific Grove, near Monterey, California, to the Beaux-Arts classicism of the Oakland Young Women's Christian Association (YWCA), begun in the same year. Her successful private practice continued during all the years of San Simeon's construction, just one of many indications of her single-minded, energetic devotion to her work. She and Hearst had collaborated previously, in 1912, on a retaining wall for a potential Hearst residence in Sausalito, north of San Francisco, though the residence itself was not built; in 1914, on a small cottage on property Hearst owned on the south rim of the Grand Canyon (demolished after the site became a national park); and most notably on the dramatic and effective Mission Revival-style Los Angeles Examiner Building in 1915.

Since Hearst was a known quantity to Morgan before she began the job at San Simeon, she knew his abilities, including his skill at visualization. Steilberg recalled, "Hearst was the only layman I ever met who could really *read* a plan."[9] And just as surely she also knew of his airy disregard for all matters financial. For Hearst, not regarding money was a convenient way of not being ruled by it. Some of Julia Morgan's friends and family felt that the advantages of this architect-client relationship were nearly all on Hearst's side. They considered Morgan overused and underpaid, and it is true that Hearst let his accounts payable for San Simeon accumulate alarmingly. By mutual agreement, he provided Morgan with a monthly allowance to pay all the construction expenses, ranging from a low of $500 per month as the project began to a high of $60,000 per month in the heavy construction periods of the late 1920s. From this sum she was expected to pay for salaries, materials, equipment, transportation, landscaping, and her own commission, which at various times in their twenty-eight-year collaboration ranged from six to eight-and-one-half percent of the construction costs. Almost immediately Hearst's allowance proved insufficient for the purpose, to her lasting frustration.[10]

AN EARLY DRAWING of "Bungalow B" with Hearst's note, beginning "Think Bungalow B would better be more like Bungalow A." The earliest cottage drawings were modeled on examples in a book of California bungalow designs.

But their relationship was far more complex than a superficial view of self-indulgent client/self-denying architect can adequately explain. Steilberg described them both as "long-distance dreamers. . . . People who belong to that breed don't think about anything but their work. It's not a virtue; it's just that they're made that way, that's all."[11] Steilberg further reflected, "There was this strange comradeship with Mr. Hearst and it was really genuine comradeship."[12] He watched them together at dinner once, and recalled, "The rest of us could have been a hundred miles away; they didn't pay any attention to anybody. It wouldn't have surprised me at all to see a spark travelling from one skull to the other, back and forth, because these two very different people just clicked."[13]

The thousands of letters, telegrams, memos, and drawings that record twenty-eight years of construction at San Simeon clearly establish that the estate was neither an embodiment entirely of Hearst's ideas nor entirely of Morgan's. It was a rare, true collaboration, remarkable in its spirit and energy. Hearst proposed the majority of the hilltop features and was far more involved than the usual client in siting structures and terraces, conceiving floor plans, choosing architectural ornament, selecting plant varieties, acquiring objects, and determining their locations. His choices were often influenced by Morgan, however, who was expert at making subtle suggestions for which she never took credit. Her duties for Hearst at San Simeon were far more extensive than those of the usual architect, in any case: through her San Francisco architectural firm, she hired all employees, kept the payrolls, ordered and oversaw the shipment of art and materials, and supervised all the details of landscaping and housekeeping.

JULIA MORGAN in 1926, at age fifty-four, when both the San Simeon project and her other architectural commissions were at their most demanding.

While she tried to temper some of Hearst's wilder notions by offering a moderating suggestion here and there, she did not keep him in check. In fact, there is almost no sense of restraint lingering about the estate at all, and a fairy-tale quality of exuberance defines La Cuesta Encantada's charm.

Julia Morgan's greatest frustration came in contending with Hearst's constant habit of changing what was already built. Almost nothing was retained in the guise in which it first appeared, neither the four houses, terraces, bell towers, nor swimming pools. Some of the construction laborers only worked for a short while before quitting in disgust: good wages did not make up for the frustration of seeing their work demolished.[14] Morgan wrote Arthur Byne, a fellow architect living in Spain, who with his wife, Mildred, sold Hearst a great number of Spanish art pieces for the ranch: "Our own relationships with him have been satisfactory.—Payment usually late, but always sure, the greatest trouble being his changeableness of mind—but in return, he compensates to some extent by allowing me to change mine now and then."[15] It was not caprice or petty tyranny that prompted these frequent changes, but Hearst's desire that his estate should keep pace with his constantly widening vision of the project.

In 1919 Hearst and Morgan boarded Steve Zegar's taxi at the railroad station in San Luis Obispo, forty miles south of San Simeon, for their first trip together to the proposed site. (Zegar later proved so accommodating and useful in transporting Hearst's guests that this single taxi evolved into a fourteen-car fleet.) Zegar recalled taking Hearst and Morgan as far as the end of the usable road up the mountain, then recommending they borrow horses from some ranch cowboys to make the rest of the trip. Morgan was not an experienced horsewoman and

she declined. Zegar's solution was to have the cowboys tie a rope to the Cadillac and pull them up the rest of the way.[16] At the top was a rough campsite, the remnant of many family summer vacations, and a hillside dotted with boulders and native oak trees. The ground sloped steeply down; the soil was poor. The site's advantages were a three-hundred-sixty-degree view and access to water from springs to the east of the hill on a mountain twice the hill's height, its peak set back far enough that "Camp Hill" seemed the highest prominence from the view at sea level.

From the beginning, Hearst and Morgan laid out the estate as a group of structures, echoing the separate tents for sleeping and dining that had long been a Hearst family tradition on the hill. Such a grouping of buildings was a rare circumstance in country-house architecture, which usually focused on one main house, not the interrelationship of several in such close proximity. At San Simeon, three small houses, each facing a different aspect of the view, make a loose semicircle around the much larger Main Building. Each house was given a formal descriptive Spanish name within the first

WILLIAM RANDOLPH HEARST, or, as his nearly forty thousand newspaper employees called him, "the Chief," c. 1930. The Castle had nearly one hundred telephones and twenty-four-hour switchboard service by the late 1920s, allowing Hearst to make San Simeon a primary residence from which he conducted business.

33

AN AERIAL VIEW of La Cuesta Encantada taken in 1936 shows both wings under construction at the back of the Main Building and, in the foreground, the village of construction workers' residences on the south side of the hilltop. Just above the staff residences is the teardrop-shaped driveway that served as the estate's entrance. The large building to the left is House A; the other two cottages are obscured by trees, but the Neptune Pool is visible in the upper left corner. The Roman Pool is below the tennis courts at the far right.

few years of construction, though informally they were almost always referred to by alphabet letters. This habit may have started when Morgan provided Hearst with alternative design options, labeling the drawings "Plan A" and "Plan B."[17] The eighteen-room Casa del Mar, "House of the Sea," which Hearst and Morgan generally called House A, was named for its long view of the Pacific Ocean to the south, and was Hearst's intended residence. The other eighteen-room house, located in the middle, was Casa del Sol, "House of the Sun," or House C, and was sited west toward the sunset. The ten-room Casa del Monte, "House of the Mountain," known as House B, was given its formal name for its view of the rugged northern Santa Lucia mountain range, and served as the Hearst family's earliest quarters. The massive central building itself was Casa Grande, "The Big House." Initially the three small houses were each planned to be single story; but additional stories were soon planned for each of them, varying their sizes. They all retained the same four-bedroom arrangement

for their central floor: two bedrooms on each side separated by bathrooms, each pair of bedrooms flanking a central sitting room. None was provided with a dining room; meals were taken in the Main Building, and in the earliest years in dining tents.

Hearst declared early on, "The main thing at the ranch is the view."[18] These four separate buildings showcased that view from many perspectives and locations, far more than would have been possible from a single structure. They also allowed for heightened impressions of both togetherness and solitude. The small houses felt remote from the Main Building and disconnected as well from each other. Their separate stories nearly all have outside entrances, so it was possible for guests to share a building without seeing one another. Certainly the single most powerful impression one receives from this interdependent plan is the notion of a Mediterranean hill town, the Main Building functioning as the cathedral at the crest of the hill, surrounded by residences at a slightly lower elevation.

Hearst's intention was to start the Main Building in the fall of 1919, beginning with it since it was self-contained. Its earliest plan featured a three-room main floor—assembly room, dining room, and a smaller sitting room they called the "trophy room"—topped with one and a half stories of sleeping quarters.[19] He wanted it finished by the summer of 1920 so that the family could occupy it on their next trip west. He proposed that the three smaller houses be constructed that fall, making everything ready for family use by the summer of 1921.[20] With construction under way, in September of 1919 Hearst and Morgan began to discuss ornamenting Casa Grande with a single tower, based on the Gothic Cathedral of Santa Maria la Mayor, in Ronda, Spain.[21] Within a few months, they were committed to this idea, even though the single tower was quickly replaced with two identical ones, still loosely based on the Ronda design. This decision influenced many of the architectural developments that followed in the next three decades.

Soon Hearst himself realized that his construction schedule was wildly impractical, considering the many difficulties Morgan faced: both labor and materials were scarce at the close of World War I; a waterfront strike had effectively stopped all shipping from San Francisco; the site itself was remote and most of the steamships would not land there; the materials, once unloaded at the dock, required a six-mile climb in primitive trucks up a steep dirt road that turned into a bog at the first rain; and winter was about to begin. Hearst was always eager to see his latest ideas for the ranch take shape, and always certain that progress could and should be more rapid. Unrealistic construction deadlines and a tone of urgency were constant through the entire twenty-eight years of the project—but occa-

MORGAN'S EARLY FLOOR PLAN of House A included a central sitting room flanked by two sets of bedrooms, with an entrance lobby to the east.

sionally even William Randolph Hearst had to make accommodations. Since it would be impractical to start on the Main Building, he resolved that the three small houses should be built first, as their sizes made them more attainable goals.[22]

The notion of the Ronda Cathedral treatment for the Main Building stayed true, however, and that decision seemed to call for Mediterranean ornament in the smaller houses. From then on the concept of bungalow design was abandoned. Hearst wanted to link these houses stylistically to the Main Building, which they planned to give not only ecclesiastical towers but also an ecclesiastical entrance, based on a church doorway entrance in the Alcazar in Seville. Both the tower and the entrance were illustrated in Austin Whittlesey's *The Minor Ecclesiastical, Domestic, and Garden Architecture of Southern Spain*, published in 1917, which Hearst bought and mailed to Morgan. He drew her attention to photographs of specific houses, patios, and churches in this and in several other books on Spanish architecture, saying that he thought they could apply Spanish ornament to "our cottages and give them a little more dignity and at the same time more distinctiveness."[23] He felt this could be done by selecting Renaissance motifs borrowed from domestic architecture to balance the sacred motifs on Casa Grande.[24]

In selecting motifs from historic buildings to use as a wellspring of ideas, William Randolph Hearst and Julia Morgan were drawing on the customary resource of architects of the period. Morgan typically met clients in the library of her office in order to peruse with them the large folio volumes of etchings and photographs that were the central inspiration for eclectic architects at the time.[25] Such a practice has in more recent decades been

Sacred forms were applied to secular building

THIS PHOTOGRAPH of a church doorway in Seville, Spain, now in the Alcazar, appeared in Whittlesey's The Minor Ecclesiastical, Domestic, and Garden Architecture of Southern Spain, printed in 1917. It was employed by Hearst and Morgan as the inspiration for Casa Grande's main entrance door.

MORGAN IMPROVED on the scale of the main entrance door to Casa Grande by using larger-sized fifteenth-century statues of Gothic wild men and also by introducing a canopied niche for a thirteenth-century statue of the Virgin to replace the iron grille that had been employed in the historic Seville doorway.

THIS PHOTOGRAPH of Santa Maria la Mayor in Ronda, Spain, also appeared in the Whittlesey book. Of this building, Hearst wrote: "It is from this tower that Miss Morgan and I took the motif for the towers at the ranch. The Cathedral is a very quaint old building—very composite in style. In fact, hardly in any style. It is attractive, however."

JULIA MORGAN'S DRAWING of Casa Grande's towers followed the inspiration of the cathedral at Ronda.

ANOTHER PHOTOGRAPH from Whittlesey's book shows an arcaded porch in Cordoba, Spain.

THE WEST FRONT of House C, Casa del Sol, was adapted from the Cordoba model.

types for a dramatic, picturesque effect.

WILLIAM RANDOLPH HEARST and Julia Morgan confer in the courtyard of House B. Morgan's longtime employee Walter Steilberg said of their relationship: "Excepting Mrs. Hearst and Miss Davies, Miss Morgan was the woman who meant most in his life. I don't mean that there was any romantic idea at all, but there was . . . a sense of comradeship [and] . . . mutual understanding which was something quite wonderful. . . . In visiting San Simeon now, I have a feeling that this place is haunted by these two great personalities."

disparaged as lacking creative impulse. But for practitioners working in a number of different historical styles, choosing the proper source was in itself a creative act, far removed from the sterility of mere imitation.[26]

Their surprising choice to pattern the Main Building on a church was made for stylistic, not spiritual, reasons. Hearst did not build a chapel on the site; he was never active in any church. There is a slight suggestion in Casa Grande's floor plan of an early Christian basilica, with the Refectory as the nave, and the west-facing Assembly Room as the transept; the problem with this analogy is that it reverses the basiliça scheme, as one enters from the vestibule off the Assembly Room, where the rear, or apse, of the church would be.[27] Hearst and Morgan employed Spanish Renaissance church architec-

ture in the same way that William Beckford and Horace Walpole employed sacred Gothic architectural imagery in their eighteenth-century English country houses, Fonthill Abbey and Strawberry Hill, respectively. Sacred forms were applied to secular building types for a dramatic, picturesque effect.

Hearst was not interested in re-creating the ornament commonly employed in the Mission Revival style, and he also rejected the historic eighteenth-century Spanish Colonial style employed in the California missions themselves. He wrote to Morgan:

The Gothic and Renaissance of Spain are so very much more interesting than the Baroc [sic] stuff of the Eighteenth Century. The iron work of your windows is already Renaissance, the first big hall of the big building

W. R. HEARST points proudly to House A (right) and House C, nearing completion in July 1923. All three cottages were supplied with electricity in the early years by a gasoline generator and a small hydro-electric plant. The septic system for the hilltop complex was located on the lower hills near where Hearst is standing. Of the complications of building on steep slopes, Morgan wrote: "I look now at all the old medieval hilltop castles with a sense of fellow understanding and sympathy with their builders."

will be in the Renaissance style, and on the whole I do not think it will be bad to have such a Gothic doorway as this Seville one, and the Gothic pinnacle towers of the Ronda church of Santa Maria.[28]

Still Hearst was far from certain about the suitability of this scheme. Eager to hear Morgan's views on the matter, he emphasized: "all these things are just thoughts, and if you do not like them we will not try to follow them."[29] He deferred frequently to Morgan's taste, especially in the early phases of their architect-client relationship: "I make a lot of suggestions and if any of them are impracticable or imperfect from an architectural point of view, please discard them and substitute whatever you think is better."[30]

Hearst continued to mull the long-term impact of whether his preference for the Spanish Gothic and Renaissance styles might be inappropriate to California's history, and he wrote to Morgan a few days after his previous letter, proposing an alternative architectural style.

I started out with the Baroc idea in mind, as nearly all Spanish architecture in America is of that character, and the plaster surfaces that we associate all Spanish architecture in California with are a modification of that style, as I understand it.

If we should decide on this style, I would at least want to depart from the very crude and rude examples of it

MORGAN'S EARLY SKETCH for a group of buildings features the Main Building in the background with a single tower patterned on that of the Cathedral of Santa Maria la Mayor in Ronda, Spain.

CG1-108
KM-C

THE SOUTH EARRING TERRACE *features the Verona wellhead Hearst presented to his mother, Phoebe, which she had displayed prominently at the entrance to her Pleasanton hacienda. Her son also gave it an important location, south of his House A.*

THE WEST FACADE of House A. Formally called Casa del Mar, it was named for its sweeping views of the Pacific Ocean to the south. The setting and climate made the choice of the Mediterranean Revival architectural style particularly fitting.

that we have in our early California Spanish architecture.

The Mission at Santa Barbara is doubtless the highest example of this California architecture, and yet it is very bare and almost clumsy to my mind.

The best things I have seen in this Spanish Baroc are at the San Diego Exposition. . . .

This style at its best is sufficiently satisfactory, though in our early California architecture it seems to me too primitive, and in many of the examples I have seen in Mexico so elaborate as to be objectionable.

Hearst initially preferred the hybrid of Spanish and Mexican Colonial architecture designed by Bertram Goodhue and Carleton M. Winslow for the 1915 San Diego Panama-California Exposition—later acknowledged as one of the first appearances of the Spanish Colonial Revival architectural style. In this taste he was following a cultural trend, since this became the most popular building style in California in the 1920s. He soon changed his mind and looked instead to the style of the Spanish Renaissance, preferring historic buildings over the San Diego World's Fair structures, and asking Morgan, "But after all, would it not be better to do

something a little different than other people are doing out in California as long as we do not do anything incongruous?"[31]

Morgan also had reservations about imitating the florid, tile-laden buildings of the San Diego Exposition, especially in matters of scale. "Two years ago work took me down to San Diego very frequently and I know the buildings well," she replied to Hearst.

The composition and decoration are certainly very well handled indeed, but I question whether this type of decoration would not seem too heavy and clumsy on our buildings, because while the Exposition covers acres with its buildings, we have a comparatively small group, and it would seem to me that they should charm by their detail rather than overwhelm by more or less clumsy exuberance.

I feel just as you do about the early California Mission style as being too primitive to be gone back to and copied. Charming as they are in mass and color, I believe their appeal is because of their simple, direct expression of their object. As I wrote you in my last letter, I believe we could get something really very beautiful by using the combination of Ronda Towers and the Sevilla doorway, with your Virgin over it and San

Simeon and San Christophe on either side. This would allow for great delicacy and at the same time, brilliance in the decoration, and I see how it could be executed without running into very great expense.[32]

Morgan and Hearst had collaborated just five years earlier on the Los Angeles Examiner Building, a textbook example of Mission Revival style, complete with domes, plain white walls, and innumerable arched openings.[33] It had been an appropriate style for a public building, but not for the private one Hearst was contemplating. Further, it was a style that had peaked: the final year of its popularity was 1915.[34] Hearst saw the historic images they

were emulating as "something a little different" from the architecture of California at the time, though today we can clearly see San Simeon's architectural style as part of the larger 1920s Mediterranean Revival movement, which borrowed from both Italian and Spanish Renaissance sources for its inspiration.

This earliest phase of the project foreshadowed the construction that followed at San Simeon. The letters and telegrams flew by the hundreds between Morgan and Hearst, who interested himself in every aspect of planning and construction, and constantly modified the direction and the results. Siting the three cottages was

A BATHROOM in Hearst's own House A, featuring a solid marble sink, gold-plated fixtures, and a seven-headed shower.

THE GARDEN between House C and House B was laid with patterns of boxwood hedges, brick pavers, and polychrome tiles.
BELOW: A MOOR'S HEAD TILE on the eaves of House C, patterned after an antique
Spanish Talavera tile published in Arte y Decoración en España.

typical of his attempts to fine-tune the growing estate. Hearst, in New York, conferred with Morgan and his childhood friend, artist Orrin Peck, who came to the hill to work specifically on this project.[35] Both Peck and Morgan advocated siting the houses lower down the hill than Hearst had initially planned, but Hearst felt that lowering them would lessen their impact, even while ensuring their better views. Hearst argued that all four structures should be considered together as part of the architectural group, linked effectively by landscaping, concluding to Morgan: "In fact, I think that when we get the cottages

built, we can lay out a plan of walks and flower beds or landscape features of some kind that will bring all the structures together into a harmonious whole."[36] The two outer cottages—House A and House B—Hearst placed on the 1,095-foot elevation line, but he decided that House C, in the center, would be best placed lower down, at the 1,090-foot level, to distance it from his own residence in House A. Construction on the three houses began in February 1920, and Hearst soon regretted his decision.[37] Just over a year later he proposed that towers be built over the bathrooms on the main

43

CONSTRUCTION WORKERS *began laying rebar for Casa Grande in the spring of 1922. Steel-reinforced concrete was the sole structural material employed in La Cuesta Encantada's buildings. It allowed them to mix materials on site, provided rapid results, and resisted California's twin threats of earthquake and fire.*

floor of House C, in order to bring its roofline up to the height of the flanking houses.[38]

Another early change of plan was Hearst's decision that House C should feature Moorish ornament from southern Spain, including a deep entrance court and round-arched windows, in addition to the two small towers decorated with openwork balcony screens. In contrast, the ornament of Houses A and B emulated sixteenth-century Spanish Renaissance motifs, themselves derived from Italian Renaissance decoration of the fifteenth century. Hearst made the most changes to House A, his intended residence. Some of La Cuesta Encantada's most striking features—its sizable libraries and dramatic mosaic-lined Roman Pool—Hearst initially conceived as improvements to House A, then later constructed on more spacious sites elsewhere on the hill.[39]

Morgan always insisted on completely modern construction materials, using steel-reinforced concrete almost exclusively. Both economical and earthquake-resistant, concrete and its possibilities for artistic expression had long been one of her interests.[40] The hill itself is in an area known to geologists as the Cambria Slab, chiefly made up of sandstone injected with Franciscan Melanges—areas of mixed rocks, primarily chert, serpentine, basalt, shale, and high-grade metamorphic rocks. The Main Building site provided a remarkably fine grade of aggregate for their concrete, and

Morgan used the area as a quarry and turned the resultant hole into the Main Building's basement foundations, which were built on hard clay.[41]

Morgan selected a construction superintendent, Herbert Washburn, to supervise on site, but traveled herself by train to San Simeon—usually twice a month, sometimes more—to oversee matters firsthand. Labor was scarce, even when the carpenters were offered the generous sum of fifteen dollars a day. Morgan told Hearst, "The San Francisco men sent down on the 'bonus' plan have nearly all come back: one turned back at San Simeon, some got to the top of the hill and did not unpack, and some stayed a week or more. They all agreed that the living conditions, money, and food were all right, but they 'didn't like feeling so far away from things.' Mr. Washburn is picking up 'country' men as fast as he can." The weather made shipping at San Simeon perilous, and the distance up the road with the materials was a daunting impediment. Morgan continued, "With the present fleet of trucks twenty-five tons a day can be hauled if all the trucks work all day on teaming. There were 600 tons in the last shipment which means

A CAST-PLASTER *ceiling corbel in the Hero Room, a lower-story bedroom in House A. This ceiling was patterned on a sixteenth-century original in the Casa de los Tiros ("House of the Heroes") in Granada, Spain.*

presentation drawing of House C shows its twin towers, which were added to the building in 1921. These towers raised the roofline on the Esplanade side and also added to the Moorish look of the building's exterior.

25 days teaming but undoubtedly there will be some rainy days."[42]

Hearst's pattern in the early years of San Simeon's construction was to arrive at the ranch in mid-summer with his family, their imminent appearance occasioning a frenzied rush to complete as many areas as possible. This building flurry also meant a depletion of construction funds.[43] These arrears were seldom made up, since it was while Hearst was in residence at the ranch that he and Morgan came up with their most elaborate future construction plans. Once the foundations of the cottages were under way, Hearst began to focus on both the interiors and the planting schemes. He also began to ship railroad cars full of art objects from New York to San Simeon, and to arrange for objects he had in storage at the hacienda in Pleasanton to be shipped to the ranch and stored in the nineteenth-century warehouse his father George had built on the bay in the town of San Simeon. In determining the style of the interiors, Hearst and Morgan looked to historic precedent once again, but not exclusively to sixteenth-century Spain. They looked as well to the country houses and town villas being built on the East Coast, and in particular to the interior designs of the architect Stanford White.

CHAPTER TWO

Widening Inspirations

William Randolph Hearst had admired the work of architect Stanford White for years. By the time Hearst was thirty-two, in 1895, he had bought his second newspaper, the *New York Journal,* and moved from San Francisco to a New York apartment to preside firsthand over his circulation battle with Joseph Pulitzer's *New York World*. Hearst's residency in New York coincided with the era when the architectural firm of McKim, Mead, and White was at the height of its productivity and influence, and when White in particular was shaping upper-class taste. Hearst was familiar with the Century Association Club, Madison Square Garden, and many of the firm's palatial town and country mansions, often fitted with spectacular interiors by White. But Hearst could only admire from afar. Unmarried and still heavily reliant on periodic doses of money from his mother, Phoebe, Hearst was not in circumstances to hire White to design a home or decorate an interior for him.

White, of course, was more than an architect or a decorator: he was an arbiter of style. Particularly in the country-house designs executed by White and his partners, Charles Follen McKim and William Rutherford Mead, from 1890 to 1906, the dual traditions of grandeur and warm livability display White's taste.[1] He relegated paintings—the focus of most previous American collecting and decorating—to a minor category in his own homes. His son Lawrence Grant White later explained, "The pictures in his collection were all interesting and decorative, but few by painters of great renown, in contrast to the numerous collections which abound in poor examples of the works of great masters."[2] White most preferred the Italian Renaissance period for interiors and often featured an antique ceiling and another element of architecture—often an ornate fire mantel—designing a room around these pieces, though not in a literal sense. Besides architectural elements, White devoted himself to Hispano-Moresque pottery, sumptuous fabrics, and Mediterranean furniture, all tastes William Randolph Hearst would later adopt. White mixed objects with such freedom because he was striving for aesthetic effect over historical accuracy.[3] The result was the kind of dense layering that occurred in historic European houses, influenced by many centuries of collecting.[4] When challenged on whether this sort of European eclecticism was appropriate in America, according to his son, White made a spirited reply: "Once, when reproached for thus despoiling the old world to embellish the new, he defended his actions by saying that in the past dominant nations had always plundered works of art from their predecessors, that America was taking a leading place among nations and

MARRIAGE CHEST. *Spanish, Catalan, late 15th–early 16th century. Walnut, tempera, and water gilding. 27 x 50 x 22 ¼"* *(68.6 x 127 x 56.5 cm). Hearst Monument Collection, Casa Grande Lower South Duplex.*

The interior lid is painted by an unknown artist with a scene of St. Peter meeting Christ on the road to Rome.

had, therefore, the right to obtain art wherever she could."[5] White even worked politically to make acquiring European art easier for Americans, testifying in 1892 before the Ways and Means Committee of the United States House of Representatives that art should enter America from Europe free from customs duties. While this proposal was not successful immediately, by the end of the first decade of the new century customs legislation was decisively in favor of Americans. William Randolph Hearst became a direct beneficiary of these reduced tariff rates.[6]

In 1907, when Hearst was four years married, successful in his newspapers, and a prominent enough citizen to have undertaken two winning political campaigns— for United States congressman from New York—and two losing ones—for governor of New York and mayor of New York City—he moved his family into the Clarendon Apartments on Riverside Drive. By this time he met the proper economic and social criteria to commission a Stanford White design, but it was too late. White had been fatally shot in June 1906 by Harry K. Thaw, the jealous millionaire husband of Evelyn Nesbit, a former paramour of White's. Scandalous accusations of White's immorality grew during the subsequent trials of the murderer (who after the first jury deadlocked was declared not guilty by reason of insanity in his second trial). Many of White's friends were unwilling to defend his memory against the awful details dredged up in court.[7] Sales of White's possessions began, held on location in his New York home at East Twenty-first Street and Lexington Avenue in the spring and fall of 1907.

Thomas Kirby, the chief auctioneer of the American Art Association—the leading New York auction house of the time—presided over the scene, which Hearst attended, along with most other prominent art collectors. Hearst bought many pieces, among them a ceiling panel formerly mounted in White's own drawing room, a composite of a central painting by a follower of the Dutch seventeenth-century artist Joachim Wtewael, titled *Angels Bringing Tidings of Christ's Birth*, which was surrounded by smaller eighteenth-century paintings of the Virtues. This ceiling, with modern extensions, was mounted years later in the Doge's Suite Sitting Room of Casa Grande. Hearst—in a bidding war with John D. Rockefeller, Jr.—also bought the two eighteenth-century Venetian weather vanes that were later placed on Casa Grande's bell towers.[8]

Hearst was still attentive to White's acquisitions and ideas many years later. In 1922, he bought from the art dealers French & Co. the finest single fire mantel in the San Simeon collection, originally from the Château de Jours in Jours-les-Baigneux, France. White had purchased it there for banker Charles T. Barney and mounted it into the New York home he designed for him at 67 Park Avenue.[9] Barney's subsequent suicide had prompted the razing of the house and storing of the mantel. In the spirit of White's taste, this mantel became the centerpiece of the Assembly Room of the main house at San Simeon. Hearst wrote Morgan: "I bought the mantel. It is really a wonderful one, and we have got to arrange to use it. This mantel and the tapestries would make any room. . . . I know you will build a hall to receive it."[10] In December 1919 Hearst had sent

WILLIAM RANDOLPH HEARST seated among his collections, c. 1905. At about this time Hearst had already begun to acquire Greek and Hispano-Moresque pottery, architectural elements, and antiquities, all categories he would purchase in large amounts in his later years.

EDITH WOODMAN BURROUGHS. CIRCE. American, 1907. Bronze. 20 ½ x 8 x 7" (52 x 20.3 x 17.7 cm). Hearst Monument Collection, Casa Grande North Wing Third Floor, Room Three.
The sorceress Circe has just turned Ulysses's sailors into swine and is snapping her fingers in triumph.

Morgan photographs of some White interiors, which served as inspiration for the interiors of both the small houses and the Main Building: "These are, of course, a little over elaborate, but I think we should have a rich gold and polychrome ceiling and rich door frames, mantels, etc. against simple wall surfaces, either imitation caenstone or a solid color material, like a red velvet. I am afraid of material down there, too, lest the rats eat it up; but perhaps with real houses rats would not get in so much."[11]

Hearst even selected a specific White residential design as a model for particular rooms. Stanford White had filled the interiors of the New York home of financier Payne Whitney at 972 Fifth Avenue with a

JOACHIM WTEWAEL (school of). ANNUNCIATION TO THE SHEPHERDS, WITH A SERIES OF SMALLER SURROUNDING PANELS BY AN UNKNOWN ARTIST DEPICTING ALLEGORIES OF THE VIRTUES. Dutch, early 17th-century ceiling painting. Wood, gesso, and tempera. Center panel 6' in diameter (183 cm). Ceiling 22'10" x 22'9" (697.3 x 693.5 cm). Hearst Monument Collection, Casa Grande Doge's Suite Sitting Room.

Art scholar Burton Fredericksen describes this piece as "one of the rare ceiling paintings from the Netherlands done in the early seventeenth century." It was formerly in Stanford White's drawing room in his New York City home on Gramercy Park. When installed in Casa Grande's Doge's Suite in the mid-1920s, the center mounting for a chandelier was covered over, and a modern painted border was devised to enlarge the ceiling to the size of the room.

49

blending of objects he had acquired on a 1905 shopping trip abroad. He juxtaposed sacred pieces with pagan ones and created modern copies in the proper spirit when there were no antique examples.[12] The rooms were completed in 1906, after White's death, and were featured in *Town and Country*. Hearst sent the published photographs to Morgan over a decade later, writing:

> The ceilings I cannot get, so we will have to copy some of these that we get glimpses of in these pictures. One advantage of the scheme in this Payn[e] Whitney picture is the height of the woodwork paneling around the wall. As I have not a great deal of velvet and do not know whether I can get much more, we might use some

A PORTRAIT of Stanford White, c. 1900, when his firm McKim, Mead, and White was designing luxurious country and city residences in the East.

OPPOSITE:
Mantel. *French, 1560. From Château de Jours, Dijon. Stone. 17' x 15' ½" (432 x 407 cm). Hearst Monument Collection, Casa Grande Assembly Room.*
    Stanford White purchased this mantel from the château's owners in the early 1900s and built it into financier Charles T. Barney's New York City home. After Barney's death in 1907, the house was demolished and the mantel was stored until Hearst purchased it from art dealers French & Co. in 1922.

Hearst was too independent to mimic White in all things.

such scheme in my Sitting Room or in the big assembly room of the large house.
    Please be careful of these pictures. I could never get them again; and please let me have them back when you are through with them.[13]

Examining the Sitting Room in House A (which Hearst referred to as "my sitting room") and the Payne Whitney scheme shows clearly that Hearst and Morgan followed the draping of the red velvet, the placement of the fire mantel, the subtleties of the low-relief gilded ceiling, and the general opulence of the room quite closely. The treatment of the Assembly Room in the Main Building, which is decorated much like the Payne Whitney dining room, with choir stalls used as wainscoting and tapestries ranked above, also clearly shows Stanford White's influence.

    Hearst was too developed and independent in his own tastes to mimic White in all things, of course. He did not emulate the baronial and Victorian touches White had used in his two personal New York residences—his town house next to Gramercy Park and his country house on Long Island, known as Box Hill—no bearskin rugs, no rubber plants in profusion. But in the joyful, eclectic assemblage of La Cuesta Encantada's interiors, the spirit of Stanford White is very much alive. In the quantity and variety of his acquisitions, to be sure, Hearst far outstripped White—and every other American collector.

THE SITTING ROOM of the Payne Whitney mansion, 972 Fifth Avenue, New York, decorated in 1906 by Stanford White.

THE HOUSE A Sitting Room was decorated in 1923 to emulate the spirit of the sitting room in the Payne Whitney mansion, designed by White seventeen years earlier.

Contending with the volume of objects Hearst bought—purchased mostly in the auction houses and art galleries of New York City and then sent by train to San Simeon from 1920 on—was a considerable challenge to Julia Morgan. Bewilderment crept into her tone in 1921 when she described the flood of pieces (destined to increase, in fact, in the later years of the twenties) to her friends in Spain, art dealers Arthur Byne and Mildred Stapley Byne:

> Under the circumstances I had probably best tell you a little more of what he is doing here. So far we have received from him, to incorporate in the new buildings, some twelve or thirteen carloads of antiques, brought from the ends of the earth and from prehistoric down to late Empire in period, the majority, however, being of Spanish origin.
>
> They comprise vast quantities of tables, beds, armoires, secretaries, all kinds of cabinets, polychrome church statuary, columns, door frames, carved doors in all stages of repair and disrepair, over-altars, reliquaries, lanterns, iron grille doors, window grilles, votive candlesticks, torcheres, all kinds of chairs in quantity, six or seven well heads (only one of these Spanish), marble and wood columns and door trims, a few good wooden carved ceilings, one very nice gilt and polychrome ceiling hexagonal in shape, one very fine rejere [a wrought iron church grille] about 18' wide and 17' high, a marble sanctuary arch from the entrance to some choir, and pictures—most of these of early type painted on wood, with a few good canvases; a number of Donatellos, lots of Della Robbias. I don't see myself where we are ever going to use half suitably, but I find that the idea is to try things out and if they are not satisfactory, discard them for the next thing that comes that promises better. There is interest and charm coming gradually into play.[14]

Morgan was working with an art collector of infinite appetite. Unlike many American collectors who turned to purchasing art after they had made their fortunes in business pursuits—such as J. P. Morgan, Thomas Fortune Ryan, and Jean Paul Getty—William Randolph

DAVID WILLAUME. WINE CISTERN. *English, 1710. Silver. 17 ¾ x 18 x 17 ¾" (45.1 x 45.7 x 78.7 cm). Hearst Monument Collection, Casa Grande Refectory.*

Wine coolers, or cisterns, held bottles of wine packed in ice. The arms of Edward Hussey, Baron of Beaulieu, were engraved on this example after 1743.

ARMORIAL BANNER. *Spanish, 17th century. Gold, silver, and colored silks. 64 x 53" (162.4 x 134.5 cm). Hearst Monument Collection, Lobby of House A.*

Reposteros such as this example, one of a pair, were square pieces of velvet embroidered with heraldic schemes. They hung in antechambers, as this pair does in House A.

Hearst's passion for art acquisition was lifelong. He had demonstrated his "mania for antiquities," as his mother described it, from his first trip abroad at age ten.[15] This passion, in fact, predated his love of journalism, coming as early in his life as had his love for the ranch at San Simeon. Orson Welles was only one of many to have grasped the fantasy potential in Hearst's love affair with objects, depicting it in *Citizen Kane* by shooting trucks and trains laden with mounds of bulging crates destined for the cavernous rooms of Xanadu. While the stories that surround Hearst's collecting, like most myths, often exaggerate, the plain truth is quite astonishing enough. In the decades while he was building San Simeon, Hearst indulged in an acquisition spree, purchasing far more objects—of wildly varied age, origin, and quality—than even he could ever incorporate within his several enormous homes.

William Randolph Hearst had been raised by his mother, Phoebe, to be both an indefatigable traveler and unstinting purchaser. The first European tour they undertook, in 1873–74, left a permanent imprint. Phoebe's yearnings for culture were strong, surely more so because she had no hope of sharing them with her husband, George, but only with her son, William. She wrote to a friend years later, "Mr. Hearst will never cross the ocean with us. Even if he should, he would disapprove of all that we might enjoy."[16] Phoebe wrote to George from Florence about young Willie: "He is begging me to allow him to take drawing lessons. . . . He is picture crazy. I do not mean to say he has any special talent, and would not wish him to be an artist (unless a *great* one) but he frequently surprises me in his expressions concerning the best pictures." While in Venice, Willie demonstrated his early acquisitiveness, with

INFANT VIRGIN. *Spanish, early 16th century. Limewood, gilt, and polychrome. 33" (83.8 cm). Hearst Monument Collection, Casa Grande Celestial Suite Sitting Room.*
The young Mary stands on clouds and cherubim as she holds a book inscribed with her special prayer, the Magnificat.

WELLHEAD. *Origin and date undocumented, possibly Italian, 16th century. Marble. 40" x 6'5 ½" x 56" (101.6 x 188 x 142.2 cm). Hearst Monument Collection, South Earring Terrace.*
Hearst and Morgan referred to the terraces below Casa Grande as "the well terraces" and displayed wellheads on them. This example was once in the collection of J. P. Morgan.

Phoebe admitting she had difficulty convincing him "there were other places to see and we could not buy *all* we saw. He gets so fascinated, his reason and judgment forsake him. I, too, acknowledge the temptation."[17] This first trip lasted eighteen months, and was followed by another when William was sixteen, in 1879. His adult life was punctuated most years by a trip abroad in the late summer. While these were buying trips in the sense that Hearst would purchase treasures from art dealers and auction galleries, he also genuinely delighted in being in a different culture. As an adult he often traveled with an entourage of less experienced companions, whom he could have the pleasure of introducing to his beloved sights. He loved every aspect of travel, it seems, with the same broad affection that colored his collecting habits.

   By the time Will went to Harvard in 1883, he was already a collector of rare books. While his years at col-lege were more important for his first journalism experi-

ence, as the business editor of the Harvard *Lampoon*, than for any academic achievements, a letter he wrote to Phoebe from Europe in 1889—a few years after he had been dismissed from Harvard for his indifferent acade-mic record and had turned himself instead entirely to the welfare of his ailing *San Francisco Examiner*—shows that he had long been developing a collector's eye and appetite.

Why didn't you buy [Leopoldo] Ansiglioni's "Galatea?" It is superb. . . . I have a great notion to buy it myself, in fact. One thing that prevents me is a scarcity of funds, as it were. The man wants eight thousand dollars for the blooming thing and that is a little over my head.
   I have the art fever terribly. Queer, isn't it? I never thought I would get it this way. I never miss a gallery now and I go and mosey about the pictures and statuary and admire them and wish they were mine. My artistic long-ings are not altogether distinct from avarice, I am afraid.

Hearst then gave his mother advice he never followed himself:

> If, instead of buying a half a dozen fairly nice things, you would wait and buy one fine thing, all would be well.
>
> As it is at present we have things scattered from New York to Washington . . . to San Francisco, more than a house could hold and yet not among them a half a dozen things that are really superb. . . .
>
> I am not going to buy any more trinkets. . . . Then when advanced in years I will not have had all that I wanted but I will want all that I have—which is better. Go thou and do likewise, Mama dear.[18]

But a life of self-restrained collecting, focused on only the finest items, was far too restrictive for Hearst, no matter how much he recommended it in his youth. In his impetuous acquisitions and his refusal to be guided by art dealers—whose influence on other American col-

lectors was huge—Hearst was similar to eighteenth-century English collectors such as Horace Walpole and William Beckford, who acquired vast quantities of wonders that reflected their personal tastes rather than the more conventional tastes of many other collectors.

The place to buy European art after World War I was America, especially following the adoption of the Payne-Aldrich Tariff in 1909, which created a favorable rate on art brought from Europe to America. Objects more than a century old and considered works of art were admitted free of duty. The immediate impact of this ruling was muted, due to World War I, but after 1918 the market in European objects—particularly from Mediterranean countries—exploded. This phenomenon coincided with changes in Hearst's fortunes and circumstances. While Hearst had been a serious buyer of books, textiles, Greek vases, and Hispano-Moresque pottery since the start of the century, he did not become a major art purchaser until after Phoebe's death in 1919. Then he had ready cash, and San Simeon to fill.

The myth persists that Hearst had acquired all of La Cuesta Encantada's contents before construction began, but in fact less than five percent of the estate's art collection was purchased prior to 1919: this small quantity consisting mainly of Phoebe's pieces that Hearst inherited, the items associated with Stanford White, a few dozen antiquities, and a smattering of architectural elements and furniture, categories of objects Hearst bought voraciously in later years. While it is inaccurate to say that Hearst stockpiled most of San Simeon's pieces for years before he built the house, it is true that Hearst and Morgan had the major items in many of the rooms determined before those rooms were constructed. Hearst's purchases were documented in photo books,

which Morgan consulted for the dimensions of specific pieces. However, the metaphor of the house as a giant jigsaw puzzle oversimplifies the case. Objects—ceilings, fireplaces, choir stalls—were very frequently altered to fit the dimensions available in the room. But rooms were also planned with specific pieces in mind, in a complicated dance of accommodation for both spaces

LEOPOLDO ANSIGLIONI. GALATEA ON A DOLPHIN. Italian, 1883. Marble and bronze. 72 x 54 x 39" (182.88 x 137.2 x 99 cm). Hearst Monument Collection, Central Plaza in front of Casa Grande.

Phoebe Hearst was a benefactor to Ansiglioni, who created three versions of this statue. William Randolph Hearst coveted it from the age of twenty-six, as he wrote to his mother. Hearst did eventually own one, which he initially considered placing in front of House A before he decided to give it a more prominent setting on the Central Plaza, facing the Main Building.

and objects.[19] Years later, Walter Steilberg reflected on Morgan's design difficulties: "Miss Morgan had to deal, not only with the visible client across the table from her, but also with these other clients who were peddling antiques to Mr. Hearst from all over the world, and her constant problem was to incorporate these things."[20]

One of San Simeon's distinctions is that there was no decorator employed to determine the locations of the pieces. In this way, La Cuesta Encantada is very different from the lavish Vizcaya, built a few years earlier, where owner James Deering served as a patron to the gifted decorator Paul Chalfin. It too was filled with a variety of antique decorative arts and architectural elements, but the pieces were placed according to Vizcaya's theme, conceived by Chalfin and Deering: a Renaissance villa occupied for centuries by one family, its rooms reflecting a long succession of stylistic changes, resulting in the Cathay room, the Espagnolette room, etc.[21] In Vizcaya's case, the decorator was the visionary—and also the spendthrift. Deering as the patron deferred to Chalfin's decisions, though he was sometimes sulky at supplying the necessary funds.[22] While Vizcaya is an extreme case of a client relying on a decorator, such a collaboration was expected in a sizable country-house project, making San Simeon's lack of one all the more notable. Steilberg recalled that Morgan "had a horror of interior decorators coming in and spoiling a house."[23] Instead, she would usually place the furniture herself, subject to Hearst's approval, relying on pieces illustrated in the photo books, after having determined with Hearst the placement of the large elements—particularly the architectural pieces such as ceilings, mantels, and window surrounds. "The furniture is going into the Doge's Suite as best we can think," she wrote to Hearst in May 1926, "so that it will be ready for you to suggest on."[24]

Hearst concurred with Stanford White's belief that America in the early years of the twentieth century was ready to assimilate the wealth of the old world and integrate it with the technology of the new. He was helped in this task by the most influential resources of the time, magazines such as *Country Life, Country Life in America, Architectural Record, Connoisseur,* and *Town*

Tiffany & Co. Table Lamp. Vase: 1889; conversion to lamp: 1891. Sterling silver, enamel. Vase: 23 x 12 ½" diameter at base (31.75 x 43.18 cm); lamp 42 x 21" diameter at shade (106.2 x 53.3 cm). Hearst Monument Collection, Casa Grande Assembly Room.

An oil-burning lamp that was never converted to electricity, this was a favorite piece of William Randolph Hearst's. It had been displayed in Phoebe and George Hearst's Washington, D.C., home.

and Country. Hearst read all these periodicals avidly, acquiring *Town and Country* in 1925 and *Connoisseur* in 1927 and adding them to his roster of magazine properties, which included *Good Housekeeping, Motor,* and *Harper's Bazaar,* among others. Throughout the 1920s and 1930s, Hearst barraged Morgan with clippings about model farms, hallway designs, gardening techniques, tennis courts, swimming pools, landscape ornament, and the proper way to lead an outdoor life, all culled from these magazines. They were the procedural manuals that translated the centuries-old traditions of English country-house life to eager American audiences, William Randolph Hearst included.[25]

European art and architecture had also shaped Julia Morgan's life. Though in her youth she had shown an interest in medicine, the influence of her cousin, prominent East Coast architect Pierre LeBrun, seems to have pointed her to architecture.[26] Morgan earned her civil engineering degree at the University of California at Berkeley in 1894, becoming one of the first women to complete the program, before the university had an architecture department.[27] In her senior year, Bernard Maybeck, a pivotal figure throughout Morgan's entire architectural career, joined the faculty. The influential architect was responsible for convincing Phoebe Apperson Hearst to institute a worldwide architectural competition for the campus design in 1899, but, most importantly for the San Simeon story, Maybeck encouraged the talented Julia Morgan to attend the prestigious Ecole des Beaux-Arts in Paris. The Ecole, estab-

lished in 1671, was the inevitable destination for many American architects studying Academic Classicism, starting with Richard Morris Hunt in 1846. Its influence was so pervasive that an entire style of American public architecture—relying on formality, symmetry, and grandly scaled effects—was called the Beaux-Arts style.[28] Maybeck, also a former student there, had learned through his European connections that the Ecole might be ready to accept women. Morgan left for Paris in 1896 and secured a place in the atelier of a friend of Maybeck's, Marcel Pérouse de Monclos.[29]

This was the usual step toward admission, the aspirant finding an architect's studio in which to work (and, in the case of many Americans, to become proficient in French) and beginning to prepare for the semi-annual entrance exams. The restriction affecting everyone's admission—whatever nationality—was that students could remain at the Ecole only until they reached the age of thirty.[30] It was common to fail the difficult entrance examinations initially, since only the top few dozen students were accepted. Hunt, as well as many other prominent American architects, failed on the first attempt: so did Morgan, at the examination in October 1897, though her performance was quite creditable, placing her forty-second among 376 aspirants. She failed

ABOVE LEFT:
WILLIAM RANDOLPH HEARST *around the time of his second tour of Europe with his mother, Phoebe, in 1879. He had an eye for art but also for mischief. His pranks devised with his boyhood friend and traveling companion Eugene Lent were uproarious enough to require Phoebe to change hotels more than once during the trip.*

ABOVE:
WILLIAM RANDOLPH HEARST *and his son John at the Alhambra in Granada, Spain, in 1934. A perpetually delighted tourist into his later years, Hearst preferred to travel with an entourage of his sons, their wives, and many other companions, surely in part so he could have the pleasure of acting the tour guide to a large audience.*

LEFT:
JULIA MORGAN *at Notre Dame, Paris, c. 1897.*

LUC OLIVIER MERSON. REST ON THE FLIGHT INTO EGYPT. French, 1879. Oil on canvas. 25 x 44 ½" (63.5 x 113.1 cm). Hearst Monument Collection, Casa Grande Celestial Suite Sitting Room. Purchased by Hearst in 1894 when he was thirty, this Orientalist painting was his earliest acquisition in the San Simeon collection.

JEAN LÉON GÉRÔME. BONAPARTE BEFORE THE SPHINX. French, c. 1867–68. Oil on canvas. 24 ¼ x 40 ½" (61.6 x 103 cm). Hearst Monument Collection, Casa Grande Celestial Suite Sitting Room. Hearst began to collect Napoleon-related pieces in the 1890s. He bought this painting in 1913. Here, Bonaparte contemplates the Sphinx while he himself is watched by his own officers, whose shadows are visible in the left foreground.

again in April 1898, and this time Monclos attributed it to prejudice among the judges, who did not want to see a young girl succeed.[31] Morgan changed ateliers at about this time, joining Benjamin Chaussemiche—a former Grand Prix award winner, the highest honor conferred by the Ecole—who became her lifelong friend. On her third try, in the fall of 1898, Morgan succeeded. She wrote to her cousin Pierre LeBrun and his wife, Lucy, with characteristic self-deprecation:

> I was working for the examinations at the Ecole again, and pretty hard. . . . When the architecture turned out well, I thought I'd wait and write you the final result, but in the oral examinations you have to wait your turn, and as [I] was the last of 392, it has kept stringing out

as to time. . . . The Judgment was given today only, and [I] am the 13th—ten French and two foreigners—they take forty in all. It's not much but has taken quite a little effort. If it had been simply for the advantages of the Ecole, I would not have kept on after M. Chaussemiche was arranged with, but a mixture of dislike of giving up some thing attempted and the sense of its being a sort of test in [a] small way, of work itself overcoming its natural disadvantages—made it seem a thing that really had to be won.[32]

Once accepted, students began in the second class and worked their way up to the first class by accumulating points granted through submitting the mandatory competition projects. Morgan advanced to the first class in the fall of 1900, when she was twenty-eight. The assignments there alternated between the submission of an *esquisse*—or sketch—typically for a portion of a building, done in the allotted time of nine hours; and a *projet rendu*—a rendered project—generally for a large public building, which consisted of several drawings, done in the allotted time of two months.[33] Morgan earned enough medals and honorable mentions to qualify for her certificate from the Ecole in 1902, at the time of her thirtieth birthday. She was the first woman ever to do so.[34]

She acquired at the Ecole a methodology that remained with her throughout her career: she learned to design by manipulating volumes geometrically and by arranging her plans axially.[35] The program at the Ecole was based on the sketch and on the concept of cutting a building apart along its cardinal axes to understand its inner structure.[36] There was no room for sloppy thinking at the Ecole, and no room in Morgan's later architectural practice, either. Walter Steilberg recalled her impatience years later with a draftsman in her office who excelled at freehand drawing. She had given him a plan to work from, and he drew a staircase that could only be ascended on one's hands and knees. Morgan's response: "Well, young man, I can't deal with fiction writers." Steilberg remembered her saying that a lot of bad architecture comes from people who get themselves in a jam and then twist themselves around to get out of it. "She felt you ought to face facts from the beginning."[37] He described her strongest design philosophy as working from the inside out.[38]

Dorothy Wormser Coblentz worked in Morgan's office from 1918 to 1922 and described it as an atelier much like the ones Morgan had belonged to in Paris. The design philosophy was the same: think the project out at the start and finish everything as you go along.[39] "She had a little desk in the drafting room, a little work table with a high back on which she had a few books; so when she was there she had a little privacy. . . . There she would sit and concentrate and produce these funny little drawings

This was a chance to assimilate many different motifs and

historic elements into an original result on the grandest of scales.

61

in which the whole story was foreshadowed, but it was just a little sketch with perhaps a little color on it."[40]

Careful study of the design philosophy of Charles Adams Platt further reinforced her Beaux-Arts training.[41] A landscape painter and etcher, Platt studied art in Paris from 1882 to 1887. Though he failed the architectural entrance examination at the Ecole des Beaux-Arts, his painter's eye worked to his creative advantage.[42] Platt's travels to Italy in 1892 resulted in *Italian Gardens* in 1894, a book of photographs and sketches of Renaissance gardens. The first landscape book of its kind, it greatly influenced American architects and landscape designers.

Platt learned the importance of axial symmetry not by following the rigorous design course at the Ecole, but by studying the layout of gardens in Italian villas, many of them abandoned and decaying at the close of the nineteenth century.[43] He also understood the interrelation-

PORTRAIT OF author, artist, and architect Charles Adams Platt, c. 1900. Morgan greatly admired his country-house designs, known for their integration of building and landscape.

SUNLIGHT hits a cast-stone garden balustrade on the lower terrace of House A. Such railings are similar to those illustrated in Charles Adams Platt's influential 1894 book, Italian Gardens.

ship between these houses and their gardens, and sought to emulate that spirit in his own designs. By the 1920s, Platt had become the most influential country-house designer of his time, a master of subtle eclecticism and creative restraint, both qualities that naturally appealed to Julia Morgan. In a Platt design, each part of the garden had a specific relationship to a part of the building, creating a series of outdoor rooms for living. He fused elements of the picturesque tradition—the

random, charming, compact schemes favored by the English—with the classical principles and formal ordering favored by the Italians, managing in this mix of two historic strains to heighten the appeal of both.[44] Platt said: "An artist should not consciously attempt to do something original. . . . He uses all the knowledge that he has been able to obtain through education and observation and practice. If he applies all this knowledge in solving his problem the individual elements of the problem itself will help to make the result original. His own individuality will do the rest."[45]

Morgan carried on Platt's tradition in her designs for the gardens at San Simeon, which similarly blend the informal aspect of English cottage gardens—a profusion of colorful flowers arranged in beds—with the formal Italian technique of careful terracing that showcases an ever-widening series of views. Though the cottages were sited first, and they and the Main Building were oriented primarily to the views, and though virtually every terrace was expanded at least once during construction, the hilltop scheme still adheres to an axial plan Morgan established in the early years. The Main Building is at the crest of the hill, facing almost due west, with a large terrace directly in front of it. Though the small houses are arranged loosely—rather than symmetrically—at a level below the front facade, this central terrace has a strong north–south axis, as well as an east–west one, both of which are emphasized by the siting of the Esplanade walk directly below. The layout is a triumph, perhaps the finest design work Morgan ever did at San Simeon: the houses retain their informal relationship to the Main Building, but the terraces and walkways give coherence to the whole. Maybeck, who remained a friend and occasional collaborator of Morgan's, visited

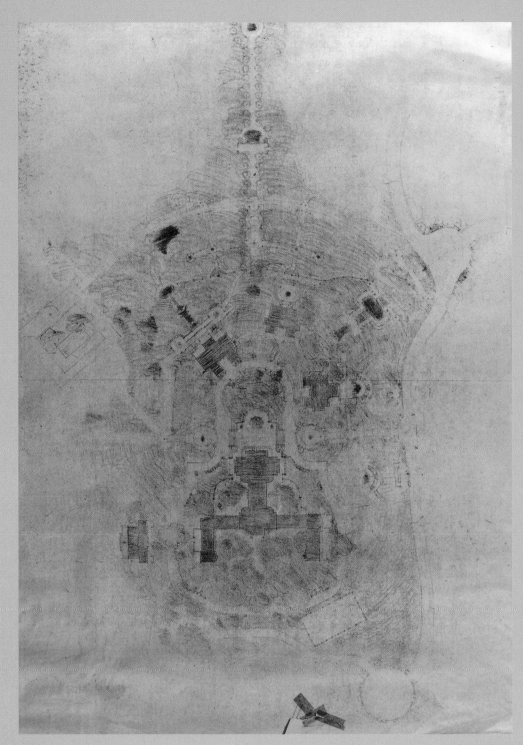

MORGAN'S HILLTOP plot plan, c. 1927, shows her interest in designing the grounds and houses along axial lines. These strong east–west and north–south axes meet at the Central Plaza, the circular terrace between the Main Building and the three cottages.

San Simeon on occasion. He admired its layout, bringing potential clients of his own to see the hilltop in the mid-1920s to demonstrate how effectively buildings could be sited on uneven ground.[46]

In her designs for San Simeon, Julia Morgan had a splendid opportunity to use her formal Ecole des Beaux-Arts training, refined after years of private practice. This was a unique chance to assimilate many different motifs and historic elements and come up with an original result on the grandest of scales. Her greatest challenge, however, came in working with William Randolph Hearst, a client who could never adhere to an architectural plan, even after he had agreed to it.

CHAPTER THREE

The Buildings Take

A severe storm shut down all of San Luis Obispo County at the close of 1921. Even Julia Morgan, never one to magnify a difficulty, wrote to Hearst in New York: "If you would like to break every bone in your worst enemy's body treat him to the trip from Cayucos to Cambria," two small towns between the San Luis Obispo railroad station and San Simeon.[1] The hilltop itself became so inaccessible that Hearst and Morgan determined to build only between April and December in the future, retaining just a skeleton crew of maintenance people, gardeners, painters, and plasterers to work during the rainy season.[2]

Hearst had hoped to be back at his San Simeon ranch by the end of January 1922, but the miserable conditions prompted him to postpone his plans.[3] He was eager to return because of his discontent with the slow pace of construction. Blind to his own role in slowing down the progress by making constant changes, Hearst simply felt that the superintendent, Herbert Washburn, was not getting enough work from the building crew. The three houses were not finished, and House A, Hearst's intended residence, was the least complete of them all. Since none of these structures had a dining area in any case, and the workmen were still far from ready to start the Main Building, Hearst proposed a new idea: constructing a self-contained English stone house to the north of the Casa Grande site. As for its architectural incongruity with the other buildings, Hearst concluded: "The Elizabethan stone English house, being English renaissance, would not be so violently different from the Spanish renaissance houses."[4] For the next few months, the English house idea appeared frequently in Hearst's correspondence, and the more he and Morgan

Shape

wrote about it, the larger the house grew. By April the plan called for a two-story house with a banqueting hall fifty feet long downstairs and six bedrooms above, built of concrete and covered with a stone facade, the decorative ornaments for which were to be supplied by two English stone houses Hearst bought for the purpose.[5] This English house was never constructed. It grew rapidly on paper from a temporary measure to a grandiose building that exceeded its site allotment, an endeavor complicated enough to rival that of the Main Building. By late April, Hearst decided to postpone the English house indefinitely in favor of commencing work on Casa Grande.[6]

As a planning exercise, the English house greatly influenced the main house. While the small houses had modern concrete construction and cast-stone exterior ornament, the Main Building was instead built the way they had planned to build the English house: of reinforced concrete with a stone facade, ornamented with some modern but also with many antique elements, and the ornament not merely clustered around the main entrance door, as previously planned, but integrated throughout the exterior.[7] Morgan also got another pointed reminder of Hearst's compulsive habit of enlarging structures in working with him on the English house. It may have been this experience, combined with the

difficulties engendered by his expansion of the little houses while they were under construction, that prompted her to move the planned location of the Main Building further east on the hill, allowing more room for future changes.[8]

When Hearst arrived at San Simeon late in April 1922, he insisted on beginning the main house immediately. Morgan had no time to prepare the structural drawings, and, since they were about to lay off Mr. Washburn, there would soon be no construction superintendent.[9] Furthermore, the small houses remained unfinished. The advantage in Hearst's mind was that he was on the hill, where he could act as the superintendent and get things moving. Ironically, he spent just one week at San Simeon—the only time he visited through all of 1922—but when he returned to New York he must have been satisfied that he had gotten the ball rolling on the project he had waited years to commence.

As Morgan readied the structural plans and looked for a construction superintendent—since the one brought in as Washburn's immediate successor left the hill within a few months—the excavation of the Main Building site began, using small charges of dynamite.[10] Many changes had occurred in the scheme since Morgan and Hearst began discussing it in the fall of 1919, all of which increased the size of the house. Though the proportions remained close to those of her original studies, every drawing had to be completely redone.[11] For instance, Hearst wanted the Assembly Room to be lengthened

65

from seventy-five feet to eighty-five feet, in order to provide sufficient wall area for a set of four large Renaissance tapestries to hang without using the space directly over the doors to the Refectory, a rare instance of the plan being altered to accommodate specific objects.[12]

All the rooms were increased in size, but the floor plan remained the same as it had been in Morgan's 1919 sketches. The ground floor of the main house consisted initially of three major rooms and two vestibules. The Assembly Room—given the same name as the social room of the many YWCAs Julia Morgan built in her career—is approached from the west by walking across a large terrace and through a west-facing vestibule that extends only half the length of the Assembly Room itself. These two spaces run north to south, parallel to the Pacific Ocean. Directly behind the Assembly Room, and

Many changes had occurred, all of which increased the size

HEARST FREQUENTLY WROTE comments on Morgan's drawings, as in this example, when he proposed lengthening the Main Building's front facade, as yet unbuilt: "I think there should be ten feet more width between the towers for the central gabled building. I think this will help rather than hurt the front elevation and it will be much better inside for the big assembly room giving that 85 ft length, and clearing the tapestries from above the doors into the refectory."

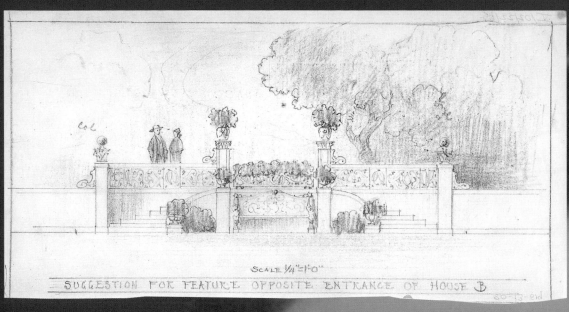

of the house. Every drawing had to be completely redone.

closed off from view by sets of double doors flanking the fireplace, is the Refectory, the name Hearst and Morgan gave the hilltop's sole dining room. It is seventy feet long but only twenty-eight feet wide, with a west–east axis, perpendicular to the Assembly Room. Behind the Refectory is a sitting room, which in the plans they alternately referred to as the "Breakfast Room," "Trophy Room," or "East Room" in the earliest years, but which they later settled into calling the Morning Room. This last, smaller sitting room runs north to south again, parallel to the Assembly Room, and at only forty-five feet long, it is slightly more than half its length. There are small bathrooms at the north and south ends of the Morning Room. This sitting room is also supplied with a small eastern vestibule of twenty-two feet, half the length of the Morning Room. Hearst and Morgan also planned from early on to have ancillary wings connected at the east end of the house: a kitchen area on the south side, which was poured in 1924 to a one-story height, and topped in 1927 with three floors of servants' bedrooms; and a pergola structure on the north side, in the area that later became the Billiard Room and Theater wing in 1929, occupying the space intended earlier for the English house.[13]

These initial plans for the public areas on the ground floor of the main house, therefore, called essentially for an interconnecting three-room structure built on a modified T-plan with no hallways, the whole one-room wide, the rooms approached serially.[14] The main reason for this somewhat unusual T-plan was likely the presence of two large oak trees just behind the site of the Assembly Room. One still survives today. Before they began to move oak trees in the mid-1920s, Morgan sited the hilltop structures around the trees. This particular accommodation engendered some surprising features in the Main Building, including the absence of obvious staircases to connect the lower and upper floors. From the earliest drawings, it is apparent that Hearst and Morgan planned only for "stair towers" as they called them: four spiral staircases at the four corners of the rectangular Refectory, which lead to the second story of the house. These stairs are practically exterior features. The western pair is approached through doors to the north and south of the doors leading from the Assembly Room to the Refectory; the eastern pair is approached from tiny enclosed porches between the Refectory and the Morning Room, located to the sides and out of view of both rooms. Staircases, so often the focal point of country-house interiors as well as a compass point to orient unfamiliar visitors with the location of the upper levels, are here practically invisible. In fact, they are more evident from the geometric projections they make on the exterior of the building than they are discernible from any rooms within the interior of the house.

There is a precedent for this general plan in an earlier house of Hearst's: the Hacienda del Pozo de Verona, his initial attempt in 1894 to build a country house in California, was also built at a depth of only one room. It featured a traditional Spanish courtyard scheme, however, with wings surrounding an open square, each room having a separate entrance from the court. The primary advantages of such a design were threefold: excellent cross-ventilation, access to views from every room, and a feeling of great privacy for the guests.[15]

Though Casa Grande's initial design lacked a central courtyard, it shared the identical advantages. The main house had excellent cross-ventilation; in fact, the greater challenge was to keep it warm, not cool, and at various times Hearst requested that some of the windows on the lower floor be sealed because of the problem of drafts.[16] The view from the ground floor was not as high a priority as was preserving the wall space to display objects in the large rooms, but the fenestration was still generous in the Refectory and in both vestibules. In the west vestibule, a large glass window is emphasized by a sixteenth-century Spanish Renaissance iron grille that allows light into the room while opening it up to the view. In the Assembly Room, two large, low windows face the south and north views of the ocean and mountains, respectively. In the Refectory, the long walls are lined with matching rows of seven clerestory windows crowned by Gothic tracery. Though the Morning Room contains no windows, the circumstance goes unnoticed because the adjoining east vestibule is made entirely of windows with more Spanish Renaissance grillework.

The small, unobtrusive spiral staircases of Casa Grande provided Hearst and his guests the privacy of separate entrances. There is a great sense of distance and mystery between the floors, since it is difficult to guess how to ascend to the upper levels of the building, or even to know for certain that upper levels exist, unless one divines it from the indication of multiple floors on the massive exterior facade.[17] Part of this sense of isolation results from the differing ceiling heights in every room on the ground floor, requiring multiple levels above. But part of it stems from the same effect of vertical isolation that was fostered in the three small houses. Except for a small and narrow staircase leading from House A's main level to the lower floor—a staircase Hearst was uncertain about, and debated not including at all in the floor plan—one reaches the additional cottage levels by going outside and taking separate entrances. Guests could therefore occupy their rooms without a feeling of intrusion. The same was true of Casa Grande.

The second floor of the Main Building—planned from the beginning—contains the Library, located above the twenty-four-foot-high Assembly Room and

GIULIO ROMANO (after designs by). THE CONTINENCE OF SCIPIO. Brussels, c. 1550. Tapestry warp: undyed wool; weft: dyed wool and silk. 15' ⅛" x 21' ⅞" (461 x 647 cm). Hearst Monument Collection, Casa Grande Assembly Room.

This is one of four tapestries in the Assembly Room from the small Scipio set, originally comprising ten pieces and woven for the d'Albon family. Here, after his victory over Carthage in the Second Punic War, Scipio returns a captive woman to her betrothed and presents her ransom as a wedding gift.

OVERLEAF: CASA GRANDE'S Assembly Room, the great hall of the house, where guests gathered at all hours, but particularly for cocktails before dinner. Its decorations primarily date from the Renaissance, including choir stalls, tapestries, and a fire mantel.

extending the full length of the main facade, fronted by a wide balcony. A small lobby entrance east of the room increases its width to match that of the Assembly Room below. Above the twenty-seven-foot-high Refectory is a row of four guest rooms called the Cloisters, running the length of the Refectory and provided with doors on both the north and south corridors, which were initially built as open-air walkways (though the south side was later fitted with removable storm windows due to the severity of the winter rains). When the Cloisters were

originally built in 1923, the four rooms were divided into eight symmetrical rooms—each with its own bath—separated by walls running down the center of their seventeen-foot width, which made them cloisterlike, indeed.

Another guest suite, on the mezzanine level of the Main Building, was also planned from the beginning of construction. At the east end of the house, above the fifteen-foot-high Morning Room, what was first called the Royal Suite comprises two bedrooms and bathrooms

CASA GRANDE'S MORNING ROOM *is a sitting room at the east end of the house that was used by guests both early in the day and late in the evening. Its entrance arch is of thirteenth-century red Pyrenees marble from Spain. The seventeenth-century tapestry beside it is one of four in the room, this example depicting haymaking, a labor for the month of July.*

flanking a central sitting room, a plan echoing the arrangement of the guest houses. After the installation of a fifteenth-century Venetian balcony off the sitting room in 1925, they called this area the Doge's Suite.

These upstairs rooms were initially all there was to the main house, in addition to the bell towers. While they were pouring the building, however, Hearst and Morgan decided to add a third-story suite of two bedrooms, two bathrooms, and a central living room in the west part of the house, above the Library. First named the Imperial Suite, this space soon became known as the Gothic Suite.[18] Nothing was built above the

Cloisters at this time. By mid-1924, Casa Grande had twelve bedrooms, three large sitting rooms (counting the Library), and the two smaller sitting rooms that adjoined the bedroom suites. Each of these spaces had a spectacular view of mountains or ocean, and large windows or balconies from which to admire the vista from the upper stories.[19]

Morgan kept Hearst apprised of all construction developments after his rapid departure in 1922, writing him in July: "The hole is growing and boxing [for the form work] should begin by the end of the month."[20] Their progress was greatly aided when she sent down

MORGAN'S DRAWING of the
Assembly Room before its construction,
showing the French fireplace, Scipio
tapestries, and Italian choir stalls on the
eastern wall. Generally, Hearst selected
the major pieces for a room, which
Morgan then worked into the design
scheme, relying on photographs and
measurements of the objects. But rooms
were almost never built "around" the
dimensions of specific items; instead,
the pieces themselves were usually modified to fit into the available spaces.

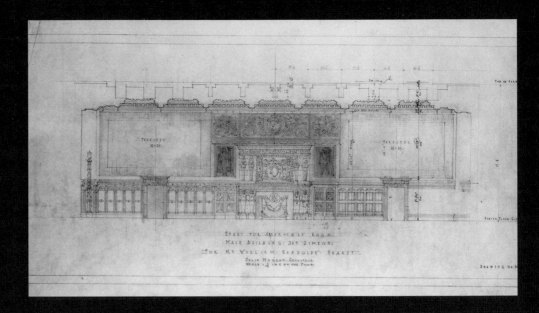

MORGAN'S DRAWING of the
Morning Room prior to its completion
shows the Flemish tapestries in place,
flanking the Spanish Gothic marble
archway.

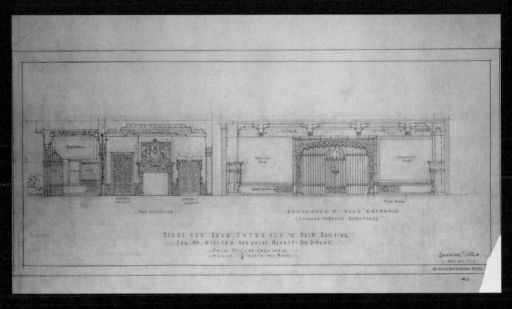

CASA GRANDE'S main floor plan, in
its earliest construction phase, before the
later additions of the North and South
Wings. A modified T-plan, the ground
floor has no central hallway or grand
staircase and is only one room wide.

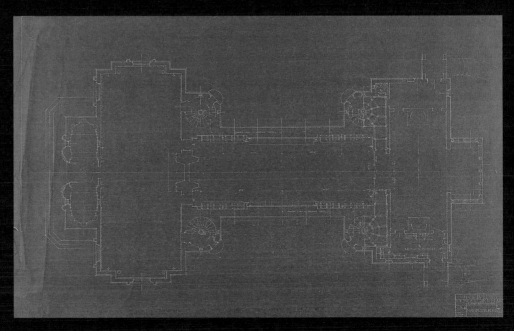

Camille Rossi, an engineer from her office in San Francisco, who served as San Simeon's construction superintendent for the next ten years. Morgan praised Rossi's leadership qualities when first describing him to Hearst; though his decisiveness—demonstrated during the first half of his tenure—turned into a troubling egomania over the second half, which may have caused her to regret her decision later. They had three thousand cubic feet of concrete to pour, at the rate of fifty yards a day, and by late August they were beginning the basement, which, divided into several vaults, encompassed the entire floor space. Morgan reported: "Mr. Rossi had the ingenuity to move the mixer along the top of the [basement] walls and fill the forms directly from the mixer without the use of barrows or chutes. . . . It is saving much time."[21] They poured straight through the summer, even though Mrs. Hearst (and presumably the five Hearst sons) came to visit while Hearst remained in New York. In fact, the weather stayed so favorable that they poured concrete nearly until Christmas, Hearst advising: "Let's make concrete while the sun shines."[22]

After a break for the winter weather, they recommenced, reaching the second-story walls by mid-May of 1923.[23] That year, Hearst and his family returned to San Simeon for the summer, arriving in June and staying through mid-August. The little houses were still not completely finished—due mostly to changes he had requested, including dividing the pair of bathrooms on the main floors of House C and House B into four, to allow each bedroom to have a private bath; decorating the lower levels of Houses C and A for guests' use; and remodeling the tower additions for House C, first constructed in 1921, to raise its roofline, then remodeled to provide two more sets of bedrooms and bathrooms for guests, with access provided by staircases placed in two of the four closets.[24] House A was finally far enough along that it appears Hearst and Millicent were able to occupy it for the first time.[25] The concrete pouring on

CASA GRANDE'S REFECTORY—the term for a dining room in a monastery—is where all the meals were served. Hearst and Morgan always referred to it by this name. Its fourteenth-century Spanish choir stalls and gilt iron church grille reinforce the ecclesiastical atmosphere—as do the silk Palio flags used for sacred festivals in Siena.

THE SITTING ROOM *of House A echoes the Renaissance opulence of the Sitting Room in House B. Hearst wanted these two houses to have similar decorations of "putti and garlands," while House C employed the Moorish decoration of southern Spain.*

the Main Building continued through the year, with Rossi and the crew—the total for the camp often numbering ninety men—ready to finish the bell towers and apply the roof tiles by late March 1924.[26]

In the nearly two years it took to pour the Main Building in its earliest form, Hearst and Morgan decided on many of San Simeon's most important features. The most pressing matter, after the interior plan, was determining the exterior facade decoration. While they adhered to their earlier decision to emulate the Ronda Cathedral tower and the Seville doorway on the west

facade, there were so many other details to address that Morgan sent Thaddeus Joy, her chief architectural draftsman and frequent representative on the San Simeon project, to New York in the spring of 1923 to meet with Hearst directly. Gaining access to Hearst was not easy, and the gloomy tone in Joy's letters to Morgan surely stemmed in part from his weariness at sitting around waiting for an audience. It might also have been prompted by Joy's disagreement with Hearst's taste on certain matters. Joy wrote to Morgan: "Main cornice brackets, soffits and frieze to be of wood. Mr. Hearst has carefully considered color effect and is confident that he will like it. . . . Mr. Hearst thinks the facades are much overloaded with ornament & that a liberal use of an eraser is of primary importance. There are too many shields."[27]

The wood cornice Joy referred to—and seemed unenthusiastic about himself—is the most striking aspect of Casa Grande's facade, after the towers. Made up of a gabled front on the west and east facades and two flat cornices along the south and north sides, it runs almost entirely around the third story and was carved in 1922–23 by craftsman Jules Suppo in his San Francisco workshop. The inspiration for the piece was a sixteenth-century northern Spanish "queer animal bracket cornice," as Morgan described it—the original entirely level, not gabled—which Hearst saw published in a Spanish art periodical.[28] She sought photographs of the piece from the Bynes, the Americans who had settled in Spain and become art experts and art dealers at the same time: "This all at the request of Mr. Hearst, who has taken a great liking to these brackets and wants them copied for a house we are building in California, on top of a mountain—many a mile from civilization."[29] Hearst and Morgan may have been influenced in their decision to modify a straight cornice into a gabled one by the ornament on the Mission Santa Barbara, which Hearst admired. Its classical cornice set between two square towers is based on an ancient drawing by

AN EARLY FRONT ELEVATION of Casa Grande. Without the wings and tower expansions, the house presents a compressed, abridged appearance.

Vitruvius.[30] Teak was rare enough for Morgan to write urgently to Hearst: "Have found on this coast at very good bargain enough teak for frieze and soffit panels, pendants and mouldings of main cornice." She continued the next day, "It is very fine stock, really beautiful material and has been in a warehouse for two years, having been brought over for the finish of a ship and not used."[31] Full-size plaster models were made first to provide a guide for the carvers to follow; the animals were fanciful, often original compositions, rather than exact copies of the antique cornice.[32] And though Thaddeus Joy may have feared that its dark color would clash when placed against the plain white surfaces of Casa Grande, the juxtaposition of wood against stone is remarkably successful, emphasizing the eclectic, creative nature of the house as a whole.

Hearst was provided with construction photographs whenever he was not at San Simeon, as well as with a series of plaster models of the estate, which were shipped to him directly in the early years and photographed when they grew too large to send. Seeing the shell of Casa Grande rise up from the crest of the hill is surely what prompted him to begin addressing the matters of planting and terraces in the early 1920s. While Hearst and Morgan had previously concentrated on landscaping the relatively small space around the three houses, in 1922 they began to discuss the creation of major landscape features that remain prominent at San

IN ADDITION to fifty-four thousand square feet above ground, Casa Grande has a fourteen-thousand-square-foot basement, which is divided into vaults used to store art objects, a seven-thousand-bottle wine cellar, and an unfinished bowling alley.

TOP: AN ALERO, or wood cornice, in Navarre, Spain, which was published in Arte y Decoración en España, gave Hearst the idea for Casa Grande's wood cornice.

ABOVE: CASA GRANDE'S first towers survived only a few years before they were heightened to account for the building's increases in scale.

RIGHT: CHOOSING A POINTED gable for the Main Building's cornice, when the historic precedent had been level, may have been an attempt to echo the pedimented front of the Mission Santa Barbara, which Hearst admired.

Simeon today. The small drive directly in front of the three little houses, first intended for automobiles, instead became a promenade, after Hearst wrote to Morgan: "Mrs. Hearst says that the driving of automobiles around the terrace road is going to spoil the big inner court as a living court. It is not merely going to be unpleasant to have the automobiles run around this paved road, but it will be additionally unpleasant to have the grease and dirt stains which automobiles leave. This she thinks will soon make the road dirty and disagreeable. I believe she is exactly right."[33] By the summer of 1923 they called this path the Esplanade, extending it around the hilltop to link the small houses to one another and also to the Main Building.

A wide, meandering path that bulged outward to accommodate the contours of the hilltop and the growing size of Casa Grande, the Esplanade was inspired by picturesque garden traditions, rather than by the axial rigor of more formal European gardens. It framed the gardens at the level of the little houses' courtyard entrances, providing a unifying element for the entire hill.[34] This was one of many solutions Morgan devised to answer Hearst's request that the grounds be brought to scale with the increased size of the structures: "The main building looms so large that the landscape architecture should be built to scale with it. I advise making approaches, stair flights, walls, and general effects with [the] big main building in mind."[35]

Both of them were very pleased with the Esplanade, which remains a delightful landscape feature. When it was being graded by teams of horses, Hearst wrote to Morgan: "It seems to give a finished touch to the big house, to frame it in, as it were."[36] Morgan reported to Hearst a few months later: "The lines and grades of the esplanade are finally established, and follow as nearly as possible your sketch on the blue print. It has been a real problem to get all around, miss all the roots and branches and not feel the fact that there are very considerable differences in grade. I have had real pleasure watching

the vista open up—wish your architectural self could have had it."[37]

No part of San Simeon bears more traces of both Hearst's and Morgan's "architectural selves" than the outdoor Neptune Pool, though the first small basin completed on its site in the summer of 1924 did not much resemble the grand version built there a decade later. Their earliest plans for a swimming pool called for an indoor plunge on the sunny south side of the hill, designed to resemble a "bath house in the Moorish style," with Arabian architecture, southern Spanish geometric-patterned ceilings, and tropical plants for landscaping.[38] The site northwest of House C—where the Neptune Pool was ultimately built—was first proposed only as a rose garden, a sloping area where Hearst wanted to build a reflecting pool for night-blooming water lilies.

The animals were fanciful, often original compositions,

The central feature of the area was to be the ancient Roman temple fragments that Hearst brought back from Italy in 1922, telling Morgan, "I have bought this and I thought it might be well to erect it in the rose garden against the trees where we were putting the pergola. . . . It would look beautiful against the trees facing the houses, with a pergola on each side."[39] Though the 1934 final version of the Neptune Pool does indeed feature these Roman temple fragments assembled together against the trees, with colonnades (resembling pergolas) on each side, the first pool built on the site was a utilitarian concrete basin, constructed with expedience rather than aesthetics as its first priority.

In the spring of 1924, Morgan was pushing the hilltop construction to completion as much as possible, in preparation for the Hearst family's summer arrival, when Hearst wrote: "I am sending back the plan of the temple

OPPOSITE ABOVE: JULES SUPPO carved the teak figures in his San Francisco workshop, where Morgan visited him frequently to monitor his progress.

OPPOSITE BELOW: THIS CORNER of the teak cornice displays a fancifully carved fish, one of dozens of animals used as corbels.

rather than exact copies of the antique cornice.

THE SOUTH SIDE of the Esplanade, a curving walk that surrounds Casa Grande and links it to the three small houses. Its completion in 1925 unified the garden scheme.

designed and built a swimming pool that was fifty-four feet long, sloping from three and a half feet to eight feet deep, equipped with metal ladders and brick decking, and completed in time for the family's visit.

This was the first summer that the buildings were finished enough for large-scale entertaining, and Hearst was eager to share his estate. Morgan had no sooner contentedly told him, "We will have all the back bills paid up by the first of April," when she was barraged with his requests that she ready the Cloister bedrooms, complete the kitchen on the south side of the Main Building, and prepare the Assembly Room for use, in addition to completing the swimming pool, all in anticipation of a huge party of guests due to arrive in mid-July.[41] In the midst of the flurry, Hearst's *San Francisco Examiner* newspaper office refused to pay her the usual construction allowance, saying they did not have sufficient funds to supply San Simeon.[42]

While these circumstances were unusual in 1924, they became very familiar to Julia Morgan in succeeding years. Hearst began to spend more time on the West Coast, and while in the beginning it was time with his family, it soon became time with the Hollywood actress Marion Davies and her many friends in the film community. Hearst's marriage unraveled: though there was

garden with the suggestion that we make the pool longer than it is, as long as we can make it in the space, and that we make it eight feet deep so that we can use it as a swimming pool. Mrs. Hearst and the children are extremely anxious to have a swimming pool, and unwilling to wait until we can get the regular swimming pools built down on our Alhambra Hill."[40] So Morgan quickly

THE NEPTUNE POOL, c. 1924, when it was hurriedly constructed in its first of three versions.

RHODODENDRONS BLOOM outside the Refectory in the shade of a large coastal live oak. Siting the Main Building around this tree and another oak that grew on the south side of the site influenced Hearst and Morgan's choice of a T-plan for the structure.

no divorce proceeding with his wife, Millicent, he began dividing his residency between the Ambassador Hotel in Los Angeles and the ranch at San Simeon. The more time he spent on the hilltop, the more ideas he developed, and the more tightly the construction budget was stretched. Julia Morgan asked Hearst in these early years about the construction pace he preferred for San Simeon: "In a general way would you say to choose economy, or speed?"[43] For Hearst there was only one answer: he wanted both.

VASE ON PEDESTAL. *18th century. Stone, 10' 9" (328 cm). Hearst Monument Collection. North Esplanade.*
One of four Italian stone vases decorated with pastoral scenes, this example ornaments the Esplanade at its north–south axis line, below the Central Plaza.

CHAPTER FOUR

Architect/Client

On the surface, the personalities of William Randolph Hearst and Julia Morgan appeared completely opposite, with the depth of his impracticality matched only by the breadth of her conscientiousness. But the similarities in their natures were far more numerous and important than the differences. As well as their devotion to art and architecture, they shared an energy and a drive for perfection that baffled and exhausted those around them. These common traits allowed their working relationship to continue amicably for more than three decades.

Their physical appearances were extremely different, of course. Hearst was a sizable man who favored hand-painted neckties and brightly colored suits. He joked that when he asked his valet to approve some very colorful neckties, the valet answered solemnly, "Well, sir, they aren't any worse than some of your others." Hearst's grandson, John Jr., reminisced, "I particularly remember one suit, a billiard-table green. Other men who wore clothes like that would have looked as though they were with the circus. But because Grandpop was so dignified, he made the clothes look dignified, too."[1] Morgan was exceptionally diminutive and dressed with modesty, as her former employee Dorothy Wormser Coblentz recalled: "She always wore a kind of a grey-blue suit and a cape, her hair pulled up in a knot, and a rather largish hat, a white blouse with a high collar and white cuffs, always scrupulously white. I'm sure the shoes were very sensible. And she looked like a nobody. She couldn't have looked less distinguished."[2]

Hearst's flamboyant newspapers led people to expect a loud personality, but upon meeting him they encountered something they did not expect: he had a soft tenor voice and a penetrating stare, which many found disconcerting. Screenwriter Frances Marion remembered that when people thought he was boring holes in them with his distant staring eyes, his mind was often far away, thinking about the press room.[3] His son William Randolph Hearst Jr. recalled: "My father was a very calm, logical person, the epitome of the old-fashioned gentleman. He often made his points with humor. . . . In public Pop was outspoken, colorful, fearless, and driven by inexhaustible energy. In private he was a caring and trusted confidant of this sometimes erring son. I loved him. At times, however, that love was like trying to hold onto a hurricane."[4] Hearst once wrote to his sons:

> Success is a frame of mind—a mental posture—an immutable conviction—an unalterable determination.
>
> Circumstances have nothing to do with success. When you have made up your mind, success is certain. But, if you only half make up your mind, you will never get anywhere.
>
> You have to know you can succeed, and be determined to succeed. You must keep your mind on the objective, not on the obstacles.[5]

In this attitude, Julia Morgan was Hearst's perfect double: "a perfectionist, and each job was a maximum effort. Nothing was left incomplete . . . nothing was left to chance."[6] Edward Hussey, another employee of Morgan's, recalled: "She never raised her voice or got angry, but she was very particular in her work. I know some big men used to quail in her presence, because she was very demanding and everything had to be right; but she did it in a very ladylike manner. She was very insistent on the work being done correctly and properly. As I understand it, some people used to rather tremble at her because of that."[7] One of many instances when Morgan focused on the objective, not the obstacles, came in the crisp response she gave Walter Huber, structural engineer for much of the work at San Simeon, when he proposed reducing the height of a room in the planned recreation wing by lowering the height of its ceiling beams. She declared this was "*not a solution*. The ceiling has in the main to stay where it is, and some way of accomplishing it be found—anything else is [a] waste of time."[8]

Morgan was a product not only of her Beaux-Arts training but also of her background as a San Francisco Bay Area architect, one of the few architects of the Arts and Crafts period who had actually grown up in the area. She established relationships with California craftsmen, engaging them to work on San Simeon both on site and in their private studios, and created the equivalent of a medieval craftsmen's workshop. Under her supervision, ironworkers, painters, cast-stone and plaster workers, tilemakers, and woodcarvers produced ornament for San Simeon, often modeled on historic precedents but always infused with their own spirit and artisanship.[9]

DOUBLE BUST. *Greco-Roman, 2nd–1st century B.C. Marble. 10 ½ x 7 ½ x 7 ¾" (26.7 x 19 x 19.7 cm). Hearst Monument Collection, Casa Grande Library.*

Hearst displayed this ancient bust in the Library, which also held his excellent collection of Greek vases.

WILLIAM RANDOLPH HEARST *and Julia Morgan beam at a movie camera in a very rare shot of them working together.*

For Hearst, the advantages of having Julia Morgan work on his projects are easy to see. Dorothy Wormser Coblentz conjectured that Hearst thought Morgan "was the only person in the world who'd never tried to take advantage of him; he had complete faith in her and she was utterly loyal to him. It was a very nice relationship."[10] Morgan's dedication to her work took precedence over her health, which began to fail in the late 1920s, doubtless due to overwork and the strain of meeting Hearst's demands. While he was blind to his role in the cause, Hearst's genuine concern after she had suffered a sunstroke on a hot summer day at San Simeon was unmistakable.

THE MOLD SHOP *on the south side of the hilltop at San Simeon, where cast-plaster and cast-stone ornaments were created using wood forms.*

Miss Morgan you *must* stop working so hard. All your friends will be really angry with you if you don't. You haven't any right to *destroy* yourself and that is exactly what you are doing. You wouldn't treat an *engine* the way you treat yourself. It is not right and it isn't *good practice.* You don't get the best work or the most work that way. You can't *race* all the time. You must *rest* some time.

Please take the boat and come abroad for a couple of months. We will see a lot of things and get a lot of ideas—and we will have a good time.[11]

It was common in the era for millionaire builders to take their country-house architects to Europe with them, both to serve as advisers on their purchases and to examine firsthand the buildings to emulate at home. However, Morgan never went abroad with Hearst. In fact, she interrupted her practice in favor of travel only when her failing health absolutely required that she do so, from 1934 on.[12]

Prior to her health problems, Morgan was steadily involved in her work at San Simeon and several other projects for Hearst, in addition to many of her most important other commissions. Equal in scale to San Simeon was Hearst's Wyntoon, a Bavarian "village" near Mt. Shasta in northern California. Bernard Maybeck had created a "castle" there for Phoebe Apperson Hearst in 1902–3, a towering green-tile-roofed, stone structure, which seemed to grow out of the surrounding forest. In the winter of 1929–30 it burned completely and Hearst immediately began plans to rebuild it. He initially considered hiring Maybeck to incorporate the stones of a twelfth-century Spanish monastery he had purchased into another soaring, green-roofed, stone-clad castle but eventually commissioned Morgan to design a group of buildings, on a more modest but still stunning scale among the stands of pines. This meant that during the 1930s, when Hearst's finances were already stretched by the Depression, he had Morgan building two physically isolated, grandly scaled groups of structures, at San Simeon and Wyntoon, while also undertaking other more minor construction projects for him in Los Angeles and San Francisco.[13]

Architectural draftsman Warren "Mac" McClure was sent to San Simeon from Morgan's office in 1929 to be her on-site representative, then was sent to Wyntoon to supervise its construction through much of the mid-

A CAST-STONE figure in the Oakland, California, studio of craftsmen Theo and John Van der Loo, modeled after the Greco-Roman double bust in the Hearst collection.

TESTIMONIALS to San Simeon's Arts and Crafts heritage are the drainpipes on all the residences, which were created from hammered copper incised with leaf forms and decorated with a ribbon band bearing the words "San Simeon."

CAST-STONE FIGURES wired for electricity are used for lighting around the Neptune Pool and the West Terrace. Though inspired by caryatids in the Italian Renaissance Villa Caprarola, these figures lend a twentieth-century Maxfield Parrish air of fantasy to the pool.

1930s. Exhausted, he wrote to George Loorz, the construction superintendent at San Simeon at the time, about Morgan's perfectionism in preparing for Hearst's arrival.

> This last week has been one of the worst I have ever put in. Personally I do not think it worth such an effort. We have worked until midnight for five nights running— and now as I write this I can see J. M. tugging and lugging porch and lawn chairs herself, but I am too tired and calloused to go out and either stop her or help her. All of the rooms have been furnished and refurnished about four times—curtains changed and rugs rolled up again until we were cock-eyed—So let the Chief come soon, says I—at least it will put a stop to this, whatever else may be in store for us.[14]

This obsession with details came from Morgan herself, not from the external demands of William Randolph Hearst.

And in all this effort there were advantages for Julia Morgan, as well. Hearst was essentially Morgan's patron; working for him allowed her access to antique materials and the opportunity to build structures almost no other twentieth-century architect could hope to create. She could never have been a society architect like Stanford White or the East Coast country-house designer Harrie T. Lindeberg: both her gender and, more importantly, her temperament precluded her from hobnobbing

socially with wealthy clients to gain commissions. Morgan had her own network of contacts, but the resulting projects were all on a much more modest scale than the ones Hearst provided. These advantages had to be weighed against the many frustrations inherent in working with such a changeable, impractical client, but those who knew Morgan best were aware of their importance to her. Flora North, who was married to Julia Morgan's nephew Morgan North, said of the non-Hearst commissions: "She got plenty of work, but it wasn't the kind of work that she had undoubtedly dreamed of doing. Hearst was probably a windfall in a sense, because she had the training for what he had in mind and the imagination and the ability."[15] Morgan also derived great pleasure from her proximity to the objects in Hearst's collections. Walter Steilberg recalled the excitement he and Morgan shared when they learned that a twelfth-century English barn Hearst had purchased was being unpacked at the San Simeon warehouses. "Miss Morgan and I could hardly wait to see it. We were particularly anxious to examine the hand-hewn beams that carried the huge roof. She loved structure, you know, and so did I."[16] When Hearst bought a particularly fine group of Renaissance objects from the home of the Spanish Count of Almenas, Morgan wrote him

A STAIRWELL leading up to the Celestial Suite: its rough concrete walls are unfinished and the impressions left by the wooden formwork are clearly visible.

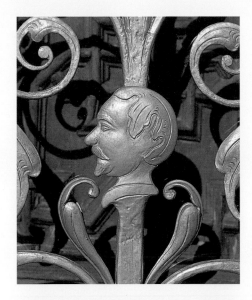

after examining the photographs of items that would soon arrive at the ranch: "Have just received the photographs of the last shipment. Am quite overwhelmed. A wonderful collection in itself. Thank you for the pleasure of it."[17]

Hearst and Morgan also shared a strong personal link long before San Simeon: their deep affection for Phoebe Apperson Hearst, Hearst's powerful mentor and Morgan's faithful patron. Mrs. Hearst and Miss Morgan most likely initially met at the University of California,

where Phoebe's home two blocks from the Berkeley campus was a gathering place for the small number of female students attending the school. Her educational benefactions were almost limitless and included every age group, from the free kindergartens she funded beginning in the 1880s to the estimated fifty thousand dollars a year she spent in the mid-1890s to send students through school.[18] All of Bernard Maybeck's students who were studying at the Ecole—including Julia Morgan—received a fifty-dollar-a-month stipend from

89

Phoebe Hearst.[19] Morgan arrived in Paris in 1896. When Phoebe visited the Maybecks in Paris to review the progress of the worldwide design competition for the University of California campus that she had asked Maybeck to oversee, she saw Julia Morgan as well, offering to sponsor her education to an even greater degree. Morgan responded:

> If I honestly thought more money freedom would make my work better, I would be tempted to accept your offer—but I am sure it has not been the physical work which has been or will be hardest, for I am used to it and strong, but rather the months of striving against homesickness and the nervous strain of examinations.
>
> Now my brother [Morgan's younger brother, Avery] is here and a place is won at the B. A., really mine now it seems, the work ought simply to be a pleasure whether housekeeping or study.
>
> Your kind words at the depot were so unexpected, so friendly, they gave and still give, more help than you can guess, and I will thank you for them always.[20]

When Morgan returned from the Ecole to practice architecture in California in 1902, she joined the office of John Galen Howard, the architect charged with implementing the winning design plan for the University of California. She immediately began working on two Hearst commissions: the Hearst Memorial Mining Building, which Phoebe built in memory of George Hearst, and the Greek Theater, which William Randolph Hearst gave to the university at the same time. By 1904 Morgan had opened her own architectural office in San Francisco. The next decade saw some of her most successful designs: the campanile, library, and gymnasium at Mills College for Women in Oakland; the reconstruction of San Francisco's Fairmont Hotel, heavily damaged in the 1906 earthquake; and the St. John's Presbyterian Church in Berkeley, now the Julia Morgan Center for the Performing Arts. Phoebe Hearst was instrumental in some key commissions, including the start of Morgan's work at the Asilomar Conference Grounds in Pacific

EDGAR WALTER. ARCADIA. American, c. 1915. Cast bronze. 35 x 22" (88.9 x 55.9 cm). Hearst Monument Collection, House A Sitting Room. Formerly in Phoebe Hearst's collection, this piece was exhibited at the 1915 Panama-Pacific International Exposition in San Francisco.

Grove, near Monterey, California, on land which Phoebe presented to the Young Women's Christian Association (YWCA) for their seasonal training center, stipulating that Morgan serve as architect for the construction.[21]

The University of California was not the only grand civic project that involved Julia Morgan, Bernard Maybeck, and both Phoebe and William Randolph Hearst. In 1910, San Francisco was chosen over New Orleans as the site of the Panama Canal Exposition, a world's fair held in 1915 that also became a celebration of San Francisco's triumphant return from the devastation of the 1906 earthquake.[22] W. R. Hearst had dreamed of holding a world's fair in San Francisco since 1891, and he immediately became an enthusiastic backer of what became known as the Panama-Pacific International Exposition. He pledged twenty-five thousand dollars in start-up money, arranged for the Liberty Bell to be transported to the fair, and erected a huge printing press to create his newspaper at the fairgrounds.[23] Phoebe was honorary president of the charitable Fair Women's Board, and allowed her art collection—with some additional items contributed by her son—to be shown in the loveliest building erected for the fair, Bernard Maybeck's stately Palace of Fine Arts. There was no Women's Building at the fair, but the YWCA's building became the structure that highlighted feminine pursuits and provided a resting place for women on the grounds. It was, however, designed by a man: Ernest Champney. At Phoebe's insistence, Julia Morgan—who had not been included on John Galen Howard's architectural committee for the Fair—was engaged to design the interior, an open plan of dining and club rooms that was praised for its hospitality.[24] When after nine months the lath and plaster buildings of the Exposition were demolished (save for the Palace of Fine Arts, which was preserved due to its

A MODEL of La Cuesta Encantada by C. Julian Mesic, Morgan's model maker, who was also a woman architect. In the early years, Morgan shipped models of the three small houses to Hearst so that he could evaluate their proposed changes. By the late 1920s (the date of this model) the model had grown too large to ship. Instead they photographed it, tinted the images with color, and sent the photographs to Hearst for his approval. Morgan once described the model as looking "like a little dream." The elaborate fountain in the foreground was never constructed.

MORGAN'S FREEHAND pencil sketch of the Doge's Suite at the rear mezzanine level of Casa Grande, before the South Wing addition was poured in 1927.

popularity), all agreed that San Francisco had witnessed an extraordinary burst of creativity.

The fair cast a permanent spell on William Randolph Hearst. He tried to bring its celebrated sculptures to San Simeon, apparently at Morgan's suggestion: "It was a wonderful idea that you had about using this material and it is going to make the hill something more distinguished than it possibly could have been under any other circumstances as we could not have hoped to have all those great artists working for us in any other way."[25] Though obtaining the rights to reproduce the fair statues proved difficult and Hearst and Morgan were not able to ornament the gardens and hillsides with them as they had planned, the fair's influence can still be seen in the final version of the Neptune Pool, which echoes in small scale the scheme of the Palace of Fine Arts: a ruined temple flanked by colonnades, the whole reflected in a lagoon.

The University of California campus and the Panama-Pacific International Exposition, or PPIE, as the fair came to be known, were two of the greatest architectural events in early-twentieth-century California. Both Phoebe's and William Randolph Hearst's deep involvement in them was a clear indicator of their dreams for, and their faith in, California. They saw it as

a twentieth-century Athens, in line to inherit the mantle of previous societies that had shaped Western art and culture.[26] W. R. Hearst declared that "no other exposition here or abroad has ever displayed so much art and architectural loveliness."[27] It was the last collaboration between the two Hearsts and Julia Morgan, because Phoebe died four years later. In early 1919, Morgan wrote to Phoebe, as she was already fighting the influenza virus that would kill her that spring: "And so through it all is the thread of your kindness since those Paris days when you were so beautifully kind to a painfully shy and homesick girl. My mother's and yours are the greatest 'faiths' put in me, and I hope you both know how I love and thank you for it."[28]

The closeness of Hearst and Morgan's association certainly did not mean that it was free of conflict. Bill Hearst Jr. recalled, "I used to listen to her and the old man go at it in her small office at the top of the hill. She and Pop had some real squawks, let me tell you, but both were so formal and low-keyed that an outsider would hardly have noticed."[29] In the letters and telegrams that record so many of their exchanges, great courtesy was always maintained. But Morgan could speak up for herself. Hearst Jr. said, "She managed to cajole, plead, demand, and warn Pop in the most courte-

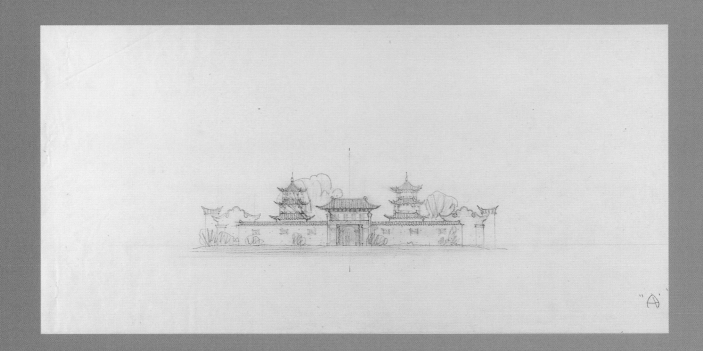

maybe it's an opportunity in disguise . . . ." Julia Morgan

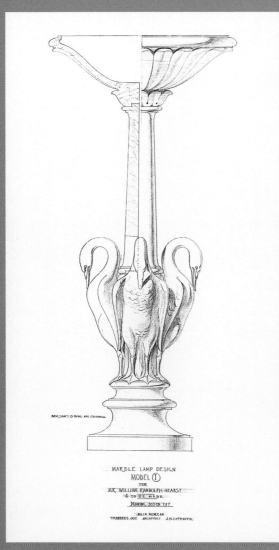

TOP: JULIA MORGAN'S *fanciful pencil drawing for animal enclosures on Chinese Hill, northwest of the Castle. These structures were never built.*

ABOVE LEFT: A DRAWING *of a swan lamp standard by Thaddeus Joy, Morgan's chief draftsman, whose specialty was creating full-size drawings of architectural ornament.*

ABOVE RIGHT: SINCE ELECTRICITY *was always available at San Simeon, night lighting of the gardens was planned from the early 1920s. Joy designed these swan lamp standards expressly for the estate.*

ous, professional language. But, if one reads carefully between the lines, she caught the old man up short many a time and indicated she would not retreat on her view unless he had a darn good answer."[30] When Morgan disagreed with Hearst, she never said so directly. Instead, she asked a clarifying question, then presented him with another alternative that was obviously superior, to which Hearst usually acquiesced.[31] As her nephew Morgan North explained it, "she wasn't going to put in a horizontal line when she knew that a vertical line would be the only thing that would be right. She would work him over by showing him sketches of his way, and showing him how it would not look as well as another way. She understood what he was groping for."[32]

Many times she lost the argument. Morgan clearly did not favor Hearst's idea of heightening the planned North Wing of Casa Grande to add a studio level, a room visiting artists could use during their stays. "To add the studio on the north wing would be virtually the addition of a third story. Would it not unbalance the Patio? A third story on the south also would bring the roof line so high the eaves would be practically on a line with those of the Main Building. Could the studio be housed in the Chinese Hill group, or possibly on the

THE NEPTUNE TERRACE, *above the Neptune Pool, with its swan lamp fixtures.*

Tennis Court development?"[33] These alternative sites both remained unfinished: the Chinese Hill was planned north of the complex, and would have held aviaries and zoo animals in pagodalike surroundings. The tennis court building, though in use by 1929, was never completely finished. The North and South Wings were indeed built with these contemplated third-floor levels, and even additional fourth-floor tower stories, which unfortunately do compete with the height of the bell towers and mar the scale of the Main Building, just as Morgan had known they would.

Surely if she had been following her own taste—which was characterized by, among other things, her interest in Chinese art, her reliance on sunlit staircases as focal points in her residential architecture, and the inclusion in her designs of many small considerate features added for their quiet charm—San Simeon would look very different. But she understood that it was Hearst's house, and her willingness to defer her own preferences, when necessary, to better reflect his gives La Cuesta Encantada its distinctive theatricality and romantic beauty. She also understood that such flamboyant design has its own special appeal. "The Hill work goes on," Morgan wrote to Walter Steilberg in 1928. "In some ways you won't know it. But I have a sneaking suspicion it is coming out pretty well in spite of everything."[34] Steilberg voiced his own frustration about the conflicting scales of the Main Building's west front, caused by the mixture of so many historic elements and motifs: "It started out as facade architecture. That was the trouble. It didn't give Miss Morgan and me a real chance to use her talents as a planner."[35] But he and Morgan's family both recognized her reasons for continuing and for creating a showcase for a different kind of art collection: "It was going to be a museum and the things in the museum . . . would be very much worthwhile for the American public to see."[36]

Morgan often quoted her great mentor, Bernard Maybeck: "If you strike a difficulty don't shy away from it; maybe it's an opportunity in disguise; and you can make a feature of it."[37] With a client as changeable and participatory as William Randolph Hearst, this advice must have sprung almost daily to her mind. As a philoso-phy it neatly summarizes the accommodating collaborative spirit Morgan brought to the job at San Simeon. On two separate occasions, Hearst sent crude drawings and scribbled notes for some of his more fanciful ideas to Morgan and signed them, "Violet le Duc Hearst," referring to the great nineteenth-century architectural reformer Eugène-Emmanuel Viollet-le-Duc, who not only championed Gothic architecture but believed in improving upon history.[38] He rebuilt many of France's Gothic cathedrals and the medieval town of Carcassone, reconstructing them not exactly as they had been originally, but in a romantic vein that he felt heightened their stylistic differences with the modern world. Hearst chose his architectural alter ego well.

Because he lived at the ranch less than half the year (and in the early years, only a few months of the summer at most), Hearst's communication with Morgan resulted in nearly a thousand individual letters and telegrams, many more than would exist if they had both been more frequently on site. Morgan often wrote her rough drafts longhand, these unexpurgated versions providing insight into how she edited herself: if emotion crept in, for example, she crossed out the sentiment before the final letter was typed by her secretary. Therefore, in April of 1920, Hearst read only the news that the steamer had been once again delayed with its shipment of cement and lumber for San Simeon and the ongoing mill strike prevented their receiving adequate materials in any case. He didn't see Morgan's personal frustration, expressed in the crossed-out sarcastic phrase, "Great life these days," which concluded her initial draft.[39]

Her letters concerning the constant money shortages were usually short and apologetic, often ending with phrases such as, "I dislike to bother you again, but have to."[40] However, she bristled at any suggestion that she had not performed a job fully. She met small criticisms—about such matters as the choice of wood to be used for fence posts—with extensive explanations. She never defended herself directly, instead just revealing the amount of research she had performed before coming to her decision. Generally speaking, she did not bother Hearst with the specifics of the everyday workings of the hilltop, saying instead, "But I must not take your time on camp detail."[41]

Morgan herself almost never spent the night at San Simeon, leaving her San Francisco office on Saturday evening and taking the night train—the *Lark*—which left around 8:00 P.M. and arrived at the station in San Luis Obispo at 2:00 A.M. She took an upper berth, which was high enough so that she could sit up and work by the light from the corridor, shining in through the curtains. Steve Zegar's taxi picked her up when she arrived, and she would appear at San Simeon in time to join the workmen for breakfast.[42] She often met with Hearst on these Sunday visits, which ended when she returned to the station that night to take the *Lark* back to San Francisco. Bjarne Dahl, an engineer in Morgan's office, recalled accompanying her on one of these trips to San Simeon: "When we got up there, she'd work with the contractor *all day long*. . . . Then it was time to go home. We'd get home the next morning, and I'd be

pooped—all tired out—and she'd go right to the door . . . and go to work."[43]

A long commute was only one of the many difficulties Morgan experienced in conducting a large construction operation—of one hundred or more men at certain times of the year—in such an isolated spot. There were many personnel problems, usually involving a lack of supervision on the job. Morgan's allegiance was almost always with the workmen. She knew how isolated they were on the hill and wrote Hearst, "I have tried a moving picture show once a week without asking you, which has been well worth the money in keeping down 'turn-over.' The operator brings his own machine, pays his expenses, and shows seven reels for $30.00."[44] She was sympathetic in the little camp squabbles and pleaded to allow the workmen to fish in the streams as a cure for their boredom but lost that argument; they had been dynamiting the trout in the streams, and Hearst, horrified, discontinued fishing altogether.[45] Morgan felt great

THADDEUS JOY (left) and Frank R. Humrich, outside a construction tent.
Joy supervised much of San Simeon's construction and generated many decorative
designs for the estate. Humrich was a decorative painter.

empathy for the workers even when she herself had been rebuffed, as in the case of head gardener H. Dodson Hazard, who had been countermanding her orders. She wrote compassionately to Hearst: "I think Hazard has tried very hard to please you, and for that reason I have humored him along although sometime ago he told me that 'his department on your orders' had, and would have, nothing whatever to do with me or my office people."[46]

Her desire to empathize and her willingness to overlook personal slights makes even more clear how difficult it must have been for her to work with Camille Rossi, the construction superintendent who started at San Simeon in 1922. His bombastic personality created dissension across the hill and exasperated Morgan for years. When, in early 1932, Hearst finally instructed Morgan to fire Rossi, he wrote to Hearst in near hysteria: "We all have to fight in order to achieve our ends. You fight for your principles in your wonderful editorials, and if at time[s] I have had to squabble with any one, it has been to get efficiency and save you money—and sometimes I wonder, does it pay to make enemies, just to save your employer's money?"[47] Hearst wavered, writing back to Morgan, "Mr. Rossi seems to be in such desperate straits that I am repenting letting him go. What do you say. Shall we try him for another year?"[48] The prospect of Rossi returning must have appalled Morgan, but she merely responded to Hearst:

> Any decision you come to in regard to Mr. Rossi I will, of course, fall in with cheerfully, but [I] believe that not carrying through will make him doubly hard to work with—he is so unbelievably revengeful and finds so many ingenious ways for indirect expression of his sentiments.
>
> I may be unreasonably tired of operating with a constant sense of contrary purpose, and not see conditions fairly or clearly as your fresh eye can.[49]

A *CEILING PANEL* in the Hero Room, House A, copied from the Casa de los Tiros in Granada, Spain. This cast-plaster panel was created in Oakland, then mounted in place, painted, and gilded.

In acknowledging her "unreasonableness," Morgan succinctly described the problem—the undermining effect of Rossi's presence—and followed up her acquiescent statement with a convincing trump card. She enclosed a letter Rossi had written to her on the same day as his letter to Hearst, in a much less hysterical vein: "Going to St. Louis [where Morgan was helping him find work] may be fine. . . . Well let us hope that everything is for the best."[50] Rossi left the hill for good. Morgan hired George Loorz as his replacement, a man she justly described as having "left a record for good work and good will behind wherever he has been."[51] Had Rossi stayed, however, there is no doubt that Morgan would have "fallen in cheerfully" with Hearst's decision, which was always her practice.

One of the most distinctive aspects of La Cuesta Encantada's history is the wide range of responsibilities shouldered by Julia Morgan as its architect: personnel, supplies, interior design, shipping, landscaping, finances, and even the welfare of the zoo animals Hearst started collecting in the mid-1920s were all under her care. The other remarkable aspect of the job was its duration. At twenty years of construction over the twenty-eight-year interval from 1919 to 1947, San Simeon took at least five times longer to build than a typical, luxurious American country house of the period generally required. By the middle of the 1920s, the small houses were completed, the gardens were laid out and planting begun, the Main Building's west exterior was completed, and the interiors of most of the major rooms were under way. In a normal architect-client relationship, it would be time for Morgan to contemplate concluding the construction phase of the buildings, which would soon be ready for large-scale entertaining. With Hearst as the client and San Simeon as his canvas, however, construction was far from over.

CHAPTER FIVE

A California Country

In the mid-1920s William Randolph Hearst started using La Cuesta Encantada year-round, and he soon discovered what Julia Morgan had known since construction began: in a winter storm, his temperate summer retreat became a cold, sodden outpost, battered by

wind and rain. The antique fire mantels installed in his House A—and throughout the estate—were beautiful, but their large sizes

when combined with small modern chimneys caused them to smoke, no matter how they were altered.[1] "We have the unsatisfying alternative of freezing to death without a fire or smothering to death from smoke," Hearst complained to Morgan.[2] Though the houses had been provided with electricity from the start of construction, powered by Hearst's small hydroelectric plant run with water from the springs east of the hilltop, a more abundant and dependable form of power for heating was clearly necessary. In 1924 Morgan proposed Hearst bring commercial electric power to the site: if he paid eleven thousand dollars for the cost of the electric line to San Simeon, San Joaquin Light and Power would credit him with the entire sum at the rate of twenty percent a year until he was repaid in full.[3] Underground cable was laid to ensure nothing would interfere with the view.[4]

Yet even with both wall-mounted and freestanding electric heaters in the rooms, keeping the buildings draft-free and dry was almost impossible when the wind blew the rain from the Pacific Ocean in gusts of eighty miles per hour. Hearst wrote to Camille Rossi in

House

February of 1927, after he had experienced a huge storm: "At present the water drives in everywhere and the wind blows in through the cracks and crevices until the rugs flap on the floor. . . . Let's have COMFORT AND HEALTH before so much art. The art won't do us any good if we are all dead of pneumonia."[5] If this particular deluge was not bad enough to drive him from the hilltop, the next one was, as he wrote Rossi the following week:

> We are all leaving the hill. We are drowned, blown and frozen out. . . .
>
> Everybody has a cold. All who could have left and the few who remain are eagerly waiting a chance to get out. . . .
>
> Before we build anything more let's make what we have built practical, comfortable and beautiful. If we can't do that we might as well change the names of the houses to pneumonia house, diphtheria house, and influenza bungalow. The main house we can call the clinic.[6]

Hearst downplayed his ire in his account to Morgan, telling her, "We had a lively time in house A last night. The storm was severe and I spent most of the night ripping off the weather stripping in my room. The darn stuff sounded like a flock of saxophones going at full tilt in a jazz band."[7] Morgan was perfectly willing to institute all the weatherproofing measures he requested, and she may have felt a bit of triumph in her boss finally experiencing one of the storms that had plagued the project from the start. "I enjoyed your description of 'A Night in House A . . . ,'" she wrote. "You always said you would like to see one of those famous storms on the Hill."[8]

Though the severity of the hilltop winters surprised Hearst, he had intended for some time to turn the ranch at San Simeon from a summer house to a year-round residence, which partly explains his many enlargements. He began to expand his plans for the gardens when the three houses were nearly finished, instructing Morgan to plant citrus trees for winter harvesting, which would ensure a year-round supply of fruit, since, "We will probably spend longer and longer periods on the hill as the construction nears completion—I hope from April until Christmas."[9]

As the Main Building started to rise above the houses at the end of 1923, Hearst realized that the grounds should encompass far more than just modest planted paths around the structures. To be in proportion, the gardens and the surrounding landscape needed spectacular features of their own.[10] Hearst had long been aware of the importance of the view of the hilltop when seen from the road below, and at Morgan's recommendation he engaged artist and landscape designer Bruce Porter to visit San Simeon in late 1922 to advise on a

THIS SATYR'S HEAD appears at the center of a twentieth-century Italian scrolled marble bench facing the ocean at the lower patio level outside House A.

tree-planting scheme for the surrounding hillsides. This consulting effort was an arduous job, Morgan wrote Hearst: "Am just back from San Simeon with Mr. Porter—that is, with what is left of him. . . . As [I] thought probable, he grasped the place as a whole and from the painter—as well as planter—viewpoint."[11] Porter approved of the siting of the small houses and could envision how the Main Building would tower above them all: "Even now, with but three of the buildings completed—they strangely magnify themselves into the bulk and importance of a city." Porter urged them to regard the perspective of looking up at the planting from the highway as equal in importance to looking down on the planting from the residence site. He recommended, therefore, that they not screen the walls and terraces with plants, but instead show the structural footings on the slopes, a practice they adhered to. He added, "The preservation and accenting of all wildness and nativeness of the surrounding country will add to the romance and surprise that awaits the visitor at the top."[12] This admonition was unnecessary: a lifetime on the land had given Hearst a great appreciation for its natural character.

A CASCADE, or water staircase, was built in the pool's second version to showcase the statues of the Nereids and Neptune that gave the pool its name.

OPPOSITE: CASA GRANDE'S north bell tower nearly disappears in the mist of a foggy morning.

By 1925, the Esplanade walk was laid and the plants largely determined, many of the palms and large shrubs, like camellias and bougainvilleas, arriving fully grown.[13] Hearst could see that his rapidly expanding estate called for "big architectural effects in the gardens." He was overflowing with ideas for flights of steps, gates, columns, lakes, cloisters, orchards, seats, shrines, temples, sundials, "lakes, pools, cascades, and every old thing."[14] The swimming pool had been hurriedly built in its first version to be available for the Hearst boys in the summer of 1924; now lengthening it and completing its

cascade, or water staircase, would give it greater dignity, he felt, while supplying it with both a heater and sand filter would make it more usable as a swimming pool. Hearst had purchased a sculpture group of Neptune and the Nereids in 1922, writing to Morgan, "I have been thinking what to do with that Neptune fountain. We ought to use it somewhere. I don't want too many décolleté ladies around the grounds and gentlemen as a rule aren't interesting. This Neptune fountain though not beautiful is quaint and although the nymphs are not over attired the dominant figure is an elderly gentleman with whiskers who lends respectability to the landscape—for those at least who don't know his record."[15] They placed the Neptune and Nereid group at the top of the cascade, which filled the enlarged rectangular basin of the swimming pool, thus providing the Neptune Pool with its name.[16]

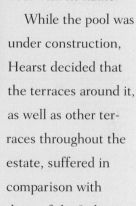

While the pool was under construction, Hearst decided that the terraces around it, as well as other terraces throughout the estate, suffered in comparison with those of the Italian Renaissance villas that Charles Adams Platt had written about in *Italian Gardens*. "Our walks and terraces are generally narrow and not formal." Hearst wanted "terraces as big as possible and the steps as wide and stately as possible."[17] By 1928 an enlarged terrace was built west of House C, in proper proportion to the enlarged swimming pool, and the Neptune Pavilion—a kidney-shaped bathhouse containing seventeen dressing rooms—was constructed into the hillside behind the top of the cascade, providing changing rooms for guests and a view of the pool from the Neptune Terrace which formed its roof.[18]

In addition to expanding the Neptune Pool, terraces were built that enlarged the scale of the gardens to correspond with the enlarged Main Building. The Central Plaza, planned from the early twenties to be a formal terrace for Casa Grande, was first poured in 1922, but a large oak was in the way. Hearst and Morgan began discussing moving the hilltop oaks, something she had done with small trees on a previous project.[19] These oaks were large, mature specimens, however, and moving them would be difficult. The first two oaks were moved in preparation for Casa Grande's North Wing construction in 1925–26. This enormous undertaking involved digging down to each tree's roots, encasing them in a concrete container, and using winches and

MOVING AN OAK required tunneling under the tree and placing reinforced girders under the main roots. Then a circular trench was dug around the tree, and a reinforced concrete band was poured around the roots. A bottom was placed under the girders, and timbers and rollers were placed beneath them. The tree was moved either on these rollers or, if the relocation was downhill, on greased skids.

house-moving equipment to drag them to the replanting sites, efforts which testify to Hearst's reverence for San Simeon's natural landscape.[20] The mature oak on the Central Plaza was moved west to allow for the terrace's expansion in the summer of 1928.[21] Another terrace expansion that was equivalent in complexity was the covering up of a staircase north of House B in December 1929, in order to build the large North Terrace over it. The stairs were sealed over by the enlarged terrace above, but they remain in place below, a reminder of the smaller scale of many of the early garden features.[22]

One of the most impressive aspects of the landscape at La Cuesta Encantada was the menagerie displayed along the road. Hearst initially proposed a small enclosure for buffalo, antelope, and deer in 1923.[23] Soon, of course, his quest for greater effects expanded this idea into a deer park and a separate buffalo and elk park, both located along the road, with a gamekeeper's lodge—planned in a Spanish style but never built—sited nearby.[24] Hearst was an animal lover, but he had never before been an animal collector, except for ranch animals and dogs. Suddenly, exotic species began to arrive at San Simeon for an elaborate zoo that evoked the menageries of Woburn Abbey and other English country houses. Morgan wrote Hearst in the spring of 1925: "The lions are beauties—about the size of St. Bernards and as well kept and groomed as human babies. It seems incredible that any living creature could contain the resentment felt by those wild cats. They have not [been] 'tamed' in the slightest."[25] Some of the animals were first kept in pens east of the estate, then in later years were moved to more spacious cages along the road. Grazing animals were given fenced-in enclosures of hundreds of acres, each tract separated by trip gates and dotted with rustic log shelters, which the guests drove by as they made their way up the hill.

To drive among groups of wild animals on the way up to Hearst's hilltop was to suspend one's disbelief before even stepping from the automobile. Morgan reported to Hearst a few years later: "I had to rub my eyes last night when out of the semi-darkness staring at the lights were grouped three ostriches, five zebras, five white deer, two

with big horns, a llama, and some speckled deer. All in a group! The giraffes are a [sic] beautiful specimen."[26] Brayton Laird, who worked for Hearst in the orchards in the 1930s, had a typical tale, driving up at night and seeing "a big herd of buffalo . . . then . . . a whole herd of elk. . . . there [were] water buffalo, wildebeest, kangaroos running around, little kangaroos jumping in and out of the pouch and they looked like a bunch of rabbits. . . . [T]here must have been five hundred animals like in [the] African plains there. . . . [Y]our headlights would light the eyes of those animals up. They'd all be looking at you and it was just like the lights of a distant city."[27]

Some of Hearst's most romantic effects were never acted on, including a plan for land east of the Roman Pool, where fourteen garages were eventually constructed. "Shall we put an observatory on Garage Hill," he wondered, "with a big telescope and study the stars in our old age? Or shall we put the observatory on Reservoir Hill? Of course Reservoir Hill is the ideal spot but rather hard to get to. Still it would give another point of *interest,* and a place to go to *see.* Then the

water could be made a pleasant adjunct. What think? Sort of romantic isn't it! Reminds one of Washington Irving's *Tales of the Alhambra.* The astrologer and the fair maiden." [28]

Though Hearst built no observatory, he found his fair maiden in actress Marion Davies. Vulnerable, unaffected, and fun, Davies captivated everyone who knew her. She described Hearst's admiration for her in the beginning as like "Svengali, or Pygmalion and Galatea."[29] She was naturally modest and may indeed have felt that, like those fictional characters, Hearst had created her as his ideal woman. Certainly he idealized her, and many felt she in return humanized him with her graciousness and charm. Maurice McClure, a construction worker at San Simeon from 1921 on, recalled, "I thought she was one of the most wonderful people I have ever met. She had a heart that was as big as the all outdoors."[30] Hollywood director King Vidor said, "She was easier to get to know and to get close to than he was. There was always a little aura of the mysterious . . . about him. . . . She was very much down to earth . . . at ease at all times with everyone. . . . And she was very generous, very charitable, and

"big architectural effects in the gardens" —
flights of steps, gates, columns,
cloisters, orchards, seats, shrines,

GARDEN STEPS, *formerly part of the White Oak Terrace, were built in the early 1920s in front of House B.*

THESE SAME STEPS *in front of House B were covered rather than removed in 1929, when the North Terrace was expanded to be in proper scale with the enlarged second version of the Neptune Pool.*

EXCAVATION *on the second version of the Neptune Pool, c. 1925.*

temples, sundials, "lakes, pools, cascades,

and every old thing."

THE SECOND VERSION *of the Neptune Pool was lined with white Vermont marble in 1927.*

FULLY GROWN TREES, *such as this Canary Island date palm, were hauled up the hill in trucks and planted in the gardens.*

TOP: A HERD OF LLAMAS *on the road to the hilltop. While the primates, bears, and big cats were caged, exotic range animals often grazed near the road, to the delight of the guests.*

ABOVE LEFT: ONE OF SEVERAL *picturesque log animal shelters, which were placed near the road so that the animals would get accustomed to staying in visible areas of the ranch.*

ABOVE RIGHT: LOOKING DOWN *on the animal pens on Orchard Hill. A mid-afternoon custom for the guests was to watch the animals at feeding time.*

very loyal to her friends and to him."[31] Alice Head, an Englishwoman whose career began at *Country Life* and who became the chief of Hearst's British magazine operations, wrote: "At large parties I have often seen Marion go up to those guests who seemed shy or a little bit out of things and in her own inimitable way encircle them with warmth and affection so that they soon became at ease with the party. Her particular kindness and attention are for the poor and humble, and I know of no more illuminating light to throw on a person's character, especially when that person is a beautiful and world-famous film star."[32]

A new era at San Simeon, with Marion presiding as hostess, seems to have begun in the spring of 1926. Hearst wrote to Morgan after a visit to the hilltop, in a tone of warm pride: "All those wild movie people prevented me from talking to you as much as I wanted to. Next time I shall go up alone and we can discuss *everything*. Nevertheless the movie folk were immensely appreciative. They said it was the most wonderful place in the world and that the most extravagant dream of a moving picture set fell far short of this reality." This was, in fact, the house's grand opening. Hearst was now sharing his beloved home with the people who were going to fill it for the next twenty years, people with whom he was at ease: they had little sense of history, still less of social standing, but they had a tremendous appreciation for effect. As the producer of more than a hundred films himself, he valued their highest compliment: La Cuesta Encantada was better than living in a movie set, its backdrops of mountain, sky, and ocean more stunning than any painted ones. These guests were quick to see its potential, but Hearst concluded: "They all wanted to make a picture there but they are *NOT* going to be allowed to do it."[33] This fantasy realm was used for Hearst's home movies but never as a movie set; it remained his private home. Morgan felt the special nature of this visit as well. "I liked and enjoyed very much the movie people," she wrote Hearst. "They are artists, and alive. It was a pleasure also to see the way those who did not go swimming went around absorbedly taking in detail. To tell the truth, I was quite thrilled myself."[34]

This new social era at San Simeon coincided with a period of great prosperity for Hearst, as well as for the nation. He responded, of course, by increasing his expenditures on San Simeon while simultaneously undertaking many new projects elsewhere. As Morgan

MARION DAVIES *and Hearst take a rest on their holiday abroad. His affection for her is unmistakable. Marion had a stutter that many who knew her said they found endearing, since it seemed to increase her natural vulnerability.*

succinctly put it to Arthur Byne, while inquiring if any medieval Spanish cloisters were for sale: "Our capacity of absorption is apparently limitless."[35] Byne obliged in the summer of 1925 by disassembling and shipping to America a twelfth-century Cistercian Spanish monastery, Santa Maria de Ovila, which though never erected there was initially planned for use at San Simeon.[36] Hearst also delegated Alice Head to purchase St. Donat's for him, a medieval castle in Glamorganshire, Wales, in the summer of 1925. He had seen it photographed in the pages of *Country Life* and decided he would like a country home in England. "We were successful, we were prosperous, we were on top of the wave," Head recalled. "Out of the current year's profits we bought *The Connoisseur,* we bought St. Donat's Castle and we bought vast quantities of antiques."[37] In 1926 Hearst hired architect William Flannery to build Ocean House for Marion Davies, a one-hundred-plus-room Georgian-style residence on the beach at Santa Monica. Morgan herself also worked on additions to

A LARGE PARTY *gathers at the main entrance of Casa Grande. Back row, from left: King Vidor, Beatrice Lillie, Richard Barthelmess, Eleanor Boardman. Middle row: Frank Orsatti, E. B. Hatrick, Edmund Goulding, Ma Talmadge, Greta Garbo, Nick Schenck, Alice Terry, Harry Rapf, Aileen Pringle, J. Robert Rubin, Norma Shearer. Front row: Hal Roach, Natalie Talmadge, Eddie Mannix, Constance Talmadge, Buster Keaton, Paul Bern, Irving Thalberg. Reclining: John Gilbert.*

Davies's Southern California home, the site of some of her most celebrated Hollywood parties.[38] The next year—probably not coincidentally—Hearst bought Beacon Towers for his wife, Millicent, who rechristened it St. Joan's. A medieval-style beachfront estate at Sands Point, Long Island, New York, this former residence of Mrs. O. H. P. Belmont was designed by Hunt & Hunt, the two sons of architect Richard Morris Hunt, in 1917.[39]

Though Hearst's expenditures on other residences increased enormously, he became more attached to San Simeon and correspondingly more concerned that its art collection reflect its prominent position in his affections. In February of 1927, he wrote to Morgan:

> A great many very fine things will be arriving for the ranch—some of them have already arrived.
>
> They are for the most part of a much higher grade than we have had heretofore. In fact, I have decided to buy only the finest things for the ranch from now on, and we will probably weed out some of our less desirable articles.
>
> I had no idea when we began to build the ranch that I would be here so much or that the construction itself would be so important. Under the present circumstances, I see no reason why the ranch should not be a museum of the best things that I can secure.[40]

Among the pieces that prompted this letter were the superb Spanish Renaissance articles Hearst purchased from the collection of the Count of Almenas, who sold his belongings in a celebrated auction at the American Art Association in New York in January 1927. The Bynes wrote the sale catalog and had tried for some years to entice Hearst into buying the entire collection.[41] Always a single-item-oriented collector, Hearst was not tempted by the chance to buy a large collection en bloc, but he did appear at the auction to select sculpture and furniture of high quality, many pieces of which were placed in his own quarters at San Simeon. This sale marked the end of the popularity of Spanish Renaissance pieces in the New York sale rooms. Hearst was one of the few collectors who continued to acquire Spanish objects through the 1930s, long after most buyers' ardor had waned.[42]

ADRIAEN YSENBRANDT (attributed to). MADONNA AND
CHILD WITH ANGELS. Flemish, early 16th century. Oil on panel,
45 ¼ x 33 ¾" (115.3 x 88.2 cm). Hearst Monument Collection, House A
Sitting Room.

The central figures of the Madonna and Child are based on Jan van
Eyck's Madonna with Canon George van der Paele, painted in 1436.
The flanking angels and the ledge have been added to this composition.
Here the Madonna wears a cloak of rich, luminous vermilion color. She
holds a goldfinch, a symbol of the Crucifixion due to the flash of red
color on its bill. The Christ child holds a parrot, symbolizing the
Annunciation. It is possible that this piece is the work of Ambrosius
Benson, who like Ysenbrandt was a painter in Bruges in the early six-
teenth century. Both artists were followers of the great Flemish painter
Gerard David.

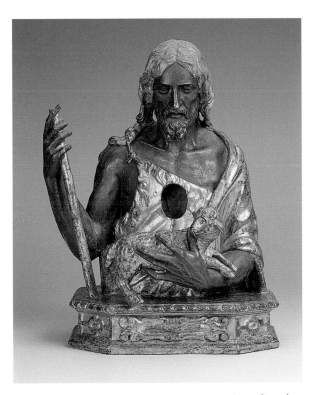

ST. JOHN THE BAPTIST RELIQUARY. Spanish, 16th
century. Wood, polychrome, gilding. 23 x 15 x 19" (58.42 x 38.1 x
22.86 cm). Hearst Monument Collection, Casa Grande Gothic
Suite Sitting Room.

A receptacle for sacred relics, this wooden bust has been
painted and gilded to resemble cast bronze and hammered gold.
Hearst acquired it from the 1927 Count of Almenas sale, which
represented the zenith of America's appetite for Spanish pieces.
While others' tastes changed, however, Hearst continued to
acquire Spanish art over the ensuing two decades.

DUCCIO DI BUONINSEGNA (school of). MADONNA AND
CHILD. Italian, c. 1300. Egg tempera on wood panel. 12 ¼ x 8 ⅝"
(31.1 x 21.9 cm). Hearst Monument Collection, Casa Grande South
Gothic Bedroom.

In this excellent example of early Sienese painting, the features of the
Virgin and Child are rendered with delicacy and emotion. This painting
was given to Hearst in 1932 by his friend Eleanor "Cissy" Patterson, the
publisher of Hearst's Washington Herald newspaper.

GOTHIC CHEST. *Spanish, 15th century. Wood, polychrome, gilding. 28 ½ x 52 ¾ x 21" (72.4 x 133.9 x 53.3 cm). Hearst Monument Collection, Casa Grande Gothic Suite Sitting Room.*

The gabled top does not lift; instead, the front is hinged as a door, behind which are drawers. Popular as bridal chests and known in Spain as arcōnes-huches, *such pieces were frequently decorated with gilded moldings and carved central panels, as is this example, which Hearst purchased from the 1927 Count of Almenas sale.*

The year 1927 marks the first time Hearst applied the word *museum* to San Simeon. It was a term he used twenty years later as well, at the very end of his residence there.[43] Hearst occasionally allowed local residents and members of various clubs to visit the estate when he was not present. A common country-house tradition that goes back centuries, it also put into practice his intention to make the house a museum. He did not make specific arrangements for the Castle's use after his death, however, and his promised weeding of its less desirable arti-

cles largely did not occur.[44] This house-cleaning declaration reiterates Hearst's unsuccessful avowal to Phoebe in 1889, "I am not going to buy any more trinkets."[45] Hearst's nature was fundamentally additive, not subtractive. The quality of his purchases continued to fluctuate, though from this date on he did increase his patronage of art dealers' showrooms, where the pieces were generally of a higher quality than at the auction houses.

Hearst used the unfinished Assembly Room both as a social room and a dining room from the summer of 1924 until mid-1926, when the Refectory had progressed enough to be usable.[46] Morgan, no doubt thinking of the enormous size of these two rooms, wrote to Hearst: "The building is going to eat up furnishings like an ogre."[47] She need not have worried that there would be a shortage of pieces, as she made clear in writing to Arthur Byne the following year, when she described the Assembly Room, where many of the objects had been placed:

> . . . [W]e have a 17' x 17' mantel from a French chateau, 16th century—an enormous wooden ceiling plain dark wood deeply paneled and carved, from a 16th century Italian palace—four 15' x 24' Scipio tapestries from the Royal Collection, Madrid—two 14' x 18' tapes-tries ditto . . . plus a set of opening trims of marble, one a fine antique—two lovely old, blue and silver valances 6' x 27'—two . . . paintings, grand scale—a carved and polychrome doorway about 23' x 23', and want a choir stall to use as a wainscot or paneling about 12' to 14' high all round the room to tie together with. Now it sounds frightful, but *it is not.*[48]

Her stout defense was an admission that the Assembly Room has a complex scheme. In fact, it is the grandest room in the estate, its combination of elements succeeding because their dominant theme is horizontality, the rectangular forms of the tapestries and choir stalls interrupted only by the Château de Jours fireplace on the east wall and the identically sized rectangular entrance-

PAIR OF MAIOLICA COVERED VASES FROM URBINO. *Italian, 17th century. Glazed terra cotta. 22" (55.9 cm). Hearst Monument Collection, Casa Grande Doge's Suite Sitting Room.*

Such istoriato ware is named for its characteristic narrative painting, usually of Biblical or mythological subjects. Among the scenes depicted is the story of Moses being placed in a box and floated down river before a crowned female, probably the Pharaoh's daughter.

CASKET. *French, early 16th century. Ebony and carved rock crystal, with gilt bronze mounts and agate and lapis lazuli ornament. 19 ½ x 14 ½ x 24" (49.5 x 38.8 x 61 cm). Hearst Monument Collection, Casa Grande Assembly Room.*

Though the function of this piece is not certain, it was probably used as a ceremonial presentation casket for gifts rather than as a jewel case or a reliquary. It was presented to Hearst in 1927 as a gift from the New York art dealers French & Co.

LEFT: ST. PETER. *Spanish, 15th century, done in 13th-century style. Wood and polychrome. 42 ½" (107.9 cm). Hearst Monument Collection, Casa Grande Gothic Suite Sitting Room.*

St. Peter is shown as the Pope, wearing papal garb and the conical tiara.

way on the west wall. Only the textiles, paintings, and fire mantel were placed unaltered in the room; the choir stalls, ceiling, and door and window frames were all extended to the necessary dimensions. In employing choir stalls as a wainscoting and tapestries above, Hearst and Morgan were once again taking inspiration from Stanford White's Payne Whitney mansion, this time from the dining room.

They were still working on completing both the Assembly Room and the Refectory early in 1927. The Refectory lagged the farthest behind because of difficulties Morgan had installing its ceiling. Hearst wanted to emphasize the Gothic nature of the room, in contrast to the Renaissance-era Assembly Room. The navelike Refectory has clerestory windows above tapestries set at the same level as the fourteenth-century choir-stall panels they used as wainscoting on the remaining walls. "I feel pretty sure the lowered tapestries will be good [in the Refectory]," Hearst predicted. "They are so in [Henry VIII's sixteenth-century English palace] Hampton Court."[49] He also wanted a Gothic ceiling, something so difficult to obtain that they initially determined that they would create a painted and beamed one, patterned after a fourteenth-century Sicilian original in the Palazzo Chiaramonte in Palermo.[50] This proved so time-consuming a fabrication that they decided to use a

Spanish antique instead, but when it turned out to be two unrelated ceilings packed together, Hearst suggested they use a Renaissance ceiling of full-length figures of saints, which they could modify to incorporate into the room: "of course it is not as good as [a] gothic ceiling but it might be better than a Moorish one."[51] The flatness of this ceiling contrasts oddly with the Gothic imagery in the grillework, window frames, and choir stalls. Morgan was philosophical about having adopted a solution that strikes a discordant note of horizontality among all the vertical lines of the room: "Perhaps the flatness forced by conditions will make this large scale ceiling tie into its surroundings as it would not with its original heavy deep beams and deep panels."[52]

Both the Assembly Room and the Refectory were visually complicated rooms for Morgan to design because of the number of antique and modern objects they contain. The East Room (later known as the Morning Room) was less tightly structured, its tapestries separated by intervals of exposed concrete, scored and textured to look like stone. Adjoining both the Refectory and the halls leading to the two added wings of the building, this space also had a more informal function: guests used it as an additional sitting room, especially late in the evenings.[53]

THE DINING ROOM of the Payne Whitney mansion in New York, designed by Stanford White, displays paneled wainscoting below and ornamental hangings above. Hearst and Morgan took this room as their inspiration for the Assembly Room's interior scheme.

THE ASSEMBLY ROOM, c. 1930.

TILE PANEL. *Persian,
Safavid Dynasty, 17th century.
Fired and glazed terra cotta.
114 x 60" (289.6 x 1524 cm).
Hearst Monument Collection,
Casa Grande Billiard Room.*

*The scene depicted, of the
Persian King Bahram Gur
killing a dragon, comes from the
tenth-century Shānāmā (Book
of Kings) of Fīrdawsī. While
Bahram Gur spears the dragon
through the head, two youths
watch in astonishment from a
nearby tree. Even the birds look
on in amazement. The scene is
repeated on both sides of the arch.*

Hearst wanted the large public rooms completed as quickly as possible so that he could use them for entertaining. The most notable guests of the decade came at the close of the 1920s, when Winston Churchill, his brother Jack, and their sons Randolph Churchill and John Spencer Churchill visited San Simeon in September 1929, one month before the stock market crash. Twenty-one-year-old Randolph wrote in his diary: "The most deliciously warm weather I have ever known greeted me on arising. . . . The house and grounds are by no means completed, though nine years have passed since it was started. Everywhere are workmen, motor lorries, and pneumatic drills."[54] Randolph's cousin, John, wrote: "Hearst treated our visit as a state occasion. Although he had been separated from his wife for some time he decided—for form's sake, I suppose—to summon her from New York to act as official hostess."[55] Millicent was indeed the hostess at San Simeon, though when the party left for Los Angeles after a few days, Marion entertained them in southern California. Of Millicent's position Winston Churchill wrote his wife, Clementine: "She has not got an easy role to play: but with 5 sons & a separate establishment some sort of arrangement is necessary & not impossible." He described San Simeon as "astonishing." "His house is

THE REFECTORY, *c. 1930, with cut flowers on the tables.
Greenhouses south of the estate raised orchids, lilies, and other flowers
that could be cut for interior arrangements. Fruit and flowers in the
gardens were not picked.*

rudely described as Monte Carlo Casino on the top of the rock of Gibraltar—but it is better than this."[56] Hearst himself Winston described as

> most interesting to meet, and I got to like him—a grave simple child—with no doubt a nasty temper—playing with the most costly toys. A vast income always overspent: Ceaseless building and collecting not very discriminatingly works of art: two magnificent establishments, two charming wives, complete indifference to public opinion, a strong liberal and democratic outlook, a 15 million daily circulation, oriental hospitalities, extreme personal courtesy (to us at any rate) and the appearance of a Quaker elder—or perhaps a Mormon elder. . . . At Los Angeles . . . we passed into the domain of Marion Davies; and were all charmed by her. She is not strikingly beautiful nor impressive in any way. But her personality is most attractive; naïve, childlike.[57]

ANTONIO CANOVA. VENUS ITALICA. *Italian, c. 1810. Marble. 6'3" x 23" x 25" (190.5 x 584.x 63.5 cm). Hearst Monument Collection, Casa Grande Assembly Room.*

According to art historian Hugh Honour, Napoleon Bonaparte first viewed the Medici Venus, a Roman statue of the early third century, at the Uffizi Gallery in Florence in 1796. It made such an impression on him that when his troops invaded Italy four years later, he claimed her as the "bride" to the Apollo Belvedere, which he had already moved from Rome to Paris. Thus, the Medici Venus, the most famous statue in the Uffizi, left Florence for Paris in 1802. The Florentine authorities asked Antonio Canova, then the most celebrated living sculptor, to create a replacement. While Canova was opposed to the practice of copying antique statues, he realized this was an exceptional case. He consented in 1803 and asked to be sent a cast of the Medici Venus. While it appears that initially Canova intended to sculpt a Venus of his own invention and additionally to execute a copy of the Medici Venus, only his own Venus, the Venus Italica, seems to have been created. Canova actually sculpted four slightly different Venuses; the example in the Hearst collection is the second he created, commissioned by the King of Spain. After the king's abdication was forced by Napoleon, Canova instead sold this second version to Napoleon's brother, Prince Lucien of Canino, who later sold it to the Marquess of Lansdowne in London in 1822. In order of execution, the Venuses of Canova are: first, the Venus Italica at the Pitti Palace; second, the San Simeon statue; third, the Residenzmuseum example in Munich; and fourth, the Hope Venus in the Leeds City Art Gallery in England. Though Hearst bought this second Venus Italica at the famous Lansdowne sale of 1930, its whereabouts were listed as unknown until only a few years ago, indicating how seldom scholars have studied the Hearst collection until recently. Its "discovery" in the spot where it had been resting for seventy years marks a gradual increase in appreciation for San Simeon's fine and decorative art objects.

The open way in which Hearst displayed both his marital and extramarital arrangements to Churchill was typical. His only concession to propriety was to have Millicent presiding over San Simeon on this important occasion. Other than the family Christmas celebrations in 1924 and 1925, and a few later family visits, after 1925 Millicent served as hostess at the hilltop only in Hearst's absence, with her own parties of guests.[58] At all other times the social tone was set by Marion Davies, who created an atmosphere as spontaneous and effervescent as her personality.

FREDERICK WILLIAM MACMONNIES. BACCHANTE. *American, 1914. Marble. 7'3" x 31" x 36" (221 x 78.3 x 914 cm). Hearst Monument Collection, Casa Grande West Vestibule.*

In 1893 MacMonnies created a Bacchante in bronze as a gift for Stanford White's partner, Charles Follen McKim, who donated it to the Boston Public Library in 1896. It was not displayed because of its immoral theme: an inebriated woman holding an infant. The ensuing controversy increased the piece's popularity, and MacMonnies created several other bronze and marble versions. This one was in Phoebe Hearst's collection at the Hacienda del Pozo de Verona in Pleasanton, California.

JEAN LÉON GÉRÔME. PYGMALION AND GALATEA. *French, 1892. Marble. 6'4" (198.1 cm). Hearst Monument Collection, Casa Grande West Vestibule.*

The Roman poet Ovid wrote in the first century A.D. of Pygmalion, the King of Cyprus, who sculpted a woman so beautiful that he fell in love with her. Venus took pity on him and brought her to life. Here Gérôme depicts the moment of her animation, which he emphasized by tinting the statue in delicate colors that have since worn away. This piece was shown at the 1893 World's Columbian Exposition in Chicago and was acquired by Hearst in 1910. Casa Grande's entrance vestibule is flanked by the MacMonnies and Gérôme statues, two important late-nineteenth-century works.

CHAPTER SIX

Marion Davies Invites

William Randolph Hearst and Marion Davies made a good pair. He had Victorian gallantry, a strong desire to educate those around him, and complete contempt for social snobbery. He was shaped by the freedoms of his youth in the West, where people measured you by what you did rather than by who your parents were, by what wealth you possessed rather than by where it came from. Hearst had always found "society" immensely boring—though occasionally

amusing. In the 1890s he wrote to Phoebe while making the crossing to Europe aboard the RMS *Lucania*:

> Lady Cunard is on board. She is at my table. She spoke about you and asked how you were. She is a nice little thing but kind of light-headed and chatters loudly with a sort of turkey gobbler by the name of Guinness who makes the soup and a gibbering idiot by the name of Van Alen who doesn't make anything except a holy show of himself. Lady Cunard asked me why I didn't go into society and I could have told her that if I had no other reason the present company would furnish enough. She isn't bad, though, she certainly shines intellectually when compared with the men.[1]

Hearst's chosen companions were newspaper people, a gritty bunch, and show people, known for their informality and frankness. Marion Davies was the blank slate whom he could introduce to art and travel and make into the world's biggest movie star. She had insouciance and a warm heart, and declared *dull* a four-letter word.[2] Beneath her surface gaiety lay tremendous openness and vulnerability. Marion seemed to those who knew her to be giving rather than grasping, though she lived in opulence, constantly receiving jewelry and other gifts from Hearst. Far from the profile of the typical gold digger, her defining trait was her generosity to friends and employees. Anita Loos, who minted the gold-digger persona with her classic story *Gentlemen*

Hollywood

Prefer Blondes, said, "Actually, jewels meant so little to Marion that her most valuable accessory could have been a safety pin."[3]

Marion was not the first performer to fascinate Hearst. He was briefly engaged to actress Eleanor Calhoun in the 1880s. Phoebe had introduced them and then forced them to part—Miss Calhoun had been acceptable as her protégée but not as her daughter-in-law.[4] She initially felt the same way about Millicent Willson, who was a twenty-year-old dancer on the vaudeville circuit when she married W. R. in 1903 on the eve of his fortieth birthday.[5] Phoebe grew fonder of Millicent, who left the stage after her marriage and began to have social aspirations. Phoebe's warmth increased especially after her grandchildren began appearing in 1904. The most distressing of all her son's attachments had been his long liaison with a waitress he met while at Harvard, Tessie Powers. Phoebe exerted gentle, then strong, pressure to separate them, but she was unsuccessful for many years.[6] Soon after Hearst came to San Francisco to take over his father's *San Francisco Examiner* in 1887, he brought Tessie across the country, installing her in a home in Sausalito. Rather than seeing her only clandestinely, as did many men who kept paramours in the late nineteenth century, he

took her to the theater, traveled abroad with her, and scandalized society by appearing in public with her, behaving as openly as he would with Marion Davies years later.[7]

Though in her older years Marion claimed she was born in 1905, in fact she was born on January 3, 1897. The youngest of five children, she and her three older sisters were raised for the stage and groomed to seek out older men who would be their patrons and protectors. Her formal education came at a convent boarding school from 1910 to 1913, with ballet lessons on the weekends. After three years at the convent, she dropped out and began to take ballet daily, and tap dancing lessons, being tutored somewhat haphazardly for a short time longer. In 1914, Marion appeared on Broadway for the first time, having moved up quickly from being a "pony girl," who danced only in the interludes between numbers in small revues, to a first-line chorus girl.

Hearst was well-known for frequenting Broadway revues and the parties that followed them, at which Marion was often seen with publisher Paul Block.[8] Marion remembered seeing Hearst at the Campbell's Studio, where she was posing for photographs to be featured in Hearst's *American Weekly.* "He had the most penetrating eyes—honest, but penetrating eyes. He didn't have a harmful bone in his body. He just liked to be by himself and just look at the girls on the stage while they were dancing. . . . I think he was a very lone-

MARION DAVIES poses against the stone walls of Casa Grande in a publicity still for M-G-M Studios, c. 1930.

some man."[9] Their relationship began in 1915, when Hearst was fifty-two and Marion was eighteen and dancing in the Broadway revue *Stop! Look! Listen!* A year later she graduated to the Ziegfeld Follies, and by the close of 1917, she made her first film, *Runaway Romany,* with the assistance of her former brother-in-law, George Lederer, and without any help from William Randolph Hearst.

For a time W. R. and Marion's love affair remained clandestine, but within a few years it was no longer a secret, with painful results. Bill Hearst Jr. wrote about it years later: "In the early 1920s my father began spending more and more time making movies with Marion in Hollywood. I wept when I began to understand what was going on. Because of the embarrassment to both of us, I never initiated the subject with my mother."[10] He speculated that if his mother had remained silent about it, rather than challenging his father and forcing him to choose between them, she might have saved their marriage. Hearst "intensely disliked unpleasantness and even indirect confrontations. . . . Despite the fact that my father was attracted to the actress, he made no commitments to her. They had not yet decided to live together. It was still possible that Mother could have prevailed."[11] This might have been filial wishful thinking: the actual solution the Hearsts adopted was to separate without divorcing in 1925. Millicent remained in New York and Hearst spent much of his time on the West Coast. They stayed in communication and were even amicable friends. Millicent shared Christmas at San Simeon with Hearst and their sons in 1928, hosted Winston Churchill in 1929, and came back again for a family visit in the mid-thirties. On many other occasions, she appeared at

MILLICENT HEARST, *c. 1910. Mrs. Hearst accompanied Hearst and their children to San Simeon for many summer visits in the early years of construction. Hearst's letters to Morgan from this period often refer to Millicent's design ideas. But after their informal marital separation in the mid-1920s, Millicent visited San Simeon only occasionally.*

the ranch in Hearst's absence, with her own party of guests. Bill Jr. said that Millicent had confided to his wife, Austine, that she would have granted W. R. a divorce, despite her Catholicism, if he had asked for it. He speculated that his father never would have sullied his mother's reputation by putting her through the ordeal that divorce represented in the 1920s; furthermore, the financial and legal problems of such a proceeding would have been considerable. "Pop didn't wish to cause my mother or us new personal embarrassment. . . . My father knew that divorce would have saved him from public attack. He chose to accept the blame attached to his life and spare the family."[12]

Though Millicent concentrated on her charities and society events, scandal nonetheless took a toll on her. W. R. was publicly attacked for the immorality of his domestic arrangements.[13] Hearst became even more of an absentee father, his loyalty to Marion over their mother a source of shame to his sons. Marion wrote, "I was always a bridesmaid but never a bride," assuming a matchmaking role among her friends and affecting a lightheartedness about her own ambiguous marital position, belied by her increasing dependence on alcohol.[14] Both Bill Jr. and Marion recalled the awkwardness of meeting at San Simeon for the first time. Bill arrived unannounced and was afraid to join the other guests, explaining to Hearst's secretary, Joe Willicombe, that he was not sure if his father would want him to meet his girlfriend. Willicombe transmitted the message to Hearst Sr., who told his son to come into the Refectory, but did not introduce him to Marion. "She just came over and said, 'I'm Marion Davies.' And I said, 'Yes, I know.' So there I was."[15] Marion showed her discomfiture behind the bravado: "It was a delightful life. I was embarrassed all the time."[16]

What Marion and Hearst were creating was not the conventional society of the time, though in years since it has become the norm: the elevation of movie stars and business associates to the social elite. "The society people always wanted to meet the movie stars, so I mixed them together," Marion recalled. "When they say that society people are higher than the stars, that isn't so. Society always wants some celebrity at their parties, and they are lucky if they can get one, because theatrical

world where they could be accepted as a couple. Hearst's reporter Adela Rogers St. Johns recalled, "Marion was there [at] the dinner, she was the hostess, she met everybody—the presidents, the governors, the ambassadors—everybody. And they all accepted her. It was a . . . throwback [to another time]. In those days, the mistress of the king had a specific position and everybody recognized it and that was that!"[19]

Marion was always warmth and compassion personified. She was a naturally unaffected hostess whose consideration extended to all the employees as well as to all

MARION DAVIES, Constance Talmadge, Hedda Hopper, and Frances Goldwyn work a jigsaw puzzle at San Simeon, photographed by Cecil Beaton. This lighthearted and very social pastime was later transformed into a metaphor for solitude and despair in Orson Welles's Citizen Kane.

people are very particular who they go with."[17] When Marion referred to "society," she was not speaking of the New York social set Hearst had always scorned. She meant "café society," the name given by Maury Paul—a Hearst columnist who wrote for his New York American under the name Cholly Knickerbocker—for the combination of swells and celebrities that began to mingle in the years between the world wars. In this set, fame counted more than family. As Walter Winchell, another Hearst columnist, put it: "Social position is now more a matter of press than prestige."[18] Hearst the press lord and Marion the movie star made a powerful combination in this group, and at San Simeon they created a

the guests, many of whom were not major stars. Friends from her showgirl days and actors who were down on their luck and not getting any parts were frequently invited to the ranch, as were all the members of her noisy family, whom Marion referred to as the Sanger Circus, after a traveling group of acrobats.[20] British photographer Cecil Beaton recalled Anita Loos telling him, "Marion is most attentive to all sorts of people. . . . I've often gone into a shop where she knows the salesgirl and the salesgirl says, 'I've had a postcard from Miss Davies this morning.'"[21] At San Simeon, Marion graciously presided over streams of guests, including Howard Hughes, Jean Paul Getty, Maurice de

THIS PAGE:

TOP LEFT: *Hollywood star Jack Mulhall reclines in the well-known "Cardinal Richelieu bed," which, though incorrectly named—it was a seventeenth-century Italian bed from Lombardy, not France—still became a symbol of opulence to the Hollywood guests, who would request to be assigned there in House B.*

TOP RIGHT: *Actress Colleen Moore pauses on her way into House B, in 1931.*

RIGHT: *Cary Grant leans against a first-century Roman grave marker on the Central Plaza.*

OPPOSITE PAGE:

TOP LEFT: *Screenwriter Anita Loos and her husband, director John Emerson, pose on the Central Plaza.*

TOP RIGHT: *Hearst among his guests, with the legendary bottles of condiments scattered on the table in the Refectory.*

BOTTOM RIGHT: *Guests gather around the Neptune Pool, c. 1931.*

A PAGE FROM the Castle's guest book, inscribed by Constance Talmadge Netcher, Townsend Netcher, Natalie Talmadge Keaton, Buster Keaton, Carmen Pantages, and George K. Arthur, and signed and dated June 1931 by William Randolph Hearst.

Rothschild, Bernard Shaw, Calvin Coolidge, Joseph Duveen, Bill Tilden, Alice Marble, Helen Moody, Ignace Paderewski, H. G. Wells, Hoagy Carmichael, Gutzon Borglund, Gertrude Ederle, P. G. Wodehouse, Will Rogers, Louis B. Mayer, Irving Thalberg, and almost every major Hollywood star of the era—Mary Pickford, Douglas Fairbanks, Jimmy Stewart, Charlie Chaplin, Buster Keaton, Gary Cooper, Bob Hope, Tom Mix, Roy Rogers, Greta Garbo, Harpo Marx, Jean Harlow, Constance Bennett, and Clark Gable. Almost equal in number with the celebrities were Hearst employees, called to the ranch for meetings with the boss they all referred to as "the Chief." Aileen Pringle, a silent-screen actress who remained close to Marion, remembered the sudden appearance of a group of editors: "You would come downstairs and you would find in the Great Hall . . . probably thirty men standing around in blue suits. It would be a surprise for us. They arrived during the night."[22]

Marion summarized the typical routine of San Simeon hospitality, which echoed the traditional country-house weekends in Britain and on the East Coast of America in the first third of the century.

> I'd go up on weekends, and there'd be twenty or thirty guests, possibly forty or fifty. The train would leave Los Angeles at 8:15 [on Friday evening] and arrive at San Luis about three in the morning, and we'd motor on up. We'd come back on Sunday to be at work Monday.
>
> Pete was the man who owned the limousines in San Luis. Several cars were needed, and it was almost an hour and a half's drive. W. R. would pay for the train and for the cars.
>
> When we arrived we'd have breakfast and a rest. Luncheon was about 2:30 and dinner about half past eight at night. Saturday night we'd watch a movie.
>
> Before breakfast on Sunday we'd play tennis or go horseback riding—the usual things, the sporting life routine. Or we'd swim. . . .
>
> W. R. would come out and join the guests and go swimming. And he played tennis and went horseback riding. He was excellent at riding.[23]

Hearst's use of San Simeon as a working home meant that much of the responsibility for the guests fell to Marion. "W. R. was a very fine host, but he was not socially minded," she recalled. "He would greet the people, then he would disappear. He would go to the architect's office, or maybe he would work on his editorials. He would pay no attention to the guests, except at mealtimes, when he would be very polite, and then he would disappear again."[24] There were times when this responsibility became wearing. Marion admitted, "When I wasn't working I'd stay at San Simeon, and then I'd wish I were working because there were so many people there and the routine got tiresome—laying the place cards and meeting the visiting characters."[25] Still, what guests most remembered about the social nature of their visit was Marion Davies: her skill at bridge, her quick laughter, her side-splitting gift for mimicry. Gretchen Swinnerton, the wife of Hearst cartoonist Jimmy Swinnerton, said, "Marion was just a cute little old girl that had no particu-

POLAR BEARS in the bear grotto, which was built in 1934 on the north side of Orchard Hill. Ice was brought in to keep the bears comfortable in the summer.

A HERD OF Grey's zebra remains on the San Simeon ranch, where they are often glimpsed among the cattle.

lar social ambitions, and he didn't either, and so I think that's why they got along so well."[26]

But no matter how warm Marion was, she could not always protect the guests from Hearst's sometimes chilly reserve. British humorist P. G. Wodehouse wrote:

> You don't see Hearst till dinnertime, and then, if you're a sensitive soul like me and sitting immediately opposite him, you might wish you hadn't seen him then. In my experience there are two kinds of elderly American. One, the stout and horn-rimmed, is mateyness itself. He greets you as if you were a favorite son, starts agitating the cocktail shaker before you know where you are, slips a couple into you with a merry laugh, tells you a dialect story about two Irishmen named Pat and Mike, and in a word makes life one grand sweet song. The other, which runs a good deal to the tight lips and the cold gray stare, seems to view the English cousin with concern. It is not elfin. It broods. It says little. And every now and then you catch its eye, and it is like colliding with a raw oyster. Mine host belongs to the latter class.

Wodehouse also cast his eye on another feature of his visit that made an enormous impression on all the guests—Hearst's private zoo and the exotic imported animals that roamed the ranch.

> Hearst collects everything, including animals, and has a zoo on the premises, and the specimens considered reasonably harmless are allowed to roam at large. You're apt to meet a bear or two before you get to the house, or an elephant, or even Sam Goldwyn. . . .
>
> No drinks are allowed after dinner, which must come as a nasty blow to many, though perhaps they might have refused them anyway after seeing that yak in the road. A man has to be a pretty tough toper not to knock off after the shock of finding yaks among those present.

THE REFECTORY at Christmas, ablaze with lighted Christmas trees and decorations.
Hearst loved best the handmade gifts he received from his guests.

Wodehouse also noted the seating arrangement at dinner, which clustered the newly arrived guests near Hearst and Marion's seats at the center of the table. "The longer you're there, the further you get from the middle. I sat on Marion's right the first night, then found myself getting edged further and further away, till I got to the extreme end, when I thought it time to leave. Another day and I should have been feeding on the floor."[27] The customary dress for dinner was not formal, requiring only business suits for the men and cocktail dresses for the women. The photographer James E. Abbé planned for more formal attire, which would have been expected at East Coast country houses. His children wrote a reminiscence of a visit to San Simeon with

their parents: "Papa put on his dinner jacket, and when we got downstairs he was the only man dressed, but he was the best dressed man in the castle that night. Mr. Hearst then came down dressed in beige tweed."[28]

Louise Brooks was twenty-one when, as a celebrated dancer and actress, she arrived at San Simeon for the first time with her husband, director Eddie Sutherland. The charms of the place were lost on him.

> After three days, Eddie said to me, "I'll be damned if I'll be rousted out of the hay by a cowbell at eight o'clock every morning for breakfast, and have my liquor rationed as if I were some silly schoolboy. Besides, there's not even a golf course here. I'm going back to Hollywood tonight." Eddie was right to the extent that

THE THEATER, *where movies were shown nightly to the assembled guests and any employees—construction, grounds, or household—who wished to join them.*

ONE OF *the Theater's cast-plaster caryatids, which bear some resemblance to the caryatids that ornamented the Women's Building at the 1915 Panama-Pacific International Exposition. Julia Morgan had designed the interior for architect Ernest Champney's building.*

the ranch was a deadly dull place for anyone who did not revel in opulence, who was not a member of Marion's stock company of guests, who was not mentally stimulated by visiting celebrities, and who wanted neither film advancement nor financial aid from Marion or Mr. Hearst.[29]

Charlie Chaplin was a frequent guest, who recalled: "The dinners were elaborate. . . . There was game of the season: pheasant, wild duck, partridge, and venison. Yet amidst the opulence we were served paper napkins, and it was only when Mrs. Hearst was in residence that the guests were given linen ones."[30] Paper napkins and another highly visible touch of informality, condiments in their bottles on the table, were a shock to many, and an immediate reminder that this was not an East Coast dining room. Actress Colleen Moore remembered: "I was amazed, of course, at all the ketchup bottles and all the condiments. We used to wonder what became of the pickled peaches with only one peach taken out of them, because every single day they were all brand new and filled."[31] Dancer Irene Castle was struck by the "hanging battle flags," actually antique Sienese banners that hung in the Refectory. "Sitting around the refectory table, you felt you should be chewing on big legs of mutton and throwing the bones to the dogs."[32] On special occasions, guests were often asked to speak after the meal. Marion Davies's niece Patricia Lake, who was married to the comedian Arthur Lake, reminisced: "It was very good training, because you would be called on, and you'd better have your wits about you." Arthur Lake then recalled that he taught Hearst how to truck: the rhythmic walk which was a popular dance at the time. "He'd get up and he'd truck on down in the big dining room there. He could do it pretty good, too, with his finger [waggling] just right."[33]

WILLIAM RANDOLPH HEARST (the son of an actual pioneer) and Marion Davies strike a melodramatic pose at their famous covered wagon party in 1933.

After dinner, there was usually a movie shown about eleven o'clock, viewed outdoors at first, a tradition that dated to Hearst's camping days with his family on the hilltop. By the early 1930s, the Theater was completed on the ground floor of the North Wing, and the guests gathered there. Actress and radio personality Ilka Chase was sardonic about her visit to the ranch, admitting about Hearst that it "may have been his reputation working on my imagination, but he scared me to death." In spite of that she never doubted his devotion to Marion, and recalled visiting when

the theater was not yet complete—the plaster was still wet—so an immense pile of fur coats was heaped at the door and each guest picked one at random and enveloped himself before entering. The regular seats hadn't been installed, so we sat in wicker armchairs; there was one wicker sofa, which was tacitly understood to be reserved for Hearst and Marion. They would sit

CHRISTMAS 1934: *pianist Ignace Paderewski stands beside an enormous tree on the Central Plaza.*

close together in the gloom, silhouetted against the screen, and bundled in their fur coats, they looked for all the world like the big and baby bears. Although there was an occasional interloper, most of the pictures shown at the ranch were Marion's, which put a slight strain on the guests' gratitude.[34]

The other memorable evening activities were costume parties, which were given both at Marion's house in Santa Monica and at San Simeon. Colleen Moore remembered that trunks of costumes arrived from the studios and guests picked their outfits according to the selected themes, including, at San Simeon, a covered wagon party, a Hawaiian party, and a Civil War party.

After dinner, there was an orchestra, I think they had come from Los Angeles. The [Assembly] room had been cleared of the carpets . . . so that there was dancing. I don't know where the furniture disappeared. We were dancing and having a great time, and then Mr. Hearst got the idea, and we got in chairs and then the guys pushed the chairs around the room. We all thought that was hilariously funny.[35]

Marion mused,

Over the years thousands of people must have come to San Simeon. But W. R. didn't really select them; I think most of the guests selected him. We'd get a little message, "I'm arriving . . ." But he never mentioned any feeling against sharing San Simeon.

Between my pictures he'd say it would be nice to kind of relax and just have a few people. We'd have about ten guests, and it would be really quiet. The place is huge and you would only feel about so big. When he wanted quiet, I wouldn't invite the ones who wanted constant merriment.[36]

There were plenty of those, as Frances Marion recalled.

We all looked upon [San Simeon] with a feeling akin to awe, for it was a monument to a man's dream, there being nothing about the home that seemed real except the humans, who spent most of their time destroying the illusion by their human behavior. . . .

Mr. Hearst presided over his three-ring circus with dignity and amusement. After dinner and the movie he would retire to the Gothic Library which he kept under lock and key and opened only for the chosen few.

Many said that Mr. Hearst was hiding out or spurning them; however, we who knew him were aware that he merely sought a few hours of respite in his quiet

PHOTOGRAPHER Cecil Beaton, who took this photograph, later wrote that when he arrived at San Simeon, "Hearst stood smiling at the top of one of the many flights of garden steps."

Cecil Beaton, a lifelong diarist, first came to San Simeon with Anita Loos and her husband to share New Year's Eve of 1931. At twenty-seven, Beaton already possessed an excellent visual sense and an unforgiving eye for social situations. "The party assembled at the station," he wrote. "Everyone was in high spirits. Tough blondes, hams and nonentities mingled with directors and magnates." After the long train ride and a drive from the station past "enormous green hillsides that made remembered mountains seem like mole hills," they "caught sight of a vast, sparkling white castle in Spain."

It was right out of a fairy story. . . .
    The sun poured down with theatrical brilliance on tons of white marble and white stone. There seemed to be a thousand marble statues, pedestals, urns. The flowers were unreal in their ordered profusion. Hearst stood smiling at the top of one of the many flights of garden steps. . . .
    My room seemed gigantic. There was a carved gilt ceiling . . . old, tinselled velvets hanging on the walls.

retreat. He always surrounded himself with the young but youth is noisy when disporting itself in pools or tennis courts. "Yet who wants to stifle those happy voices," he often said. "Not I."[37]

Not that Hearst wasn't sorely tried at times. Cary Grant told of being a " 'bombardier' in a biplane" flown by Bill Hearst Jr: "Bill purloined and piloted Herb Fleishhacker's airplane at San Simeon one morning and induced naïve me to come along." Bill Jr. recalled: "Cary was foolish enough to come with me. . . . We got the kind of paper bags one found at the corner candy store and filled them with flour. We buzzed around and threw the bags on the hangar's asphalt roof. It was great fun because you could see where they hit." Neither young man realized that even the small bags frightened the guests and damaged the hangar's roof. When they returned to the house, "Cary's bags were packed and on the front porch, which was the way Mr. Hearst let a guest know he was no longer welcome. Someone interceded, however, and Cary was allowed to stay."[38]

A TRICK SHOT from Life *poses Jimmy Stewart in front of the towers of Casa Grande on his 1938 visit.*

The view from the window revealed a panorama of pale green mountains, blue, misty hills, and a silver sea in the distance.

In Marion, Beaton saw a woman "pretty as a Greuze, and what a character! She is kind, humble, shrewd, blindly generous and madly inconsequential. . . . never alone, always surrounded by a gang of twenty or thirty hangers-on."

That weekend party included Anita Loos and her husband John Emerson; Marion's nephew, screenwriter Charles Lederer, at the time a youth of eighteen; actor Eddie Kane; British ambassador Moore; and actresses Colleen Moore, Doris Lloyd, and Eileen Percy. On the second night, the guests gathered in the Assembly Room before Hearst's arrival, where there was an unfortunate incident:

> Eddie and Eileen now danced a frenzied apache together, making a beeline for a gold, carved chest so priceless that Hearst would not allow a telephone to be on it, nor anyone but the head housekeeper to dust it. The dancers dashed at the forbidden object, opened the lid and jumped inside. On the bottom was a bowl of water to preserve the wood from warping. Splash went Eddie Kane; splash followed Eileen Percy. Marion closed the lid on them, then jumped on it to keep the prisoners inside. The bottom of the chest caved in. Water poured from underneath. And at that very moment Hearst most typically came back into the room. He watched the tableau with a deathly white expression.
>
> There was a distinct coolness after that. A chastened group moved on to the terrace to see something of the new Clara Bow film. Then we hurriedly departed to catch our train.[39]

Such antics were surely one reason Hearst limited the amount of alcohol served to his guests. Prohibition was another. Casa Grande had a seven-thousand-bottle wine cellar and kegs of beer in the pantry, and these

BENEATH *the Assembly Room is the wine cellar, with a seven-thousand-bottle capacity.*

beverages were served at dinner, but hard liquor was controlled. Cary Grant recalled that before the nine-o'clock dinner was announced, guests arrived in the Assembly Room for "one weak martini—or two if you were quick." He added, "I would sometimes bring a bottle or two in my suitcase and unpack quickly. You couldn't let the servants find any extra liquor."[40]

But the primary reason for Hearst's concern was Marion herself. Bill Jr. said, "Perhaps Pop felt that Marion's heavy drinking—she became a hardened alcoholic—may have been his fault because he had not married her. This caused him much soul-searching and grief in his final years."[41] Hearst drank almost no hard liquor, though it was a hard-drinking era with little understanding of addiction, and newspapermen drank more heavily than most. Many guests recalled that Marion stashed bottled in the ladies' room, secure that she could not be disturbed there. "I will always remember the night when Mr. Hearst came and threw our robes and our toothbrushes and toothpaste in [to the bathroom]," Hearst reporter Adela Rogers St. Johns said. "He just opened the door and . . . said, 'If you girls are going to stay in there all night, you'll need these!'"[42] David Niven was a frequent guest from the mid-thirties on, and while at the time he participated eagerly in the illicit pre-cocktail hours and helped sneak alcohol to Marion as did many guests at the ranch, he felt differently about it later. "It seemed fun at the time to stoke up her fires of outrageous fun and laughter, and I got a kick, I suppose, out of feeling that I had outwitted one of the most powerful and best informed men on earth, but what a disloyal and crummy betrayal of someone who had shown me nothing but kindness and hospitality and what a nasty potential nail to put in her coffin."[43]

MARCEL LOUIS MAURICE COURBIER. GIRL FEEDING LAMB. *French, 1929. 43 x 65 x 23 ½" (109.2 x 165.1 x 59.7 cm). Hearst Monument Collection, North Esplanade.*
Cecil Beaton noted the contrast between the antique and modern statues in San Simeon's gardens: "Some of the statues, I noted with surprise, were not up to scratch, even cheapjack. Perhaps it was by intent; we'd been so overpowered by Donatellos and Della Robbias that it made the place come alive to see a nymph with bobbed hair eating an apple."

Hearst gave Marion everything he could, but he did not make her Mrs. Hearst, and he was unable to make her Hollywood's top movie star. His well-meaning meddling in her film career—insisting that she stay with costume dramas when her natural bent was for comedy—and the inflated claims of her talents printed in his newspapers reduced Marion's worth in the public's mind, exactly reversing his intentions. Frances Marion, a celebrated screenwriter who worked on many of Marion's films, said: "Mr. Hearst may have been a genius at newspapers but he just did not understand motion pictures. Lavishness doesn't guarantee a good picture. Marion was actually a natural-born comedienne but Mr. Hearst smothered her under extravagant stories and overdone backgrounds. In other words, you could not see the diamond in the setting."[44] Marion herself had a very low opinion of her talents: "I couldn't act, but the idea of silent pictures appealed to me, because I couldn't talk either. . . . W. R. always said to me, 'Never read any bad reviews about yourself. Read only the good ones.' Of course I thought, What if there are no good ones? Then I'm really in the dumps. I'd rather read the bad ones than the good ones anyway, because at least there are more of them."[45] She was embarrassed at the

size of the publicity machine pressed into service to promote her films. "The old saying is, 'It pays to advertise.' I suppose that's all right, but I used to feel I had too much."[46] She stuck with her film career, even though relatively few of her movies were financial successes, and she relocated from M-G-M to Warner Bros. Studios in 1934 because Hearst felt she was being skipped over for parts. Marion shone in the three comedies she made at M-G-M with director King Vidor—*The Patsy, Show People,* and *Not So Dumb*—where her true gaiety and effervescence transferred onto the screen.

In the thirty-six years they were together, Marion treasured their mutual loyalty. "I was always on W. R.'s side, so there was nothing to argue about. And W. R. was always on my side. That's why I liked him so much."[47] They certainly disagreed over Marion's abilities on screen, however. After Hearst's death, in recording her memoirs, Marion sadly concluded: "All my life, I wanted to have talent. Finally I had to admit there was nothing there. . . . W. R. argued with millions of people. He thought I could do anything. . . . He thought I'd be the best."[48] But onstage at San Simeon, it's hard to imagine how anyone could have performed better.

In the second half of the 1920s, so many projects were under construction on the estate that it was difficult to complete any one of them or to show clear progress. Morgan wrote to Hearst in the fall of 1928, when his arrival was imminent: "The men have never worked harder, or with better spirit—so what is undone is so because it was more than could be done in the time. I used to be amazed in laying out seating plans [for auditoriums] to find out how rapidly the seatings increased with the increase in diameter. It is like that on the Hill, as we go out from the center, the work to produce any effect increases amazingly."[1]

One of the most visible effects on Casa Grande was the decision to veneer its exterior in limestone, cut and grouted to appear as massive blocks. Morgan wrote to Arthur Byne: "We finally took the bull by the horns and are facing the entire main building with a Manti stone from Utah, about the color of Caen stone or of the similar Spanish stone most of the carved Gothic 'antiques' have been made of."[2] The stone unified the building's front and side facades considerably, blurring the lines between the antique and modern elements and giving Casa Grande its familiar gleaming white color. Morgan was very pleased with the result, which, she wrote to Hearst, "is going to be the making of the building."[3]

Actually, the interiors of the building were even less completed than its exterior. Though there were almost always scores of household servants, secretarial staff,

Expansion

and guests to feed several times a day, the Kitchen was not among the first structures built on the hill. There were plans from early on to put the Kitchen in the south wing of the Main Building, near the Refectory, but it was not poured until two years after construction on the main house began and was not actually usable until 1927. Prior to its completion, a camp kitchen on the grounds was used for food preparation.[4] A variable number of staff worked in the kitchen, usually including a chef; an assistant chef; a pastry chef; a "help" cook, whose duty was to cook for the servants; a dishwasher; a butler; and waiters and maids. The butler wore a suit and the waiters wore white jackets, while the women generally wore white dresses.[5]

Twelve bedrooms were poured in three stories above the kitchen in 1927, and these rooms primarily accommodated the female members of the household staff. The male house servants, construction workers, and gardeners lived in barracks and cabins on the south side of the hill. This servants' wing was generous in the size of its bedrooms and in the number of bathrooms, though it was sparely furnished with modern, department-store pieces and lacked wall-mounted electric heaters. Its staircases were also narrower and steeper than those in

CASA GRANDE, c. 1927, with the towers scaffolded. The lower towers were raised and the space formerly meant for bells was converted to two bedrooms. Through nearly thirty years of risky hilltop construction, there were no fatalities among the building crews.

the rest of the building. The large and cheery "Help's Dining Room," where the office staff, watchmen, and all the household help ate, was located off the Kitchen and was capable of accommodating as many as thirty-five people at round tables. An egalitarian custom uncommon in other country houses was that the Castle staff were invited each evening to sit in the back rows of the Theater and join Hearst, Marion, and their guests in the nightly film viewing.[6] In the early years there were conflicts among the staff, chiefly because Morgan's infrequent site visits and the lack of supervision, coupled with Hearst's frequent absences, led to both staff infighting and inactivity. By the late twenties, Morgan had successfully hired a group of servants who worked better together. Once an effective staff was in place, Hearst brought with him those in upper positions when he relocated to the Ocean House, San Simeon, and Wyntoon, leaving a housekeeper in permanent residence at San Simeon to supervise the remaining workers, many of whom were laid off in his absence.[7]

Breakfast for guests was served informally, from nine o'clock until noon, without Hearst or Marion present. Guests came in to the Refectory and placed individual breakfast orders with the staff. Lunch, which was buffet service sometime between two and four o'clock, was served when Hearst and Marion appeared at the table.[8] Dinner varied between seven thirty and nine o'clock each evening, depending on when Hearst appeared in the Assembly Room. The food was American and simple,

The three cottages are grouped asymmetrically around the Main Building. Both swimming pools are on the north side of the hill, which inclines more gradually than on the south side. The road was very little changed from the early years of construction. It delimited the hilltop site, whose buildings and terraces gradually grew out from the central portion of the hill to meet it. The road ends at the South Terrace, where guests disembarked and walked to Casa Grande up two flights of steps—unlike most country houses, where the main entrance was reached by automobile.

OPPOSITE PAGE:

Casa Grande (the Main Building) contains roughly 115 rooms: twenty-six bedrooms, thirty bathrooms, twelve servants' bedrooms, ten servants' bathrooms, fourteen sitting rooms, two libraries, two dining rooms (one of these for servants), one theater, one billiard room, one kitchen, one pantry, and a dozen miscellaneous rooms. The three cottages contain a total of twenty-two bedrooms, eighteen bathrooms, and four sitting rooms. The approximate size of the Main Building is 54,000 square feet, plus a basement of 14,000 square feet. Including the three cottages, the indoor Roman Pool, and all the other structures the enclosed space of the estate covers approximately 110,000 square feet.

SITE PLAN

1. Casa Grande
2. Casa del Mar (House A)
3. Casa del Monte (House B)
4. Casa del Sol (House C)
5. Neptune Pool
6. West Terrace
7. Esplanade
8. Central Plaza
9. South Terrace
10. North Terrace
11. Recreation Building (Roman Pool)
12. Switchboard Office and construction crew residences
13. Garages and Workshops

CASA GRANDE, FIRST FLOOR

Stage

Theater

Projection

Billiard Room

Morning Room

East Vestibule

Pantry

Kitchen

Refectory

Assembly Room

Vestibule

CASA GRANDE, SECOND FLOOR
LIBRARY AND CLOISTER BEDROOMS

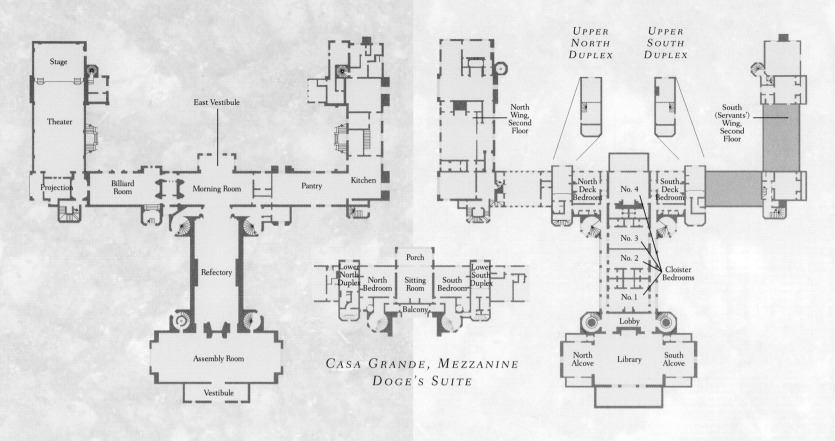

UPPER NORTH DUPLEX

UPPER SOUTH DUPLEX

North Wing, Second Floor

South (Servants') Wing, Second Floor

North Deck Bedroom

South Deck Bedroom

No. 4

No. 3

No. 2

No. 1

Cloister Bedrooms

Lobby

North Alcove

Library

South Alcove

CASA GRANDE, MEZZANINE
DOGE'S SUITE

Lower North Duplex

North Bedroom

Porch

Sitting Room

Balcony

South Bedroom

Lower South Duplex

CASA GRANDE, THIRD FLOOR
GOTHIC SUITE

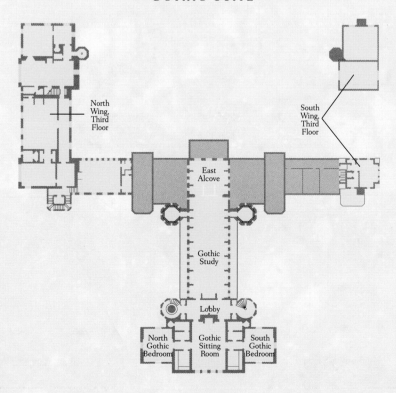

North Wing, Third Floor

South Wing, Third Floor

East Alcove

Gothic Study

Lobby

North Gothic Bedroom

Gothic Sitting Room

South Gothic Bedroom

CASA GRANDE, FOURTH FLOOR
CELESTIAL SUITE

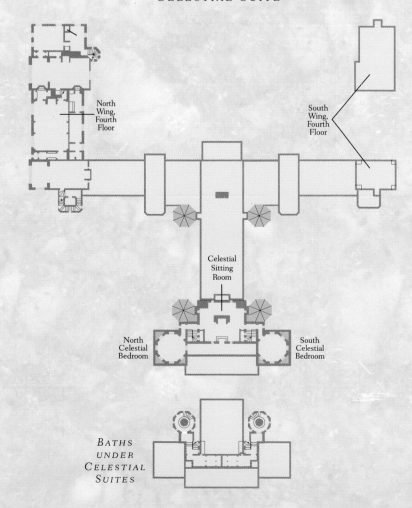

North Wing, Fourth Floor

South Wing, Fourth Floor

Celestial Sitting Room

North Celestial Bedroom

South Celestial Bedroom

BATHS UNDER CELESTIAL SUITES

not French and sophisticated. Turtle soup was a common first course, and roast turkey appeared frequently. Orchards and vegetable gardens on the ranch supplied much of the produce, and Hearst's dairy and poultry operations supplied the milk, eggs, and fowl, including pheasant. Ranch staff raised and hung the beef and venison, aging the meat in the walk-in cold-storage lockers in the basement area beneath the kitchen.[9]

Hearst himself would occasionally take a turn in the kitchen at San Simeon. Gretchen Swinnerton taught him how to fry chicken and make biscuits for dinner. At the end of the lesson, she recalled, "He had me put my hands in the flour . . . and go up and pat them on his back, and he walked into the Assembly Room and he said, 'Well, I got the general idea of baking.'"[10] More frequent were his attempts at Welsh rarebit, melted

THE BLUE ROOM, a larder off the Pantry, was used by the head chef as an office. Though the number of staff fluctuated with the size of the guest lists, there were typically twelve to fifteen household servants. Many of the staff rooms were decorated with wall paintings.

THE PANTRY was first poured as an addition onto the south side of Casa Grande in 1924, then remodeled and lengthened in 1927. Chilled beer kegs were kept in the cabinet in the foreground; the tables were Monel metal and used for warming food.

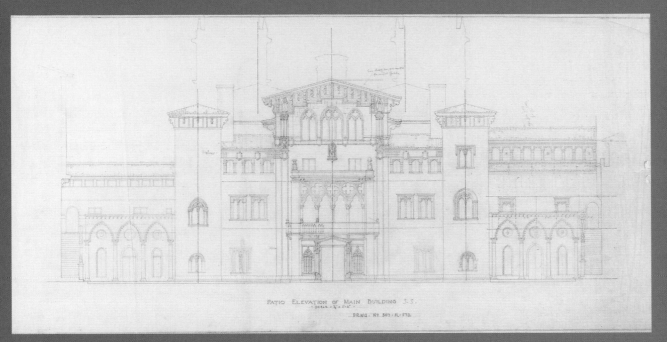

MORGAN'S *elevation drawing of Casa Grande's rear courtyard shows the marble loggia of the Doge's Suite and the continuation of the Venetian ornament in the ground-level Billiard Room and Pantry arches.*

cheese and ale served over toast, which he made often enough to write about in his newspaper column: "You cannot trifle with the sentiments of a Welsh rarebit. You have to make up your mind and move rapidly and on schedule. You have got to strike while the iron is hot. Otherwise you may have a perfectly good and useful synthetic substance for auto tires, but it will not be a Welsh rarebit."[11] A favorite entrée of Hearst's was pressed duck, which required that the duck be served very rare. This was not to Adela Rogers St. Johns's taste, and she remembered telling him, "This duck is going to walk right off your plate if you don't look out!"[12] Adela also could not understand why she had to dress and go to the Refectory for her morning coffee, rather than having it brought to her in her room. When she asked Marion about it, she replied, "W. R. did not approve of breakfast in bed. . . . [H]e thought . . . that the wonderful walk through morning dew and freshness with the sparkle of the sea below and mountain air blowing from above . . . was a good way to start the day." Adela agreed, but was sure she would have enjoyed the experience more "with one cup of coffee under my riding britches or my tennis skirt."[13]

The Doge's Suite was the first bedroom area completed in the Main Building, and guests who were assigned there (a task usually shouldered by Hearst's

secretary, Joe Willicombe) took it as a compliment. According to Colleen Moore, "Newcomers got the C House, then moved up to the Richelieu bedroom, if they behaved themselves; then into the 'Big House,' and finally into the Doge's Suite. When you slept in the Doge's, you knew that you had 'arrived.'"[14] Planned for the mezzanine level above the Morning Room from the

MARION DAVIES *feeds the pigeons in St. Mark's Square, Venice. Hearst contemplated keeping pigeons on his Venetian-style rear courtyard but never acted on his intention.*

earliest phase of construction, it was first completed in 1926, then remodeled in 1931 due to the addition of the North and South Wings onto the back of the Main Building, which attached at the Doge's Suite and blocked its former windows.[15] Its sitting room contained the painted Dutch ceiling formerly in Stanford White's New York home, and also a Venetian loggia that faced the eastern view of the hills and the back courtyard of Casa Grande. Hearst had wanted the entire back courtyard area (which they planned in the thirties to contain an art gallery that later evolved into a plan for an enormous Great Hall, never commenced) to be decorated in a Venetian

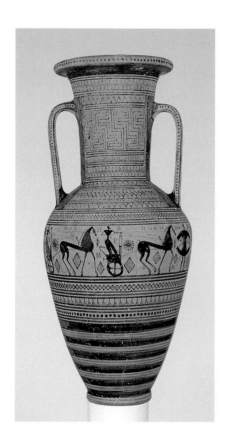

ATTIC-GEOMETRIC NECK-AMPHORA. *Dipylon Workshop, 740–735 B.C. Painted ceramic. 23 ½ x 8 ¾"* *(59.69 x 22.25 cm). Hearst Monument Collection, Casa Grande Library.*

Hearst acquired this piece in the Puttick and Simpson sale of Cecil Baring, Lord Revelstoke's vases in 1935. An excellent example of Late-Geometric pottery, it features a spirited frieze of charioteers in addition to its geometric patterns. Hearst bought his first Greek vase in 1901 and continued to purchase them over the next fifty years.

THE LIBRARY CONTAINS *four thousand books and a portion of Hearst's collection of ancient Greek vases, which was once considered unrivaled in the twentieth century.*

THE LOBBY of the Library shows the contrast between the finished paneled walls and the rough concrete stairwell beyond. Though guests and staff used the elevator in Casa Grande's northwest stairwell to reach the main floors, mezzanine levels in the building had no other access than winding concrete stairwells, many of which were left as poured. This lobby is lined with mostly modern wood panels, patterned after antique examples that were also incorporated into the scheme. Its ceiling is an additional portion of the sixteenth-century Spanish ceiling in the Library itself.

THE UPPER SOUTH DUPLEX, *one of the four loft-style bedrooms created from former open spaces at the back of Casa Grande. Hearst's initial idea was to design these spaces above the first floor to bring light into the upper stories from both sides. Within months of the start of construction, however, these two high and narrow shafts were converted into four bedrooms, in an excellent example of Morgan's ability to find an effective and creative solution to a difficult design problem.*

style. He wrote to Morgan about the tops of both wing extensions: "The towers I think can be carried up prettily and made as tall as the architectural requirements demand. We can put pigeons in them and feed the pigeons in the court as they do in Venice. "[16]

One of the most important areas in the Main Building was the Library, located on the second floor directly above the Assembly Room. A stately and gracious spot, its formality contrasts with the more informal atmosphere of most of Casa Grande's public rooms. In the mid-thirties, Hearst moved his superb collection of ancient Greek vases—which he began acquiring in 1901—into the room. Its more than four thousand books were reading copies, rather than rare volumes, as the bibliophile A. E. Newton recalled after his visit. "Someone knocked on my door and asked if I wanted to ride, motor, shoot, golf, swim, or play tennis, and he seemed very much surprised when I said, 'Not if I can help it.' He bowed, as who should say, 'This is liberty

hall,' and presently I began to wander over the mansion . . . seeking what I knew I should find—the library. I came upon it at last, a noble room . . . filled with books, not collectors' books, but just such books and magazines as one would expect to find in the house of a country gentleman."[17]

The rest of the second floor is occupied by the Cloisters, originally eight little rooms, soon changed to three bedrooms in a row running west to east above the Refectory, and a fourth bedroom in the back, raised up above a mezzanine formed by the Doge's Suite below, which for some years was divided into two spaces occupied by Hearst's youngest sons, David and Randolph. This last bedroom was formerly flanked by two open decks that were converted into two more bedrooms in the early thirties.[18] Each Cloister bedroom contained two beds, two baths, and a central closet shared by both occupants. Long corridors line both sides, providing sweeping views. At no other spot in the Main Building is its unusual plan more visible: looking from one open corridor to the other—a width of less than thirty feet—one gazes straight through the house and to the vistas beyond. According to Marion, the Cloisters were assigned to the young unmarried starlets, while the bachelors were given the Duplexes, two-story bedrooms at the back of the house, with no elevator connection to the main floors. "W. R. was right, in a way. There were young girls, and they could have gotten involved. The moonlight is very efficacious there . . . he was very careful." She wryly concluded: "And there was one good thing about it—nobody stayed too long."[19]

The Duplex rooms she referred to were four altogether, one atop the other in two unconnected sets, each unit containing a loft-style bedroom built above a sitting room and bath. Located in areas initially planned to be "light wells"—high openings in the upper stories that were created when the two Wing additions were built onto the main house—these Duplexes are an excellent example of Morgan's skill in facing a design

LOOKING ACROSS to the north bell tower from the south brings into view the expressions on some of the cast-stone faces. The bell towers also contain large tanks that hold the water supply, brought from mountain springs high above the hilltop.

A CORNER OF HEARST'S *South Gothic Bedroom when he was in residence.*

THE ENTRANCE *to Hearst's own Gothic Suite on the third floor of Casa Grande.*

HEARST'S *South Gothic Bedroom was ornamented with a fourteenth-century Spanish Gothic ceiling from the northern city of Teruel. A portrait of his mother, Phoebe Apperson Hearst, painted by Henry Clive, an illustrator for Hearst's magazines, hangs to the right of the bed; a photograph of his father, George Hearst, hangs to the left.*

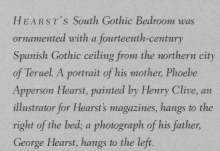

THE GOTHIC SUITE *Sitting Room when Hearst lived there.*

The north Gothic Bedroom.

challenge.[20] Hearst decided, in a quest for more bedrooms, that these spaces should be filled in. Morgan made four unusual and effective guest suites out of two spaces forty feet high and twelve feet wide.[21]

By 1926, Hearst had decided to move out of House A and into Casa Grande, choosing the entire third-story Gothic Suite for his own.[22] When the plans for Casa Grande were first drawn, it was to have had only two stories, with the wooden cornice above the second story and the bell towers—which had no access—above that. Adding the third level in 1923, which was first called the "Imperial Suite," greatly improved the proportions of the building.[23] The stunning views from this story must have attracted Hearst, who moved in with Marion Davies in 1927. His taking occupancy there meant that Casa Grande was now a home, not just a series of upstairs guest bedrooms and downstairs public rooms. Its distinctive wooden gable framed his own quarters. His selection of the third story meant that the elevator became a priority: it was installed inside the northwest stair tower in 1928. Morgan arranged for some of the fine Gothic sculptures from the Almenas collection to be placed in the suite, and told Hearst just before his arrival: "You will be able to step in [the elevator], press the Gothic Suite button, and not be surprised to find moved up there quite a good many of your fine things—it's really scrumptious up there."[24]

The most impressive part of the suite is the Gothic Study, directly above the Cloister bedrooms. It was an afterthought rather than a part of the original plan, as was so often the case in San Simeon's construction, but here the result shows no trace of having been cobbled together. Hearst had talked to Morgan about using the low-ceilinged storage space east of his Gothic Suite as a

study as early as 1926. Morgan was interested in the possibilities of the room, but worried about the effect:

I am wondering if you will ever be satisfied with the limited height of the room. It has bothered me at all hours—and has brought this suggestion: Suppose we take off the roof from stair tower to stair tower [of the Cloisters] . . . from wall to wall over the study proper. Then put back a [raised] roof. . . . This would give a little clerestory all along each side of the room for windows. The new concrete slab for the roof would be supported by steel trusses resting chiefly on the present study walls.[25]

THE NORTH Gothic Bedroom when Marion Davies was in residence.

This was a reversal of roles: customarily it was Hearst who proposed such major changes in construction and Morgan who tried to keep him in check. Now, Hearst sounded the note of caution: "I telegraphed you my fear of the cost of raising the roof on the house. . . . I imagine it would be ghastly. In fact, it might be possible to build a whole new house—such as we purposed erecting on the North and on the South of the Big House—for what it would cost to make this roof an ideal habitation. I am awaiting your figures."[26] Morgan lobbied uncharacteristically heavily for the plan, assuring Hearst that the total cost would not exceed six thousand dollars, and that after the roof raising the "cost for finishing would be about [the] same . . . and effect many times as fine."[27]

She was absolutely correct: the room is a triumph. They removed the roof from the Cloister bedrooms in 1931, lengthening the eastern end of the study. Steel girders were put in place to carry the roof and then disguised by plastered concrete arches painted with scenes inspired by the paintings in Sicily's fourteenth-century Palazzo Chiaramonte, planned much earlier as decorations for the Refectory's ceiling beams. A fifteenth-century geometric Spanish ceiling was placed between the arches, its reddish tones providing the palette for the modern paintings, done by an artist in Morgan's office, Camille Solon, in a childlike style. The clerestory window panes were tinted a rosy pink, suffusing the room with a soft glow.

The Gothic Study became the center of Hearst's business affairs. John Hearst Jr., said of his grandfather:

> After the post-dinner movie, Grandpop would excuse himself, tell the guests the place was theirs and go to work. He kept an eye on every one of his newspapers and his method of working was unique. The papers were spread on the floor of his study in long military lines and Grandpop would move among them, poking them with a foot and marking in red crayon the things he liked or didn't like. When he had finished, he would dictate messages to his various editors. Then the teleprinter on the direct wires would start chattering, 'The Chief says . . . .'[28]

A PORTRAIT OF WILLIAM RANDOLPH HEARST,
painted in 1894 by his lifelong friend Orrin Peck,
hangs in the Gothic Study.

THE GOTHIC STUDY, *where Hearst met with advisers,*
displays some of his finest metalwork and statuary.

As well as holding nearly four thousand books and some
of the finest Germanic metalwork in Hearst's collections, the Gothic Study served as a meeting place for
Hearst and his advisers, who were accustomed to their
boss's night-owl habits. Presiding over these conferences
was one of the few portraits Hearst ever posed for,
painted by his childhood friend Orrin Peck in 1894,

when W. R. was thirty-one. The vigor of his gaze brings
to mind an article he wrote much later in life:

> The reason we do not have tranquil lives—any of
> us—is because we do not WANT tranquil lives.
> We would rather be worried than BORED.
> Who wants "quiet study and thought and the enjoy-
> ment of trees and flowers" as a regular regimen?

As an occasional relaxation, yes. But as a constant and exclusive occupation, no. . . . Beware of tranquillity. It proclaims the toppling-over stage. . . .

Life is action. Sport, as well as work, is contention. All nature strives and vies, not to attain tranquillity but a more effective degree of activity.

Nothing that is alive and vigorous is tranquil—not the birds nor the beasts nor the poor fish nor human beings nor nations. Whatever begins to be tranquil is gobbled up by something that is not tranquil.[29]

The other most effective addition onto the Main Building during this busy period came in 1926 when they raised the existing bell towers, increasing their height to improve the building's scale and turning the resulting hollow spots, where the bells had been intended to be placed, into bedrooms. The Main Building had grown so much that the early towers were completely out of scale. Furthermore, heightening the towers allowed for a greater number of bells, thirty-six of which were installed in the early thirties. The tile on the towers provides Casa Grande with one of its most distinctive features, and it is the one element that has the strongest parallel to the 1915 San Diego Exposition buildings, which, for a time, Hearst thought of emulating for the Main Building's facade. Hearst also showed a sophisticated understanding of the towers' impact when lit at night, the light piercing the openwork surface. He wrote Morgan: "This will give us an opportunity to see the effect from a distance as well as nearby."[30] Hearst talked early on about these spots as "wonderful sleeping porches," since experience with the guests had shown him they would need far more bedrooms than were available in the mid-1920s.[31] An unforeseen consequence was that there was now a higher level in the house than Hearst's own, and that it had to be reached by a narrow staircase, about which Morgan told the portly Hearst: "The only point which will require that you keep thin will be at the entrance from the top of the old stair tower—to this new hallway."[32]

Guests who stayed in the Celestial Suite had no choice but to travel through an unfinished staircase before they reached the finished turret stair that led them up to their quarters, a fact not lost on the author

and bon vivant Ludwig Bemelmans: "The only vacant and airy spaces—and they come upon you suddenly as you open a door—are unfinished corridors, lofts, stairs, and passages where the cement seems still to be wet and bears the grain of the wood mold in which it was poured. Sticking out everywhere are iron staves, like walking sticks, that you see in unfinished concrete construction work."[33] Another curious feature was that since the bedrooms—bathed in light by the shafts that stream through the modern openwork window grilles— were the exact size of the previous bell towers, there was no room for a closet or bathroom. Instead the bathroom and a small closet were awkwardly squeezed in on a lower landing. Bemelmans wrote about his puzzlement with these arrangements:

> The bed stood in the center, a fourposter of tremendous weight, and again carved and painted. On the wall were curtains twenty feet in length, gold brocade, with draw cords so that you could pull all of them closed and find yourself in an octagonal tent of gold. . . . But there was no place to hang your clothes, so I hung mine on the wire coat hangers that a former tenant had left hanging on the arms of two six-armed gold candelabra . . . on either side of the bed. On these I hung almost everything; the rest I put on the floor.[34]

This work on the upper stories of Casa Grande, filling in and finalizing areas that had been poured in the early twenties, was a tremendous drain on Hearst's finances. A statement of accounts Morgan made in May of 1932 showed that he was more than one hundred thousand dollars behind on the construction costs, and, furthermore, Morgan had not paid herself a regular commission since 1928.[35] Such realities did not slow Hearst, who was eager to complete the upper stories of Casa Grande so that they could move on to completing the North Wing and creating the Great Hall, which was intended to stretch the one-hundred-fifty-foot length of the back courtyard and to contain tapestries, mantelpieces, and part of his extensive armor collection.[36] As he mused to Morgan at about this time, "Everything seems to be going well, but slowly—everything except the years."[37]

CHAPTER EIGHT

Hearst as Grandee

It is easy to look at William Randolph Hearst in traditional terms, as a host of a lavish country house, an energetic art collector, a journalist with strong political opinions. But it is important to look at him as he saw himself, and a large part of his identity came from being a Californian, embracing a social informality that was, as he described his choice of architecture for San Simeon, "something a little different than other people are doing."[1] His nonconformist position was strengthened by his choice of companions and by the western social structure and customs at the ranch, which harkened back to those of a California hacienda during the Mexican period.

It would be hard to find a more enthusiastic booster of California than William Randolph Hearst. He wrote to Phoebe from a train on one of his trips to the West:

> We have just arrived in God Blessed California. The light is real sunlight, not artificial light, the heat is real sun heat, not steam heat, the Colorado river is real mud, the Yuma desert is real dirt, and the Indians are mostly real dirt, too.
>
> Some people may object to the horned toads, the cacti and the tarantulas but I like 'em. I like 'em not for what they are but for what they may become. The horned toad will soon be replaced by the Eastern tourist, the cactus by the orange grove, and the tarantula by the real estate agent. Most old Californians prefer the horned toads, the cacti and the tarantulas, but I am for progress and reform. I think California is the best country in the world and always will be no matter who comes into it or what is done to it. Nobody or no thing can shut out the beautiful sun or alter the glorious climate. The horned toad and the Eastern tourist alike bask in the light and warmth, the cactus and the orange grove grow in the generous soil, the tarantula and the real estate agent alike live off the tenderfoot.
>
> Hurrah for dear old California.[2]

This letter was written just for Phoebe's pleasure. But Hearst also wrote an essay about the greatness of California, which he printed on the back of his personal stationery at the *Los Angeles Examiner,* comparing the state's land mass to Great Britain's and Italy's, predicting

Its present population of 5,000,000 resembles that of the builders of Britain in pioneering energy and determination to push its products across the seven seas. One California city alone—Los Angeles—is planning accommodations for a city larger than London, with its seven and a half millions. It will locate these millions between a range of picturesque mountains and the open beaches of the Pacific Ocean, where its climate is unsurpassed during any season of the year.[3]

William Randolph Hearst saw California as a place of unlimited potential. He was interested in expanding the commercial prospects of its major cities, but not of San Simeon itself. That was his private preserve, the spot he and his family could have developed into a thriving commercial port if they had chosen to. Hearst preferred to leave it as much as possible as it had been in the nineteenth century, its vast ranchlands and absence of cities a reminder of the way the rest of California had looked before development started to boom in the 1920s.

The rich western tradition that Hearst nurtured at San Simeon was a nineteenth-century vision. His grandson John Jr. said: "People have said that Grandpop ran the ranch like a huge free hotel, with guests coming and going as they pleased. That wasn't true. The original GH ranch, which had been bought by my great-grandfather,

was the last of the old-time Spanish land-grant *haciendas* and it was run just as the *hacendados* had run their places. There was a huge hospitality for everyone under its roof, but at the same time a kind of country simplicity."[4] Colleen Moore described an example she witnessed of such simplicity:

> Mr. Hearst was tall and of a commanding appearance. Everyone called him "Mr. Hearst." Even Marion called him "W. R." . . . I think that one of the greatest shocks of my life came one day when we were out horseback riding. A little old Mexican hand [named] Pancho [Estrada] rode up to Mr. Hearst and called out, "Willie, come over here and ride with me. I want to show you a pasture." That night I found out that Mr. Hearst and Pancho Estrada had been raised together on the ranch and had been close friends since childhood. Mr. Hearst built a beautiful Spanish house for Pancho in the village of San Simeon. He must have been the only man in the world to call the Chief "Willie."[5]

Don Pancho Estrada was the oldest son of Julian Estrada, owner of the Rancho Santa Rosa before George Hearst began buying portions of it in 1876. An honored friend of Hearst's, he taught all five Hearst sons—and eventually their children—to ride, rode himself as Grand Marshal in the local parades on a horse with a silver Mexican saddle, and was a living link with the Mexican period of San Simeon's history.[6] Before Hearst built on the hilltop above San Simeon, he wrote to Phoebe on one of his family's camping trips: "George is off fishing with Pancho. Pancho used to be my compan-

A CAST-CONCRETE bird corbel on the Pergola, the long, landscaped bridle path located northwest of the hilltop structures.

Mr. Hearst and Pancho Estrada had been raised together.

154

He must have been the only man to call the Chief "Willie."

LAYING THE CONCRETE pipes that were used as the Pergola columns, with Casa Grande in the background. These pairs of columns, spaced eleven feet apart, eventually covered a distance of just over a mile and were landscaped for leafy shade on the trail ride.

GNARLED GRAPEVINES still grow around the Pergola columns today.

ion, but now I never see him any more, now that the children are here. He is either riding with John, fishing with George, or teaching William how to throw the riata, and in some way spends his time with them. It takes me back to the time, forty years ago, when I was a child on the ranch, and Pancho used to look out for me. How old is Pancho, anyway?"[7] This man was not merely an employee: he was an honored reminder of the Spanish-Mexican heritage of the land, one whom Hearst treated with concern and solicitude.[8]

Estrada was a frequent riding partner for Hearst, and one of the most beautiful places for riding on the hilltop itself was the Pergola, a columned arbor that Hearst had planned from the earliest days of construction. He asked Morgan what she thought of the idea in 1920, saying pergolas as walkways beneath the guest houses would be "very effective," but wondered if they would be "architecturally correct."[9] Perhaps he was worrying about using them because small pergolas were a common feature of southern California bungalows, and they had decided against using the bungalow style. Pergola antecedents were Italian, however, as Morgan must have explained to him when she showed him photographs of pergolas in Amalfi and Taormina. He wrote: "The double

row [of columns] will give opportunities for splendid vine and flower effects. We can also grow grapes and such things on 'em."[10] In spite of his interest in this idea, which resulted in various plans to incorporate pergolas around the future Neptune Pool site as well as the little houses, they did not build a Pergola until 1928–37, when the mile-and-a-quarter-long landscape feature was created on a hill north of the Castle. Morgan told Hearst: "You certainly have 'the longest pergola in captivity'—and I'm wondering about the disposal of the crops."[11] It was surely the only one made with hollow concrete pipe, hauled eleven at a time by truck out to the site, then topped with cast concrete lintels.[12] They planted it with grape vines over the lintels, and espaliered fruit trees between the columns, placed at a distance of eleven feet apart, ensuring a mass of blossoms in springtime and a cool green tunnel to ride through, out of the heat of the sun, in summer.

Some of Hearst's guests reacted to his love of the outdoors and of riding with dismay. Colleen Moore recalled wanting to stay in the Assembly Room: "We'd curl up in front of the sofa and gossip, and talk, and pretty soon Mr. Hearst would come in. He would say, 'Come on now, get out and get the fresh air,' and he'd make us all

go out . . . horseback riding. It was just dreadful."[13] Adela Rogers St. Johns and Hearst editor Cissy Patterson were experienced horsewomen, however, and they both recalled the San Simeon trail rides and picnics on horseback with fondness.[14]

There had been stables at San Simeon since George Hearst bought the land in 1865 and built a three-eighth-mile racetrack there to run his thoroughbreds.[15] Racehorses and stud farms were of no interest to Will, however, who wrote to his father, then a United States senator, in 1888: "Please telegraph me whether or not it is true that you have paid forty thousand dollars for a colt. If you have, I shall let everything here [go] to thunder and come East and take care of you. In the meantime, you had better get a nurse. I mean this. . . . If you insist upon squandering all your money, I will stop working and see what I can do in that line myself. But you simply want to become notorious, I think. I can suggest cheaper methods and some that will reflect less on your intelligence."[16]

W. R. was interested in raising and riding horses, not in racing them. He began raising Arabians in 1919 and funded an expedition to the Middle East in 1945 to seek Arabian horses to add to the American gene pool.

OPPOSITE LEFT: MARION DAVIES looks calm enough here, but many guests' accounts confirm that she was not an enthusiastic horsewoman.

OPPOSITE RIGHT: CECIL BEATON and Anita Loos pose just before setting out on a trail ride. Beaton wrote: "Anita and I decided we would ride. It was a brave moment, as I hadn't been in the saddle since St. Cyprian's school. Riding clothes were soon lent me; I fancied myself enormously." He soon regretted consenting to ride. At first he rhapsodized about the beauty of the ranch, the distant Castle, the bounding deer and antelope. Then one of his riding partners galloped ahead, leaving him the responsibility of closing one of the gates that was used to segregate the zoo animals. His horse shied, the rope that operated the gate pulley raced over his ungloved hand, and the skin of his palm got a very bad rope burn. Ahead was a two-mile ride back to the house, an unsuccessful bid for sympathy from the other guests, and a miserable whiskey-fueled evening spent observing the other guests' antics while his hand "throbbed like a tom-tom."

ABOVE: A PICNIC along the trail at the ranch. These lavish affairs involved an advance crew of chefs, a group of dude wranglers who led the guests on horseback, and sometimes a mariachi band to provide entertainment at the site. Hearst delighted in such outdoor revels of traditional California hospitality, though the guests were not always as hardy in the saddle as he was. Cars were often dispatched to drive the tenderfeet back to the hilltop.

RIGHT: MISSION *San Antonio de Padua, founded in 1771, the fourth of the twenty-one missions in California.*

BELOW: THE MILPITAS HACIENDA *at Jolon, c. 1935. A massive and stately residence, which employed picturesque Mission Revival architectural ornament, it almost completely eclipsed the actual Mission San Antonio de Padua down the road.*

OPPOSITE: A STAIRCASE *inside the Milpitas Hacienda, draped with one of the Navajo rugs from Hearst's outstanding collection.*

Hearst also raised Morgans, Appaloosas, Palominos, and Morabs, a Morgan-Arabian cross.[17] Hearst's daughter-in-law Austine remembered the "horse closet," which contained "dozens of complete sets of everything from jodhpurs to boots to caps to hacking jackets to—you name it. There was probably no guest in the history of the place who had been too fat or too tall or too whatever to be outfitted." Hearst himself rode on a silver saddle and acquired a fine collection of Mexican silver saddles, just like a true grandee would own. There were three stables on the estate: the quarter horses for the ranch hands were stabled at the bottom of the hill near the airstrip; the champion Morgans and Palominos were kept several miles south of the Castle, on land Hearst owned near Pico Creek; and the horses guests used for their trail rides came from a forty-stall stable east of the Main Building.[18]

Marion did not share Hearst's love of riding. Gary Cooper used to encourage her by talking about horses. "He knew I was afraid of them, but he adored horses. He said, 'If you love a horse, a horse loves you.' I said, 'That doesn't prevent a horse from getting mad and biting me on the toe.'" She explained, "I was afraid of horses because when I was about twelve I'd had an accident. The horse started to run and I let go and landed on some logs and broke the end of my spine. I was in a

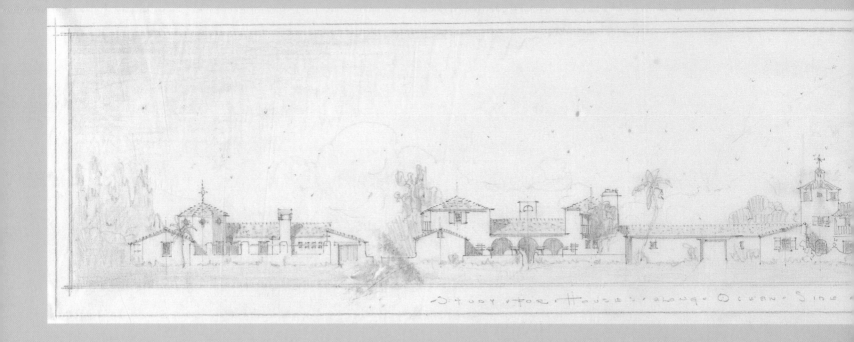

THE MISSION REVIVAL-STYLE *warehouse designed by Julia Morgan in the hamlet of San Simeon, 1930.*

TOP: "SKETCH FOR *a Group of Houses in San Simeon Village," designed for Hearst's staff, c. 1928. Hearst wanted "our little Spanish village" to be in harmony with the hilltop architecture of La Cuesta Encantada.*

plaster cast for about three months."[19] Many of the guests attested to Marion's terror on a horse; this may be one reason why the longer trail rides often featured cars to take the riders back home.[20]

King Vidor recalled an overnight trek with several stopovers that had been intended to make the ride easy for inexperienced guests.

Pack mules carrying tents and camping equipment were sent ahead to establish camps. By pushing resolutely onward, W. R., at the head of the long column, managed to reach the first night's camp by noon. The group, consisting largely of tenderfooted cowboys and tender-bottomed women imported from the most comfortable drawing rooms in the world, slid from their damp saddles and lay on the solid earth in exhaustion and thankfulness. A good dry sherry followed by terrapin soup began to revive low spirits and ease aching muscles, and we all looked forward to an afternoon of rest in the shade of tall oaks. But W. R. was in an active and adventurous mood. He ordered tired horses resaddled and the group reassembled for an early start toward camp number two.

It seemed to give him a secret and perhaps sadistic delight that being senior in years he was yet the most sturdy.[21]

Having a destination to ride to was one reason for the construction in the early 1930s of the Milpitas Hacienda, on the northern portion of Hearst's ranch.

Morgan's response, when she visited the site near the Mission San Antonio in 1925, was "What a wonderful beautiful domain."[22] In 1930, fifteen years after the Mission Revival style had peaked in California, they began to build an enormous complex in that style, located just down the road from the actual San Antonio Mission, but greatly upstaging it. Meant to serve as a bunkhouse for the upper reaches of the Hearst ranch as well as a destination to ride to on horseback, the Hacienda comes close to a fantasized perfection of the Mexican period.[23] With a frontage 225 feet long, its domes, square towers, bells, arcades, and sparkling white walls were a composite of all the Missions rolled into one.[24] Morgan wrote of the huge edifice she designed: "Many tourists are mistaking the new buildings for the Mission—it was really quite amusing this last visit."[25] It was a remarkable architectural choice, considering that Hearst described the architecture of early California as "crude and rude" when he and Morgan were determining San Simeon's architectural style.[26] The Hacienda's effectiveness is derived from its vast setting, acres of unspoiled land which recalled California in the early nineteenth century.

For the many tenderfeet who did not relish the prospect of a long horseback ride, Hearst had George Loorz build the Burnett Road, a twenty-mile-long all-

A CHOIR STALL *propped up for photographing outside the warehouse at San Simeon.*

The Arroyo de la Cruz, or Valley of the Cross, seen from the hill at San Simeon. This giant valley is a watershed through which the winter rain travels to the sea.

weather road that stretched all the way from the San Simeon hilltop to the Hacienda. Loorz was proud of the road, which took two years to complete, writing to one of the former construction crew: "I drove from the Milpitas house to the hilltop in 1 hr. 15 min. yesterday morning. Not bad eh! Mr. Hearst and about 40 guests drove over last Saturday for a fine Spanish picnic with 20 Spanish entertainers at Milpitas. All had a lovely time and most of them flew back."[27]

In his role as grandee, Hearst built employee quarters in the town of San Simeon, which he called "our little Spanish village."[28] The four houses rival the three hilltop cottages in size and charm. These were quarters for the key members of his staff, including George Loorz and Pancho Estrada. In 1931 Morgan also built three modern metal storage buildings and another Mission Revival structure, a huge concrete warehouse located next to the nineteenth-century one on the ocean. Its arches, bell, and vast white stucco walls evoke a village church, and it is often mistaken for a mission.

A true hacienda and a true country house both required a large amount of land and a working farm. Of course, cattle ranching had been under way on the land since at least the 1830s. In 1921, for instance, Hearst ran four thousand head of cattle and rented out the two

thousand acres of the southernmost Santa Rosa ranchland to two dairies. Though he was advised to develop a hog farm and a goat and sheep operation, Hearst never did so. [29] While it was desirable for the development to be profitable, it always remained a private, not a commercial, enterprise. The plans for a model farm for San Simeon—including chicken and pheasant houses, a duck pond, cow and horse barns, and a bunkhouse for the ranch hands—were completed piecemeal from 1922 through the 1930s. Hearst wanted the farm to be in an elaborate period revival style, in this case employing Basque architectural details, which were both Swiss (perhaps a nod to the Italian-Swiss dairymen of the region) and Spanish, but the cost seemed too high. He eventually settled for a less luxurious scheme, mostly done in the Mission Revival architectural style.[30] The bunkhouse was the last thing finished, in mid-1937, when Hearst told Loorz to divert construction crews from the hilltop to its construction site, down near the original ranch house his father George had built: "I want the men to have their house. We have so much house here that we can wait."[31]

William Randolph Hearst wanted to develop small areas of the land, in ways such as constructing a Hacienda in the hills as a riding destination, surrounding his own hilltop with gardens and exotic animals for his guests' amusement, and building a cattle, horse, poultry, and dairy operation below. In general, however, he did not want to alter the natural and traditional character of the landscape. A major fire in July 1930, started by a spark that escaped a trash incinerator, burned many acres. Though the buildings at the top of the hill were safe, the fire traveled from the southern hills down to the animal shelters and into the ranch area. Hearst received the news at Bad Nauheim, a German spa where he often took the cure in late summer. Wyntoon had burned only seven months before, which must have intensified his response to yet another fire. Still, his main concern was for the landscape, not the structures. "Think fire very serious; would rather have building burn than trees."[32]

In the grandee tradition, Hearst continued to magnanimously host great numbers of guests, including such celebrated figures as Calvin and Grace Coolidge, who arrived in February of 1930.[33] The most memorable guest of the decade was Bernard Shaw, who came with his wife and stayed for four days in March 1933. Hearst had invited him to San Simeon in 1927, in a characteristically western fashion: "Let me herewith extend you [a] formal and fervent invitation to be my guest and ride the range with me in California."[34] Shaw refused both this request and another one from about the same time inviting him to meet Hearst and Marion in England. He told his secretary that he had "never heard of Marion Davies, and would not go to a little dinner at the Savoy if she were all the 11,000 virgins of St. Ursula rolled into one. I am no good for games of that sort."[35] Nevertheless, he was charmed by her when he finally met her in person. Though the legend that Shaw proclaimed San Simeon "the way God would have done it if he'd had the money" is untrue, Shaw did make a critical evaluation of Hearst. Bennett Cerf spoke with Shaw after his visit to the ranch, and wrote: "He couldn't understand why America didn't worship Mr. Hearst, because, as he put it, Hearst had all the qualities that America supposedly adored. He said, 'Why is he feared and hated and made fun of, when he's got power, money, rather good looks, a beautiful girl—and a wife who lets him get away with it?' "[36]

Basil Woon, a writer who worked for Hearst, described San Simeon around the time of Shaw's visit. Grasping the importance of Hearst's relationship with the land, Woon advised: "If guests are wise, they get up early, for the mornings are the best part of the day. I remember, one morning, taking a horse out across the hills. Some five miles from the ranch I saw another rider, W. R. himself. He was riding slowly, his head sunk down, his attitude one of brooding. Now and again he half rose in his stirrups and his eyes swept the horizon—an emperor looking over his domain."[37]

Believe it or not,—Pepi this is the spot

To bring up your favorite beau

On a warm summer night,—when the stars steady light

Is dimmed by the moons golden glow

When the languorous breeze,—as you sit neath the trees

Is laden with scent from the flowers

And the castle nearby,—lifts its mass to the sky

And the lights glimmer down from the towers

If he doesn't get sappy,—and tell you how happy

A word from his sweetheart would make him

He is just a big dunce,—and devoid of romance

And the best thing to do is to shake him

—WRH FECIT

HEARST WROTE this verse as a gift for Marion Davies's young niece, Pepi Lederer. It is both an indication of Hearst's sentimental view of the ranch and the only recorded instance of him calling his estate "the castle." He signed the poem with his initials and the Latin fecit, *employed by many Renaissance painters to indicate authorship. There is a sad coda to this cheery poem: Pepi committed suicide at age twenty-one in 1934, a loss that affected Marion deeply.*

CHAPTER NINE

Financial Havoc

By the mid-1930s, even William Randolph Hearst could not ignore the Great Depression any longer. Firing Camille Rossi and hiring George Loorz to replace him in 1932 brought calm to the hilltop staff for the first time in years, but now the new worry for the crew was having enough work. Loorz's construction skills were formidable, but he did not have nearly the opportunity to exercise them that Rossi had been given in the previous decade. In fact, George Loorz often did not know how much building would go on or how many men he

would be able to hire. Hearst almost had to shut San Simeon completely for a few months in the spring of 1933 due to his money shortage.[1]

Part of the problem stemmed from Wyntoon. After it burned in early 1930, Hearst's finances and creative interest were divided between Wyntoon and San Simeon. Morgan found her energies divided also, as she traveled frequently to these remote sites five hundred miles apart to design their lavish features in architecturally different styles: northern European for the former, southern European for the latter. The Wyntoon insurance money provided cash for some rebuilding, but not on the grand scale Hearst desired.[2] Warren McClure, who worked on both projects, wrote:

Wyntoon was interesting but not on a par with the ranch. A few words about the depression and its curtailing effect on San Simeon. . . . The crew was reduced by ¾ or more but work went on under something called a budget allowance which irked Mr. H. He usually got the budget padded. . . . My little shack office was in the East court and W. R. H. spent hours in it everyday. I recall Miss Davies popping in at times with the question, "What are you kids cooking up now?" The "cooking up" was usually something akin to the Vatican or Windsor Castle, to the later disconcerting of Miss Morgan and the treasury. None told him nay however.[3]

In the midst of this construction turmoil—and surely also because of it—Julia Morgan's health declined. Ear infections had plagued her from childhood, and a serious one during her student years at the Ecole des Beaux-Arts may have done permanent damage.[4] The fall of 1932 found both Morgan and Hearst ill, Hearst undergoing an operation on his esophageal diverticulum in a Cleveland clinic and Morgan having surgery to overcome yet another ear infection. At first, Morgan seemed to be recuperating well. She requested a plane ride to view the construction whenever Hearst could arrange it, saying, "It will be mighty good to see San Simeon again."[5] He immediately consented and telegrammed her with solicitude: "Dear Miss Morgan I think if you drank a bottle of English or rather Irish stout every day it would do you a lot of good stop you eat so little the porter would give you strength stop may I send you some Dublin stout sincerely W R Hearst."[6] Morgan attempted a lighthearted response in verse, since Hearst was skilled at writing amusing poems, but her efforts at rhyme were as ungainly as Hearst's clumsy architectural sketches: "The kindly doctors probe and drain and cannot develope [sic] a single pain."[7]

Unhappily, Morgan's optimism was premature. She wrote Hearst a week later about the bandages she had to wear: "Personally, am still a turbaned Turk for some obscure reason, but have lots more strength, and energy."[8] Hearst, too, at age sixty-nine, required some additional time to heal, as he wired Morgan: "I certainly am truly and truthfully coming along finely; in fact I leave for [the] west on Sunday; I just thought it was not right to have one member of the firm have all the troubles."[9] And while Morgan responded, "It is indeed good to know that you have been successful in your own 'come back' and I'll pattern on your sketch as far as possible," she went on to explain the complications of her surgery: "What happened to me was, that not healing, the innermost ear chamber became reinfected and the miserable sequence of operations all had to be gone through again."[10] Morgan's whole inner ear was removed in the second operation. Permanent damage also ensued when the surgeon accidentally severed a facial muscle, giving her face a decided droop on one side. "The doctor never sent her a bill and she realized that in some respects he was more hurt than she was," Morgan North recalled. "She used to send a present to him every year at Christmastime." From then on, Morgan was even more reluctant to appear in public, describing herself in architectural terms as "so unsymmetrical."[11] The operation had also ruined Morgan's physical equilibrium. George Loorz wrote to Warren McClure at Wyntoon:

She was quite strong, that is she lifted heavy chairs etc. but Oh the equilibrium. I think she staggered more than ever. While we [were] going thru one of the tapestry boxes in the Vault she simply fell into it. She said, "I

A CAST-STONE head on Casa Grande's south tower, ornamenting the exterior at the level of the Celestial Suite.

" 'What are you kids cooking up now?' The 'cooking up' was usually

certainly have a jag on tonight." Again she was sketching something leaning on her elbow on a table and went flop down with her face on that. Each time I merely put my arms around her, pick her up bodily and set her in the nearest handy spot and go right on with the business. It is really pathetic.[12]

While most of George Loorz's projects at San Simeon were forced to proceed at a very modest pace, occasionally there was a flurry of activity, as when Hearst decided at the last minute to celebrate his seventy-first birthday with a Civil War party at San Simeon in April of 1934. Marion had been filming her last movie with Metro-Goldwyn-Mayer, a Civil War spy story called *Operator 13*, perhaps prompting the theme. The large party of guests required the temporary completion of upper floors in the North Wing, which had been poured by Camille Rossi in 1930. A four-story, L-shaped wing that connected to the Morning Room, it lay almost completely unfinished except for the Theater, which Morgan had completed by 1931 so that the nightly tradition of a movie screening at eleven o'clock could continue in greater comfort than it had in the early years, when the

films were shown outside.[13] Loorz had supervised the completion of the first floor Billiard Room, which dragged on until November 1933.[14] There things stood until Loorz got the word that thirteen more rooms were needed. He wrote to his partner, Fred Stolte, when the dust had cleared:

Well, we are settled down again to a more even program. Perhaps you have heard of the grand rush for his Birthday Party.

One week before his party they called me at 8 P.M. while I was having dinner with the folks at the Lodge. The order was to try to get all of the rooms in the Recreation Wing completed temporarily for occupancy in time for the party.

You remember that dead concrete wing over the Theater with nothing in the openings but tar paper storm covers. Besides that the floors were full of antique stone for later use in the openings of this wing etc. One of the rooms was my paint shop with filled shelves.

Anyway within six days we turned the place over to him furnished with all rooms, closets, bathrooms, including showers, ready for use. That is 11 rooms complete with baths and closets and 2 tower rooms quite comfortable for use but no bathrooms. . . . Note that the form wires were still in place and had to be cut thruout. The ceilings were painted, the concrete exposed walls

something akin to the Vatican or Windsor Castle." WARREN McCLURE

were painted and the floors, rough concrete tinted. Hand rails galore up and down the steps. In fact, they turned out to be very comfortable.[15]

Such frenzied preparations were not good for Morgan's health. In fact, she went abroad with her sister Emma to relax and recover, from November 1934 through April 1935. While traveling to Europe was routine for many American architects, it was almost unprecedented for Morgan. She had refused invitations both from Hearst and from the Bynes before, pleading that her obligation to care for her family (she had an invalid mother) and the ongoing nature of her work prevented her from leaving.[16] When Hearst learned of her plans he wrote her a long letter, revealing both his familiarity with Europe and his solicitude toward Morgan:

The member of the family is a fine idea, and the lady is apparently just the one you should have with you.
If you pardon me for butting in a little bit, I am going to see that you get a comfortable cabin on the boat so the trip will really do you some good.
Then when you land, please land at Naples, and I will have our correspondent get a nice automobile for you

and your relative to take you down to Pompeii and Sorrento and Amalfi and to the temples at Paestum then back to Naples and then up to Rome.

There followed a complete Baedeker of towns to visit on her way through Italy to the Alps, on to Munich, then through the Rhine to France, and then by boat to England. Sensing the possibility of her objections, he concluded: "I hope you will take the time to make the trip right and not to hurry; . . . The automobile is going to be my automobile, as I have some stored in England, and I am naturally going to attend to everything in connection with it; and all you have to do is just sit in it and be a good girl, which I know is very hard for you to do. Please let me try to help make this trip agreeable."[17] Morgan acquiesced. On her return from Europe in April, McClure reported to Loorz: "I think she looks very much better and am sure the trip helped her. However her improvement will prompt her to become very active again, I'm afraid, and will undo a lot of the good the trip may have done."[18]

Funds finally grew so short that Hearst shut down most of the construction in 1935, working only on build-

167

ing an airfield at the bottom of the hill and finishing out-door projects. Electrician Louis Schallich wrote to Loorz from Wyntoon: "Should have written you a letter from here before but in the past month this place has been a mad house. We have been working day and night and everyday. . . . No doubt, with the big pay roll up here, it has cut your force down at San Simeon."[19] In 1936 there was a brief rally, when Hearst provided more money for

hilltop construction, but again what was supposed to have been spent on San Simeon alone had to stretch to cover projects at Wyntoon as well.[20] At this time, Loorz worked to complete in a more permanent way the bed-rooms and sitting rooms of the North Wing, including the three floors of bedrooms above the Billiard Room that had been finished only temporarily for Hearst's 1934 birthday party. The upper stories above the Theater

were lengthened to accord with the length of the ground floor, and antique ceilings and fire mantels were installed throughout the rooms.

Meanwhile, Hearst traveled abroad for the summer, oblivious to his finances. He wrote Morgan, bursting with ideas:

> One thing which San Simeon really needs is fountains.
> I mean fountains which *fount*. . . .
> After seeing Villa d'Este again I realize what water would do for San Simeon. It would double its beauty and charm. In the midst of a dry land we would have an oasis of beautiful fountains.
> The work must be done on a grand scale and there must be not merely statuary and basins but *water*— spouting tumbling water. . . .
> Enclosed are some photographs of Tivoli.
> Maybe they will affect you as they did me.[21]

In Hearst's eyes, San Simeon was unequal to the Tivoli Gardens of the Villa d'Este outside Rome in just this one aspect, and since La Cuesta Encantada was his version of a Renaissance villa, he was anxious to remedy the defect. Money had never been tighter; the demands on the water supply were already enormous; and the amount of water they would have been able to reserve in the dry summers was minuscule. In fact, they never built a major fountain on the hilltop. Some of its most prominent unfinished areas are the fountains planned for the enlarged North and West Terraces. Nevertheless, grand water features provide San Simeon with two of its most distinctive elements, its swimming pools, both of which were under construction in the money-tight years of the 1930s.

THE BILLIARD ROOM, finished by 1934, was ornamented with a ceiling, tile panels, and a tapestry that all have gaming themes. While such a room is a traditional feature in a country house, there is little evidence that Hearst himself used it, though guests reported playing games there.

THE NORTH WING under construction in October 1930. The Theater and Billiard Room make up the first floor, topped by three floors of guest bedrooms. This Wing was intended to connect to the South Wing opposite, either by a separate art gallery or by a Great Hall that would have stretched the length of the eastern facade.

The Roman Pool was built long after the first version of the Neptune Pool, but it had been planned from an earlier date. In 1920, Hearst mentioned a swimming pool at the ranch for the first time, writing to Morgan that he wanted a Moorish house on the hill (which became House C): "I think it would be a pleasant variation and we might make a plunge somewhere near this house and get a good effect and combination with it."[22] By 1923 Hearst referred to "Bath House Hill—which we might call Arabian Hill, to be more poetic," as a picturesque place on the south side of the hilltop for a domed structure with a Moorish pool topped by an antique Spanish ceiling.[23] Because this "plunge" was going to be such an involved construction project, in 1924 they resolved to convert a fountain pool into the first version of the Neptune Pool temporarily as a stopgap measure.

SUZANNE MUZAUNE. NYMPHS AND SATYR. *French, 1931. Carved marble, 67 x 103" (172.2 x 264.7 cm). Hearst Monument Collection, East Esplanade.*

Three spirited nymphs are shown in high relief, stealthily playing a joke on the satyr. The nymph on the left holds a musical instrument while the one on the far right leans down to steal the satyr's pipes as he slumbers unsuspectingly. Inventory records show that Hearst bought this piece directly from Muzaune. It is one of several twentieth-century pieces by women artists in the San Simeon collection.

TWO SEKHMET FIGURES AND TWO SEKHMET HEADS. *Egyptian. Head on the left, 18th Dynasty; three others, 19th Dynasty. Granite. Full figure with vein of feldspar, 5'10 ½" x 20 ½" (179.1 x 52.1cm); ¾ figure, 45 ¼ x 17 ¾" (114.9 x 45.1 cm); chipped head, 19 x 19" (48.3 x 48.3 cm); head with sundisk, 23 x 10" (58.4 x 25.4 cm). Hearst Monument Collection, South Esplanade.*

These four pieces date from the New Kingdom. Sekhmet literally translates as "the powerful." Depicted with the body of a woman and the head of a lioness, she was the bloodthirsty protector of Ra, the sun god.

TENNIS COURTS. *In 1927 Hearst decided to excavate beneath the tennis courts to create the Roman Pool. The glass insets at the nets bring light into the pool below. Tennis star Alice Marble recalled the first of many visits: "On my first day, Mr. Hearst was my partner. Teach [Marble's coach, Teach Tennant] played opposite us with Charlie Chaplin, and all the guests turned out to watch. At sixty, Mr. Hearst seemed ancient to me, but he played beautifully."*

In the middle 1920s Hearst considered creating a saltwater pool on the hill, and then a very exotic winter pool, housed in a building of glass and gilded iron: "The temperature of the hot-house, and of the pool, too, would be warm on the coldest bleakest winter day. *We would have the South Sea Islands on the Hill.* . . . Here we could serve tea or poi, or whatever the situation called for. The pool, of course, would be the main attraction; and we might put a turtle and a couple of sharks in to lend verisimilitude." Hearst concluded this fantasy excursion with a simple statement that encapsulates the philosophy underlying much of San Simeon's ornament: "This, except for the sharks, is not as impractical a proposition as it might seem. It is merely making a hot-house useful, and making a pool beautiful."[24]

The Roman Pool as it was built in the 1930s does create a richly exotic world, but of the Byzantine empire, rather than of the Alhambra or the South Seas. In the

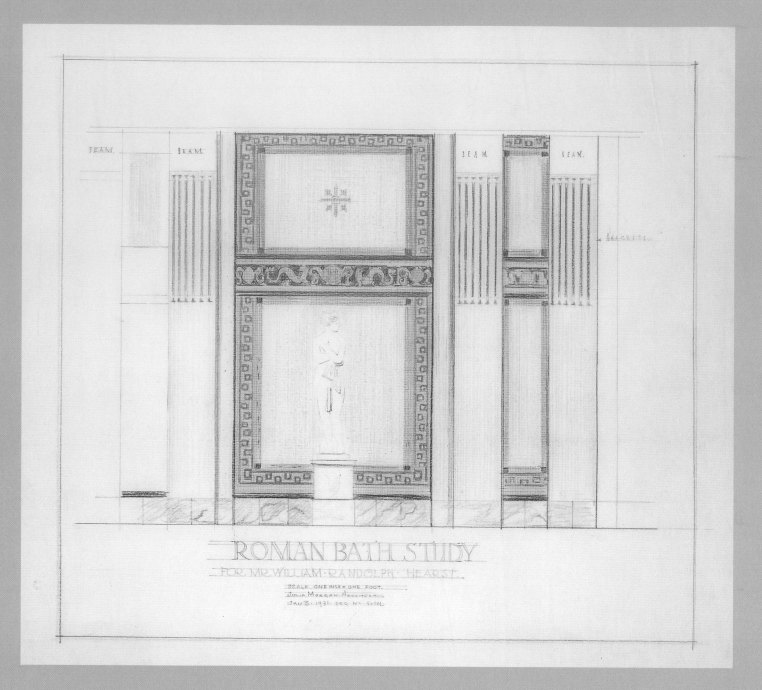

ROMAN BATH STUDY
FOR MR. WILLIAM RANDOLPH HEARST
SCALE ONE INCH = ONE FOOT.
JULIA MORGAN, ARCHITECT
JAN 3 1931 DRG NO 50581

Hearst had admired the fourth-century mosaics of Ravenna: "We have decided on the

spring of 1927, Hearst decided to build a gymnasium underneath the tennis courts, which had been constructed at the east end of the Esplanade in 1925.[25] These courts were one of the most important recreational features at the ranch, used frequently by Hearst, a skilled tennis player who played often with champion Alice Marble.[26] As a part of the gymnasium beneath, two separate swimming pools were planned, heated to different temperatures, as ancient Roman baths were.[27] These two pools evolved in the design phase into one T-shaped pool, its small alcove a shallow three and one-half feet deep and the eighty-one-foot-long central pool ten feet deep throughout.

ABOVE: A STUDY for the Roman Pool shows Venus Italica against a tiled wall. The drawings were created by Camille Solon, who also painted Casa Grande's Gothic Study arches.

OPPOSITE LEFT: THE ROMAN POOL under construction, revealing newly cast concrete arches.

OPPOSITE RIGHT: A DETAIL of seahorse tiles in the Roman Pool.

On his travels, Hearst had admired the fifth-century mosaics of Ravenna, particularly the mausoleum of the emperor's daughter Galla Placidia, decorated in cobalt blue and gold Venetian glass mosaic. In the summer of 1928 he wrote to Morgan: "In regard to the indoor pool, we have decided on the brilliant blue mosaic small tile and the gilt tile and the border of fishes with gold."[28] The tiles themselves were laid onto four-by-four-foot sheets of paper in San Francisco, then brought down to San Simeon and grouted in, a process that took from 1932 to 1935.[29] Joseph Giarritta, one of the tile setters on the job, remembered Morgan checking on the progress once a week.

> When I first started setting the mosaic, I had a section up, the mortar was still soft. Miss Morgan said it looked too perfect, and she wanted us to try to figure a way to make it look older but still look perfect. I suggested I bang my fist in it in different parts of the panel, change the smooth face of the mosaic with the small depressions here and there. She said, try it. I did, and she said that's just what she wanted. I continued that procedure all along until we finished the pool.[30]

The mosaic designs were created by Camille Solon, the muralist who designed the painted arches in Casa Grande's Gothic Study. Hearst was frustrated by Solon's changes of mind and wrote to Morgan in exasperation, blissfully unconscious of his own perpetual alterations: "Mr. Solon is wonderful as a designer and colorist, but he slows up the work tremendously by continual changes in the scheme and program. . . . The design is settled and satisfactory. I am going to take the liberty of insisting that it be unchanged. . . . Mr. Solon will be valuable if he does not interfere. If he does, I would suggest, Miss Morgan, that you find need for him in San Francisco."[31] One of Hearst's own willful and autocratic changes of mind was to salt the water in the pool once it was completed—a terrible idea from which no one could dissuade him, as plumber Alex Rankin recalled:

> One day Mr. Hearst gave Mr. Willicombe, his secretary, an order: "Put salt in the water." He wanted salt. So Willicombe came down to me in the pool and said, "I've

brilliant blue mosaic small tile and the gilt tile and the border of fishes with gold."

ordered a ton of salt to go in the pool, Mr. Rankin." I said Mr. Willicombe, you can't put salt into this pool. The pipes are not designed for it. He said, "Mr. Hearst wants salt water in the pool." Nobody could tell Mr. Hearst you couldn't do it. I said you are going to ruin the pipes, the pumps and things. He said, "How much salt do you think we should have in the indoor pool?" I said, do you want it like ocean water? He says, "Yes, something like that." I said, one ton of salt, you will know something is in the water, but you probably won't know what's in it. And he said, "How much do you think should be there?" I said, about 18 to 20 tons, by volume. And he thought I was nuts. So he went on the phone, and he called up the two salt companies, Leslie Salt, and Morton Salt, and they told him yes, it should have at least 18 tons, 20 tons might be better. About a week later I see a big truck and trailer come in loaded right to the top with half ground rewashed rock salt to put in

THE ROMAN POOL, inspired by an ancient Roman bath, was lined with one-inch-square Murano mosaic tiles of glass and twenty-two-carat gold. Its single depth of ten feet in the main basin discouraged inexperienced swimmers. It was apparently used much less frequently than the Neptune Pool.

THE DIVING PLATFORM is approached by stairs hidden behind the wall.

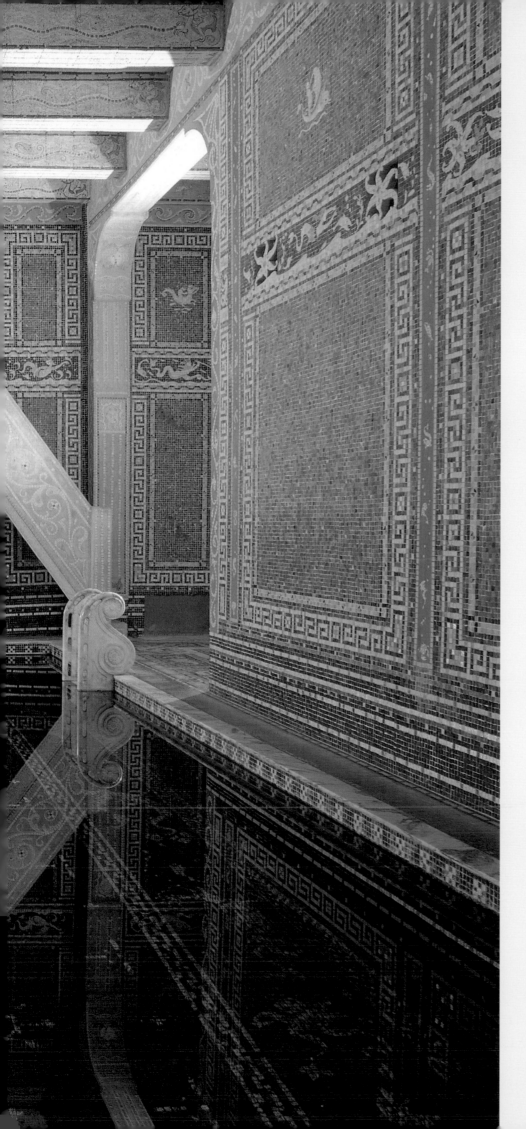

the pool. . . . Later on, the heat exchanger where the copper tubes and steel comes together, it ate it all out. The pump broke and inside of the pump, the cast iron, was like cheese. You could cut it with a knife.[32]

The Roman Pool was used infrequently, according to the recollections of former guests and staff. It seemed remote because it faced east, a direction guests had little occasion to explore on the hilltop, since the four houses all faced the other three compass points. Furthermore, its ten-foot depth likely deterred all but the experienced swimmers. But it is a place of spectacular beauty, both by day and by night. Part of the Roman Pool's breathtaking effect comes from the shining uneven surfaces of the Murano glass tiles set into the massive walls and floor, and part comes from the ambience of a subterranean grotto. Though the pool is above ground, it is set below the tennis courts and abuts the hillside beneath them, giving it a cavernlike feeling. The greatest beauty of this serene and opulent space comes from the water itself, so clear and still that it seems a shining mirror, reflecting the alabaster lamps and marble statues above and below its surface.

One such magical spot would be a great distinction, but, of course, San Simeon has two. The final version of the Neptune Pool was constructed in 1934–36, just after the Roman Pool was completed. The Neptune statue, which in the pool's second version stood at the top of the cascade, was removed in the early thirties, as was the cascade itself. In its place was built an upper pool intended for a group of statues—never installed—of Neptune in a chariot pulled by rearing horses. The *Birth of Venus* group was placed in the lower pool, and four groups of *Nymphs and Swans* were located on the deck of the basin, which was itself enlarged substantially by the addition of a border of white Vermont marble,

THE BIRTH OF VENUS *SCULPTURE GROUP by Charles Cassou, 1934, stands opposite the Roman temple at the Neptune Pool. A marble Neptune riding in a chariot drawn by four rearing horses was sculpted by the same artist, but it was never installed as planned in the upper area behind the Venus group.*

skillfully extending the length of the main pool basin to 104 feet. The width of the main basin is fifty-eight feet, or ninety-six feet counting the alcove area. The pool is three and one-half feet deep at its shallow western end and ten feet at its eastern end, the basin holding 345,000 gallons of water.

Charles Cassou, the Parisian sculptor who created most of the pool's modern statues, recommended that Morgan consider introducing other lower sculptural forms into the pool to extend the line from the Venus grouping out further into the water, since the pieces, to his eye, appeared too tightly compressed in their setting. He suggested perhaps the addition of fish or tortoises as low elements, which would preserve the scale.[33] This suggestion was not only ignored, but would have been

WHEN EMPTY, *the Neptune Pool basin reveals its white marble floor. Light refraction from the 345,000 gallons of water that fill the pool makes its basin appear blue.*

truly impractical. Cassou was accustomed to thinking of fountain groupings, but Hearst and Morgan were building something unprecedented: a decorative pool worthy of a Renaissance villa (which, in fact, also evoked the second-century villa of the Emperor Hadrian at Tivoli) that was also a heated and filtered basin of water for swimming. Freestanding low statues would have been obstacles with which an unsuspecting guest could collide. Rather, the temple and other sculptures all stand outside the water and reflect down into it.

The Roman temple itself is a composite of fragments, some ancient Roman, others modern, and the back wall is a few slender feet of concrete, decorated with a cast-stone frieze that borrows elements from the Parthenon's frieze. The Neptune Pool breaks the rules of Classical architecture, but this grouping of old and new elements provides La Cuesta Encantada with an indelible image, part Maxfield Parrish, part antiquity, which expresses the deeply romantic, composite nature of the whole complex. The notion of taking the past and improving on it, which Hearst and Morgan admired in Stanford White's designs and carried on

BERTEL THORVALDSEN. RELIEF OF HERCULES AND HEBE. *Danish, 1807–10. 62 x 58" (157.4 x 147.3 cm). Hearst Monument Collection, Casa Grande Assembly Room.*

Hercules was a mortal who was changed into a god after his success at performing twelve labors. He is shown here as a deity, indicated by the fillet encircling his hair. He sits on a rock that is covered by his lion skin while Hebe, the Greek goddess of youth, presents him with a phiale, or drinking bowl. This relief is likely an allegory of Strength, part of a set of four reliefs displayed in the Assembly Room, the other three of which are allegories of Wisdom, Justice, and Health. Hearst bought all four in 1938 at Sotheby's in the sale of Victor Rothschild's London town house, one of many large liquidation sales of British collections that occurred in the era between the wars.

through the 1940s, has no better example. Though no gushing fountains bring outstanding water effects to San Simeon, the Neptune Pool transforms the hill in just as original a way: here the Hollywood stars and starlets—living versions of idealized statues—disported themselves in a magical setting of mountains, water, and stone.

As they were finishing work on the Neptune Pool came the now-familiar directive: Morgan was to shut down operations at San Simeon and Wyntoon on

October 1st, 1936, because of Hearst's lack of money. Hearst explained to Morgan: "The reason was taxes which are becoming confiscatory and will be worse the coming year. . . . The election wasn't much help, was it?"[34] While Hearst had backed Roosevelt enthusiastically in the 1932 election, releasing the delegate votes he had controlled for John Nance Garner of Texas on the fourth ballot in order to swing his support to Roosevelt and give him the nomination, he unsuccessfully backed Alf Landon in 1936. His disaffection with FDR stemmed in part from the Wealth Recovery Tax, passed in 1935, ensuring that Hearst moved into a seventy-five percent tax bracket. And the fifteen percent state taxes in California grew so high that Hearst feared he could not continue there as a resident, instead having to limit his total time in the state to one day under six months of each year. "Heaven knows," said Hearst to the local press, "I do not want to leave California. No one does, least of all a native son whose father was a pioneer."[35]

When Hearst actually left San Simeon in 1937, however, it was not because of taxes but because of the collapse of his financial empire, a toppling that had been coming for years. He seems to have had little warning, writing to Morgan in late May of 1937, "I have suddenly been called to New York."[36] Just four days later came a letter stopping work entirely at San Simeon, for the first time.[37] All construction ceased, the last project being a Mission Revival–style bunkhouse Loorz was building for the ranch workers near the original family

house at the bottom of the hill. The extensions and real-locations of funds were of no use to Hearst now. He was facing complete financial ruin, and San Simeon construction was not the only thing that had to stop. All building projects were halted. At seventy-four, Hearst had lost control of his empire. He returned to San Simeon only a few weeks later but completely altered in mood. Loorz wrote to Morgan after having spoken to Randolph Apperson, a cousin of Hearst's who served as ranch manager for San Simeon: "[F]rom Randy I learn that Mr. Hearst is a pathetic, broken man. . . . Apparently his creditors are quite anxious to hurt him if they can. Further a government tax investigation seems eminently possible. . . . I am glad to hear that Randy reports Miss Davies to be very considerate of him, to be his only real comfort. They are here on the hilltop alone. She stole him away from New York as he seemed so worried and confined there that she feared he might not stand it."[38]

Hearst moved between San Simeon and Wyntoon while the great contraction of his finances began. It continued for the next eight years. Morgan took the work stoppage as an opportunity to return to southern Europe, this time on a freighter, in the summer of 1938. Hearst wrote her gloomily from Wyntoon: "Certainly I would like to make such a trip myself, but I guess I will have to stay here and try to make enough money to put up another house—or to finish those already begun."[39]

THE ROMAN TEMPLE at the Neptune Pool is made up of fragments of ancient Roman columns, bases, and capitals, extended and supported by poured concrete. The figures of Neptune and the Nereids, originally three-dimensional statues, were set into concrete in the temple pediment to look like a carved relief. This temple may have been inspired by the Italian Renaissance temple of the Villa Aldobrandini at Frascati, illustrated in Edith Wharton's influential Italian Villas and Their Gardens. *It is not an exact re-creation. Rather than follow the classical orders, Morgan designed a fanciful adaptation of the classical style that was picturesque rather than exacting.*

Chapter Ten

Hearst Besieged

This time none of Hearst's budget padding or money juggling would help. He was facing financial disaster, an indebtedness of nearly a hundred million Depression-era dollars, or ten times that amount in current values. He began his public financing bid in 1930 with the sale of Hearst Consolidated stock, the capital of which he drew on liberally for his many expenditures.[1] By 1936, both his circulation and advertising revenues had dropped precipitously

because of anti-Hearst boycotts over his strong opposition to Roosevelt's re-election. Hearst's long habit of operating newspapers that were unprofitable could not continue. He owed nine million dollars alone to the Canadian paper manufacturers who supplied his presses with newsprint, and seventy-eight million additional dollars to the banks who had floated his previous loans.[2]

The primary reason for his towering debt was his own improvidence. Hearst had joked once to his friend Gretchen Swinnerton, "Did you ever hear of the feller who insisted on calling a dollar bill a 'William'? He said he wasn't familiar enough with it to call it 'Bill.'"[3] Hearst and his money were now on similarly distant terms. John Francis Neylan, Hearst's personal attorney who served as his financial adviser through much of the 1930s, said, "I never knew a man who valued money less than Hearst."[4] He had tried hard to ignore the Great Depression, but by the late 1930s, optimism in the face of contrary evidence had finally failed him as a strategy.

Marion watched the financial troubles mounting. "Mr. Berlin [chairman of the Hearst Corporation board of directors] would say, 'Now, don't buy so many antiques.' And W. R. would say, 'What's that got to do with the price of eggs?'—he got that phrase from me—and that would stop them. And things would go on just the way they were."[5] When his empire finally crashed, Marion acted decisively. She discovered from Bill Hearst Jr. that unless Hearst scraped up a million dollars immediately, he would lose everything. She ordered her business manager to sell her stocks, bonds, and jewelry, then presented Hearst with a check for the million. At first he would not take the loan, but he finally consented, giving her shares in his publishing company for collateral. Marion said, "When I see anybody in trouble, I'll fight like hell to get them out. Especially someone I love very much."[6] Marion also requested help from Cissy Patterson, publisher of Hearst's *Washington Herald,* who lent Hearst an additional million dollars at five percent interest.[7]

From 1936 on, Hearst was under tremendous emotional as well as financial assault. Arthur Brisbane, his columnist, business partner, and close friend, died on Christmas Day, 1936. Hearst was so upset that he actually stopped buying art for a while, a development that

WILLIAM RANDOLPH HEARST *abroad with his adviser, Judge Clarence Shearn, whose job it was to steady Hearst's toppling empire in the late 1930s.*

the beleaguered Alice Head in London and John Francis Neylan in New York discussed with relief, Neylan concluding that "every day that it lasts is just that much profit."[8] Marion retired from films the following spring after making four disappointing movies with the Warner Bros. Studio, having left M-G-M three years before because Hearst felt she was being unjustly passed over for parts. The *New York Times* acidly reviewed a worn-looking forty-year-old Marion in her final role in *Ever Since Eve,* released in June of 1937: "After playing the eye-batting ingenue for more years than it would be polite to mention, Miss Marion Davies apparently feels she has mastered the role sufficiently to begin her cycle all over again."[9] Marion reflected: "I just didn't want to work in pictures anymore. I'd been working awfully hard for quite a long time. At that time Mr. Hearst was about seventy-eight or so, and I felt he needed companionship. He was having some financial troubles at the time, too, and he was more upset than people realized. I thought the least I could do for a man who had been so wonderful and great, one of the greatest men ever, was to be a companion to him."[10]

Another loss that shook both Hearst and Marion badly was a serious plane crash at the San Simeon coastal landing field in February 1938. Lord and Lady Plunket of England and Hearst pilot Tex Phillips died at the scene. Phillips had tried to land in the fog, thinking that he did not have enough fuel to fly the 120 miles to Santa Barbara.[11] Marion was at the ranch with Hearst

JEAN LÉON GÉRÔME. ANACREON WITH
BACCHUS AND AMOR. *French, c. 1878. Cast
bronze. 35 ½ x 15 x 16" (90.2 x 38.1 x 40.6 cm). Hearst
Monument Collection, Casa Grande Lower South
Duplex.*

*The Greek poet carries both the young Bacchus, the
god of wine, and Amor, the god of love, who embraces
him. Gérôme created a painting, a full-size marble
sculpture, and several signed bronzes on this theme.*

when the Plunkets flew up, bringing bobsled champion
James Lawrence—the only crash survivor—with them.
When Hearst first heard that the plane was having trouble, he went quickly down to the office to check on it,
certain that, whatever the problem, his regular pilot
would be able to handle it. Hearst got a severe shock
when he reached the office and found his head pilot
standing there. Phillips, the backup pilot, had begged
to make the trip solo in order to qualify for his full
license.[12] Marion recalled:

> When I thought the Plunkets should have arrived—it
> took only an hour to fly up—I went down to the phone
> in the office. I looked out the window and the sky was
> very bad. . . . The next thing I heard was this terrific
> sound. He had tried to land, but thinking they would hit a
> mountain, he had given the damn thing the gun and it had
> gone shooting up and then straight on down, in a nose-
> dive. Then I saw the flames. . . . To look at a crash, to
> know that your friends are in it, is a terrible experience.
> . . . I didn't get over that shock for quite a long time.[13]

The losses piled up. Newspapers were sold. Real
estate was sold, beginning with the Clarendon
Apartments in New York in 1936.[14] An inevitable part
of the retrenchment was the sale of over half of Hearst's
art collection, much of which was stored in warehouses
in New York and San Francisco, in addition to pieces displayed in Hearst's several enormous houses. As a buyer,
he had always frustrated dealers by resisting their influence. They had also been exasperated by his tendency to
collect in dizzying numbers of categories and to dicker
over the selling price as well. Germain Seligman, an
influential Paris dealer, wrote about Hearst as a collector:

> The buying methods of this dynamic personality were
> very strange. Nobody I have known showed simultane-
> ously such a voracious desire to acquire and so little dis-
> crimination in doing it. Hearst often purchased superb
> examples of real aesthetic merit, but he also acquired
> hundreds of items of no artistic or historic interest. . . .
> Contrary to the majority of men of business acumen,
> Hearst loved to dicker, a practice of dubious value in
> the art world, leading rather to bargaining than to bar-
> gains. Thus through the years I did business with
> William Randolph Hearst, I never derived from it the
> true enjoyment I felt with his great contemporaries. . . .

The dealer wishes to feel himself a guide and mentor, and, because he recommends and encourages the purchase of an object he considers fitting, he is willing to assume a special moral responsibility. But when, contrary to a dealer's better judgment, the client purchases less fitting items, the art dealer loses interest in the client.[15]

Hearst delighted in dickering, paid small amounts for many of his selections, and always made up his own mind on purchases, to the despair of the art dealers, whose interest in steering him to certain objects, however, was seldom without bias. Art dealer and collector Armand Hammer wrote of Hearst: "He bought everything, from the archeological sweepings of ancient societies—the equivalent of salt and pepper shakers—to its greatest and most glorious masterpieces."[16]

HEARST HAD IGNORED money troubles during all of San Simeon's construction years, but, in 1937, his situation was so desperate that it demanded a drastic restructuring. On Hearst's habit of overspending on his art collection, Jean Paul Getty, a guest at San Simeon in 1934, once wrote: "I suppose I have much in common with Hearst. I, however, have always spent ninety-five percent or more of my money on my business, while Hearst was the other way around."

FRANZ WINTERHALTER. PORTRAIT OF EMPEROR MAXIMILIAN OF MEXICO. German, 1864. Oil on canvas. 39 ¼ x 33" (99.7 x 82.1 cm). Hearst Monument Collection, House A Right Back Bedroom.

Maximilian (1832–1867) was the younger brother of Franz Josef, Emperor of Austria. Maximilian married Princess Charlotte of Belgium in 1857. Napoleon III sent Maximilian to the newly invaded Mexico in 1864 to legitimize the Emperor's reign. Maximilian was unsuccessful and was executed in Mexico by firing squad in 1867.

FRANZ WINTERHALTER. PORTRAIT OF EMPRESS CHARLOTTE OF MEXICO. German, 1864. Oil on canvas. 39 ½ x 29 ⅝" (99.1 x 75.2 cm). Hearst Monument Collection, House A Right Back Bedroom.

Hearst bought this pair of Winterhalter portraits in London in 1938, when he was facing the worst of his financial woes.

MARION DAVIES's last film role was in Ever Since Eve *for Warner Bros., 1937. A reviewer for the* New York Times *wrote that its creaky plot and Marion's inappropriate casting as the perpetual ingenue made the film "almost a collector's piece—a rummage collector's, pieced together out of thread-bare scraps of farce basted with some of the most synthetic dialogue ever coined by man and uttered with embarrassing self-consciousness by Miss Davies." It was a sad closing chapter to her long film career.*

Hammer about the details of the sale, he then suggested Gimbel's, at that time considered a second-rate department store. This may have been Hearst's most egalitarian moment, but it was not intentional. The collector who had taken great pleasure in besting the dealers at their galleries and in championing the ordinary American in his newspapers was not happy to have those very same Americans picking through his art collection in the Gimbel's fifth-floor men and boys' sportswear department. Hearst wrote to Richard Berlin that the sale was going to be "a most fatal mistake. . . . You will get nothing from the sale of any consequence . . . nothing compared to the injury inflicted upon your remaining art objects by this method of selling them over the bargain counter."[18] A small consolation, which helped Hearst to accept the ignominy, was that Fred Gimbel also owned the prestigious Sak's Fifth Avenue,

When his empire finally crashed, Marion acted decisively, sold her stocks,

Faced with imminent ruin, he had no choice but to sell. The sales began badly, starting with Hearst's English silver auctioned through Sotheby's in London, November 17, 1937. Much of it had been bought in Great Britain originally and showcased at St. Donat's. When purchasing it, Hearst had aroused the ire of the British dealers by ignoring the "ring," the informal group who kept prices artificially low by not bidding against each other at the actual auctions, then having a private sale of their own to redistribute the pieces later. Their vengeance on Hearst was to keep the prices so low at his own sale that he lost at least one hundred thousand dollars on the objects.[17] American sales began in 1938 through two New York galleries, Parrish Watson and Parke-Bernet, beginning with books and Hearst's Americana collection. The results were a similar disappointment. The market was terrible in the Depression, and the dealers either stayed away or bid ridiculously low amounts.

Armand Hammer had already had some success in selling his own Russian art collection in various department stores, and the Hearst Corporation turned to him. When Macy's, initially interested, could not agree with

and the paintings were sold there. More than half of Hearst's outstanding Greek vases were sold, but most of San Simeon's vases and other pieces survived the weeding process, the warehoused items providing the bulk of the objects that came from the ranch.

The promotion leading up to the sale was enormous, and neither Hearst nor Gimbel's had to spend a cent on it. Hammer told the *New York Times:* "The collection ranges from everything to everything. Just imagine walking into the Metropolitan Museum of Art and finding price tags on every piece. That's the only way I can describe it. The prices will be quite reasonable. Everybody will be able to afford to buy something from the Hearst Collection."[19] Hammer also gave *The New Yorker* a tour of Hearst's five-story New York warehouse, stuffed with objects. The reporter wrote:

> Mr. Hammer also said that the average Gimbel's customer is really in the market for armorial objects, whether he knows it or not. "We will sell daggers for letter-openers, parts of armor for paperweights, and shields for foyers," he said. . . . Mr. Hammer advised me not to get the idea that everything in the sale was going to be expensive, and by way of setting me straight on

this point he showed me an Early American yarn-winding reel, marked $10.50, and a mangy Georgian fireplace brush bearing a tag on which $3.00 had been crossed out and $2.95 substituted. . . . In general, the prices Mr. Hammer gave me left me with the impression that if Mr. Hearst got back ten cents on the dollar he would be doing well.[20]

Hearst himself tried to put the best face on it. He told a writer for the *Saturday Evening Post:* "I am not disposing of all my art collection, only about half of it. The remainder I propose giving to museums. You know I am not merely an art collector but a dealer in art and antique objects"—a surprising statement, considering that Hearst had never resold anything previously.[21] Profit was the furthest thing from his mind in art collecting. And while the Gimbel's sale did not make a profit when compared to Hearst's purchase prices, it was

a success in raising the targeted goal of eleven million dollars for the corporation less than one year after the liquidations had begun.[22]

The contrasts between Hearst's extravagance and the nation's desperate poverty grew harder to ignore during the Depression. If William Randolph Hearst was finally feeling financially pinched, sympathy for him was rare. Even the loyal George Loorz said, "He would like to start work on the outside pool, start a new reservoir etc but told me yesterday, 'I want so many things but haven't got the money.' Poor fellow, let's take up a collection."[23] Two savagely critical biographies appeared in 1936: Ferdinand Lundberg's *Imperial Hearst* described its subject as "the weakest strong man and the strongest weak man in the world today . . . a giant with feet of clay"; and Oliver Carlson's *Hearst, Lord of San Simeon* called him "a religious fanatic without religion, or rather . . . a

bonds, and jewelry, and presented Hearst with a check for a million.

WILLIAM RANDOLPH HEARST *meets with his advisers in the Assembly Room. To his left are three of his sons: George, Randolph, and David. Hearst continued to visit San Simeon through the cash-strapped years of the late 1930s, and he also continued to conceive complicated remodeling schemes that Morgan knew he could not afford to undertake.*

Hearst fanatic."[24] Hearst had hired Mrs. Fremont Older to write the authorized and wholly laudatory biography, *William Randolph Hearst, American,* earlier in the same year, perhaps in response to the unfavorable accounts under preparation.

Actually, fictional criticisms—which were fueled by the fact-based ones—ended up being far more enduring in their damage. The earliest set the tone for all the rest, when in 1936 John Dos Passos described Hearst by name as "Poor Little Rich Boy" in one of the closing sections of the final volume of his "U.S.A." trilogy, *The Big Money.* In prose as elegant as plainsong, Dos Passos sketched a failed emperor:

> Caesar's life like his was a millionaire prank. Perhaps W. R. had read of republics ruined before; . . .

perhaps he could too easily forget a disappointment [by] buying a firstrate writer or an embroidered slipper attributed to Charlemagne or the gilded bed a king's mistress was supposed to have slept in. . . .

And more and more the emperor of newsprint retired to his fief of San Simeon on the Pacific Coast, where he assembled a zoo, continued to dabble in movingpictures, collected warehouses full of . . . the loot of dead Europe,

built an Andalusian palace and a Moorish banquethall and there spends his last years amid the relaxing adulations of screenstars, admen, screenwriters, publicitymen, columnists . . . .

Until he dies

the magnificent endlesslyrolling presses will pour out print for him, the whirring everywhere projectors will spit images for him,

a spent Caesar grown old with spending never man enough to cross the Rubicon.[25]

THE UNFINISHED rear courtyard of Casa Grande, site of the proposed Great Hall, which was never built. Though reminders of interrupted construction projects are evident throughout San Simeon's gardens and buildings, perhaps no part of the estate demonstrates its unfinished nature better than the east facade, where antique window frames and a Venetian loggia are set into brick and concrete walls.

Hearst's excesses at his San Simeon ranch were more briefly but just as harshly portrayed by John Steinbeck in *The Grapes of Wrath* in 1939. As the Joads lurch their way in an ancient converted Hudson automobile carrying a dozen people and all their possessions from the dust-laden Oklahoma prairie to California, they begin to realize that this promised land will bring them no deliverance. The climate is all it was supposed to be, but the work they hoped for does not exist. The first person they meet in California tells them about a millionaire who can only have been William Randolph Hearst: "'They's a fella, newspaper fella near the coast, got a million acres. . . . Got guards ever'place to keep folks out. . . . I seen pitchers of him. Fat, sof' fella with little mean eyes an' a mouth like a ass-hole. Scairt he's gonna die. Got a million acres and scairt of dyin.'" Casey, an ex-preacher who was traveling with the Joads,

ABOVE: ARMOR FOR MAN AND HORSE. *Italian, Milan. 1565. Steel, copper, alloy, leather, and textile. 6' 4" x 8' x 3' 9" (193 x 243.8 x 114.3 cm). Ex-Hearst Collection, The Nelson-Atkins Museum of Art, Kansas City, Missouri.*

Hearst purchased this armor for a man and horse in 1933, writing to Julia Morgan: "I think you must be a Sibyl, with the gift of prophecy. You always drew the big hall that we propose to make at the ranch with two horse armors. I did not have the horse armors but I got two today and they are beauties. There is no reason now why we should not go ahead with the hall—of course in due time—when the horse armors have been paid for." But the money troubles intervened and the Great Hall was never built. This horse armor was instead sold at the Gimbel's sale.

RIGHT: *IN AN ADVERTISEMENT from his periodical* The Compleat Collector: A Monthly Message of Good-Will from Dealer to Collector, *Armand Hammer promises bargain prices on Hearst's armor collection, made even more appealing when the buyer used Gimbel's Easy Payment Plan.*

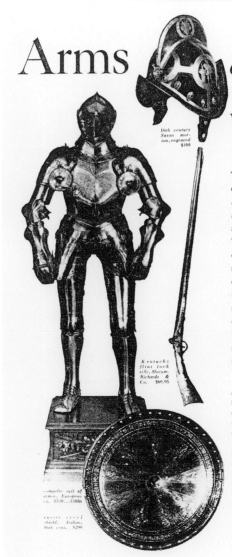

Arms and Armor

FROM THE COLLECTION OF

William Randolph Hearst

And Other World Famous Collections

The reductions on these pieces are so enormous as to be barely credible. *Yet in many cases we have a complete record of the original purchase price.* (Only recently we sold a sword for $600 that originally cost $12,000!) There have, of course, been few collections of arms and armor that have approached the magnificence or the magnitude of the Hearst collection. Its fame is international. Since the collection has been on our floor we have sold to museums and armories and to private collectors who have long waited for this treasure to be released to the public. All items subject to prior sale. Use Gimbels Easy Payment Plan. Small service charge.

complete suit of armor, Mid-European, ca. 1530........$3886
half suit English piping armor, James I period......... 167
closed helmet, engraved, Italian....................... 828
morion-cabasset, engraved, Italian.................... 132
engraved morion, Italian, 16th cent.................... 195
Saxon morion, engraved, 16th cent.................... 498
circular shield of russet steel....................... 299
2-handed Flambert blade, 16th cent.................... 119
2-handed sword, mid-European, 16th cent.............. 99
shirt of riveted chain mail, ca. 1490 349
steel blade, chased decoration, 16th cent............. 84
walking sword, fluted blade, 16th cent................ 219
Wheellock Tschinke, inlaid, 16th cent................. 179

GIMBEL BROTHERS

33rd Street and Broadway

189

dismisses such a man swiftly: "If he needs a million acres to make him feel rich, seems to me he needs it 'cause he feels awful poor inside hisself. . . . I ain't trying to preach no sermon, but I never seen nobody that's busy as a prairie dog collectin' stuff that wasn't disappointed."[26]

In the same year, Aldous Huxley wrote *After Many a Summer Dies the Swan*, a novel whose title is a line from Tennyson's poem "Tithonus," about a man in love with the Dawn. He wishes for immortal life to keep pace with her unending freshness but forgets to wish for eternal youth, decaying more with each passing day. The novel's main character, Jo Stoyte, is a millionaire who lives in a hilltop castle in California, an enormous place filled with a muddle of art from all periods, put together in utter ignorance. The library empty of books "because Mr. Stoyte had not yet brought himself to buy any," the "thirteenth-century stained glass in the eleventh-floor W. C.," the indoor pool, the morning room, the vast estate all exemplify the boorishness of its owner.[27] Stoyte's companion is the young and beautiful Virginia Maunciple—first glimpsed sitting at her own soda fountain—without question modeled on the ice cream-loving Marion Davies. Huxley had actually changed the character's last name from Dowlas, so that it would not resemble Marion's stage name or real last name— Douras—too much.[28] Stoyte is so obsessed with remaining youthful that he hires a Lothario named Dr. Obispo to conduct scientific experiments in the basement to unlock the key to eternal youth. There is no evidence that Huxley was a guest at San Simeon; his characterizations appear to have come through his friendship with Marion's close friend Anita Loos. Huxley described his novel as a "phantasy, but built up of solidly realistic psychological elements; a wild extravaganza, but with the quality of a most serious parable."[29]

Huxley celebrated the novel's conclusion at a July 1939 party in Los Angeles, where he met Orson Welles for the first time.[30] It is, of course, in Welles's film

EXCEPT FOR ITS HILLTOP SETTING, La Cuesta Encantada has little similarity to Welles's fictional Xanadu, which was based on Mont St. Michel and was intended to convey a remote severity completely absent in the real San Simeon.

Citizen Kane, released in 1941, that the most indelible images of William Randolph Hearst, Marion Davies, and San Simeon itself were created. And what could finally be more appropriate and ironic than having the image of a media tycoon rest not on history but on a media event, staged by someone who was in many ways similar to Hearst. When Orson Welles, already accomplished as a writer, radio personality, stage director, and actor, came to Hollywood at age twenty-four, he was exactly the age William Randolph Hearst had been when he took over the *San Francisco Examiner.* And Welles was ready to stir up a similar amount of fuss. Welles had Hearst's level of energy, Hearst's improvidence, Hearst's understanding of the potential of movies.

The enduring influence of *Citizen Kane* on Hearst's reputation can be observed in the simple fact that many Americans are still under the impression that it was filmed at San Simeon, as if it were a straightforward documentary. Almost sixty years later, viewers continue to regard it as a biography of William Randolph Hearst, not as a scathing indictment of the role of the press lord in America. Perhaps Hearst never saw *Citizen Kane.* Bill Hearst Jr. said that he did not. "I asked him myself—or somebody asked him in my presence, because I know I was there—whether he had seen it and he said no, he hadn't. [Pop believed that] if they made up a lot of stuff and if it was supposed to be him . . . and they made him out inaccurately, . . . there was no point in seeing it. And if they made him out accurately he might be embarrassed."[31] His press machine took many unsuccessful measures to stop RKO from releasing the film. Though there is little direct evidence concerning Hearst's own role in the campaign, it is unlikely these efforts would have been made without at least his tacit approval. *Kane* showed only in a small number of theaters and was not a commercial success. Welles said that he had expected Hearst to fight it. "He was dead right. Why not fight? I expected that. I *didn't* expect that everyone would run as scared as they did."[32]

Whether or not Hearst saw it, he must have felt that, in spite of Welles's protestations, this film was far more a personal assault than it was a composite portrait of an American press lord. Even barring the inconsistencies

—for instance, Charles Foster Kane was born poor, then abandoned by his parents and raised by the representative of a bank—it was far too specific a portrait to be mistaken for any other person, even after Welles and his screenwriter Herman Mankiewicz—who, unlike Welles, had been a guest at San Simeon—removed many references and incidents that they felt were outright libelous.[33]

Some critics now feel that *Citizen Kane* is most memorably a portrait of Orson Welles himself.[34] But that interpretation is too subtle for most viewers. Instead, they have cast San Simeon as Kane's dark and cavernous Xanadu, whose foreboding exterior sheathed a heartless, soulless interior. Many of the building shots were filmed at Balboa Park, the site of the 1915 San Diego Exposition, which Hearst had, in fact, admired and discussed as an early inspiration for the Spanish Colonial Revival architecture of La Cuesta Encantada. The interior scenes—all shot on a sound stage— showed deserted and echoing rooms in which Susan Alexander Kane gloomily worked jigsaw puzzles. In the public's mind, San Simeon became not a lighthearted palace but a forbidding fortress, its "No Trespassing" sign, next to an elaborate wrought iron initial "K," the first and last images viewers saw of the film. The jigsaw puzzles were real enough, though they were a group activity rather than a solitary pastime, as Marion reminisced in her memoirs: "We'd do the jigsaw puzzles for hours in the main living room. Twenty of us would be around and we'd pick out the pieces. It was childish, and I wouldn't do it now; it's awfully hard on the eyes. But we had a big table and everybody'd get in and there'd be arguments and little flirtations because the men would get in and pick out a piece for a girl and give her a wink. . . . It was fascinating. It was also a good way to waste time."[35]

Citizen Kane attacked Hearst on his most vulnerable side. He had always ignored slurs. Wry comments about the worthlessness of his art collection abounded in this time of liquidation sales. But to portray Charles Foster Kane's second wife—Susan Alexander Kane—as an opera singer who could not sing, an uneducated incompetent for whom Kane had to buy a career, permanently colored the public's view of Marion Davies. Almost

unknown is that it was *Chicago Tribune* newspaper publisher Robert R. McCormick who shamelessly promoted untalented opera singer Marion Claire in 1939.[36] Still, there is no doubt that Hearst had tried to build Marion Davies a career through overpublicizing her, and the public had no trouble substituting actress for singer. Also real enough, and surely the hardest thing for Hearst to bear, was the depiction of Susan Alexander Kane as a pitiful drunkard. To have the greatest weak-

ness of the woman he adored paraded before the public this way must have devastated Hearst. Even Aldous Huxley had not been so cruel. His Virginia Maunciple was a sweet-tempered vacuous innocent, but he did not make her a boozy moron. Welles apparently felt some kind of remorse over this portrayal of Marion, at least long afterward. In 1975, fourteen years after her death, he wrote the foreword to her memoirs and took care to refute the interpretation that Susan Alexander Kane was

IN THE REAR courtyard of Casa Grande, where construction ceased suddenly in 1937, a crabapple tree blooms.

meant as a portrait of Marion Davies. He carefully sketched the differences between them, pointing out that Susan Kane had been a nobody when Kane discovered her, whereas Marion was a famous beauty with her pick of beaux. As Hearst's mistress instead of his wife, Welles pointed out, Hearst courted and valued her, and she was "never less than a princess." The "lonely fortress," as he described Xanadu, had no relationship to the many pleasure domes Hearst built, where "the Beautiful People of the day fought for invitations. . . . [Marion] was never one of Hearst's possessions: he was always her suitor, and she was the precious treasure of his heart for more than thirty years, until his last breath of life. Theirs is truly a love story. Love is not the subject of *Citizen Kane*."[37]

All this sentimentalizing came far too late, as Welles undoubtedly knew. It seems unlikely that Marion would have had such a low opinion of her own career if she had not been ridiculed in *Citizen Kane*. She said, at the end of her memoirs, that she had not seen it, and that she bore Welles no malice. "W. R. never went to see *Citizen Kane* either," she wrote.

> The Hearst newspapers put a ban on it, as far as publicity went, but W. R. wasn't little that way. His theory was that no matter what anybody said, no matter what they wrote, you didn't read it and you didn't listen.
>
> W. R. said, "Yesterday's newspaper is old news." But plenty of people talked about *Citizen Kane*. They would say that it was terrible and I had to go see it. But we never did.
>
> I had no anger toward Orson Welles. After all, everybody is created to do their very best, and he probably thought that was his way to make money. Who was I to say I didn't like the way he did his picture? I was not built that way. I like to keep the waters calm.[38]

Orson Welles's tardy apology for his depiction of Marion Davies says nothing about the one character trait—her use of alcohol—that confirmed it as her portrait. But he does finish his introduction to her memoirs this way:

> As one who shares much of the blame for casting another shadow—the shadow of Susan Alexander Kane—I rejoice in this opportunity to record something

which today is all but forgotten except for those lucky enough to have seen a few of her pictures: Marion Davies was one of the most delightfully accomplished comediennes in the whole history of the screen. She would have been a star if Hearst had never happened. She was also a delightful and very considerable person.[39]

All the controversy surrounding the making of *Citizen Kane* sealed the matter in the public's mind decades before Welles's retraction: Marion Davies was a pathetic flop, San Simeon was a ridiculous monstrosity filled with meaningless objects, and William Randolph Hearst was essentially finished. Early in 1939, *Time* placed Hearst on its cover and announced one of the greatest ignominies of all: "One of the many little-known facts about William Randolph Hearst's fantastically tangled affairs is that his rival Los Angeles publisher, Harry Chandler of the *Times,* holds a mortgage on San Simeon." Hearst had taken out the note on San Simeon in 1933, and was now in peril of losing the estate completely. Chandler agreed to extend the mortgage, but as *Time* crowed:

> The Hearst who mortgaged San Simeon to get $600,000 for spending money has for the past two years been employed as editorial director of his own newspapers, and last year his salary from the Hearst Consolidated papers was cut from $500,000 to $100,000. No longer ruler of the empire he built, Hearst has only two desires concerning it: 1) to have some of it survive him; 2) to keep his job. Nearing 76, the man who was the most spectacular publisher and spendthrift of his time wants to die a newspaperman.[40]

Hearst was at San Simeon at the time, devising new building schemes that he had neither the manpower nor the money to execute. Julia Morgan, having returned from her lengthy freighter trip through southern Europe, wrote to Warren McClure about the latest scheme, which was to build a sitting room on the top floor of House C to connect its two small bedroom towers: "If Mr. Hearst asks, am working on the possibility of putting the room upstairs over the sitting room of House C. There are a good many sides to it. If you don't have to take it up, don't."[41] She knew there was no money left to build anything at all.

CHAPTER ELEVEN

Hearst's Final Return

In the 1940s, Hearst and Morgan both found themselves left behind as America's tastes in art and architecture changed. The avant-garde of the thirties became commonplace in the forties, and Hearst the art collector deplored the new "modern art." He sounded off in an editorial column in 1941:

What have we in American art today to compare with . . . [the] great creations of the Gay Nineties? Nothing but some meaningless hentracks defacing clean canvas and made by fakers for fools. If we can laugh at the Gay Nineties, just imagine the convulsions of raucous laughter that will rock the frames of future generations when they look at the pitiful productions of the so-called modernistic art of today.[1]

Morgan was similarly unenthusiastic about modern architecture, also known as the International Style, the American version of which began in southern California in the 1930s with the designs of Richard Neutra and R. M. Schindler. The austere aesthetic they created, while revolutionary at first, was influential enough to change the course of mainstream American architecture by the end of World War II.[2] Her niece Flora North thought Morgan found the modern style "so cold that there was no place in [the home] for things of sentimental value."[3] The craftsmen she and Hearst had employed to create San Simeon's elaborate decoration were not needed for modern buildings. Morgan tried to reassure John Van der Loo, who with his father had designed and executed most of the ornate cast-plaster and cast-stone relief work at San Simeon: "I do think trained and capable people will be at a premium before long again—Ornamental work will have different types of sculptured forms and will tend to longer, more centralized and grouped, rather than spread, overall uses—as was popular twenty years ago—but will require expert craftsmen just the same." Because of Hearst's finances, she would not be able to employ him soon at San Simeon, however. "I had hope for all the . . . San Simeon groups," she wrote, "there is so much ornamental and decorative design involved—Now that is in a future no one here can even guess as to."[4]

In the early days of World War II, there was some fear of coastal invasion, particularly after the Union Oil tanker SS *Montebello* was sunk by a Japanese submarine four miles off Point Piedras Blancas on December 23, 1941.[5] Hearst moved from San Simeon to Wyntoon, and hilltop building ceased. With San Simeon under blackout and no hope of building anything in America during the war, Hearst turned to a property he owned that seemed out of the reach of the conflict—his large Mexican *rancho*, Babicora.[6] When Will was in his early twenties, just out of Harvard, George Hearst offered him the management of this cattle ranch of nearly a million acres in Chihuahua, Mexico. Though the land was briefly occupied in 1916 by Pancho Villa during the Mexican Revolution, Hearst still retained ownership of thousands of acres and traveled there occasionally, including in the winter of 1941.[7] Through 1943 the seventy-one-year-old Morgan designed a large adobe ranch house for Hearst on the site, flying to Mexico to examine the land and supervise the construction firsthand.[8] She thanked Hearst for the adventure the trip provided her, and he responded: "I am glad the trip was not a trial to you—IF it was not. I 'sort of' suspect it was in part at least."[9] In truth, Morgan was frustrated by the circumstances of building Babicora. Flora North recalled her saying: "Nobody is left in my office and I can't get any supplies, and how can I do anything?"[10] The project was plagued with manpower and material shortages, communication difficulties, and bad weather. Heavy rains turned the adobe bricks they were making back into mud.[11] Hearst, thrilled to have a project, planned so many additions—towers, extra bedrooms, and a swimming pool—that the cost estimates ballooned to five times the initial amount.[12]

This time he did not get away with it. The corporation was paying for the construction of Babicora, probably as a balm to the battered Chief to keep him happy

AN ANTIQUE *Spanish lion statue serves as the finial on the staircase in the North Upper Duplex.*

and occupied, and the accountants insisted that he stay within the original budget.[13] Edward Ardoin, the project engineer, complained to Morgan: "If Mr. Hearst would only wait until this war is over, we could duplicate what he wants built for at least half of the price and do a better job."[14] Hearst answered Ardoin that they couldn't wait: "[W]e do not know how long the war is going to last. And we do not know how long I am going to last."[15] By the winter of 1944 Ardoin was disgusted enough with the trouble-plagued project that he no longer even answered Morgan's letters.[16] And there the Babicora adobe languished. Morgan went back to Mexico herself in the spring of 1944 and spent two months, but work on the *rancho* ceased with little but the foundations constructed.[17]

The other Hearst project that occupied Morgan's time during the war years was even more frustrating than Babicora. The monastery Santa Maria de Ovila, which Hearst had acquired in Spain in 1931 with intentions to use at Wyntoon, sat in crates in a warehouse in San Francisco until his art liquidations began. Hearst considered giving the monastery to the Los Angeles County Museum of Art but decided instead to sell it to the city of San Francisco to be erected in Golden Gate Park as a medieval art museum, in the tradition of the Cloisters of the Metropolitan Museum of Art in New York.[18] Morgan's design was one of her greatest projects, a structure that respected both the site and the historic building materials. But powerful Hearst opponents protested the idea in the press. A series of arson fires in 1941 and 1942 burned the carefully coded wooden

crates in which the thousands of stones sat, even burning the markings off the stones themselves. Morgan prowled the wreckage, trying to document what she could of the pieces. Walter Steilberg recalled: "Now there is evidence of the drive of that little lady and the persistence of her dream. . . . This thing was all in ruins and everything, and yet she went out there day after day and made sketches of every little detail that she could get to."[19] Morgan was greatly disappointed by the failure of this project, writing to Steilberg in 1945: "You know how much has been put into Santa Maria de Ovila in the years—interest, study, funds, etc." She felt that the Cloisters in New York failed as an architectural conception, probably because it was too sterile. Her dream for San Francisco was to "re-create a spirit, because we knew and felt something of the original builders' urge."[20] It was all for naught. The stones were abandoned in a heap behind the M. H. de Young Museum, and many of them were gradually carried off or used in landscaping projects. A northern California Cistercian order reassembled some of the fragments at their abbey in the small town of Vina in the 1990s, but Morgan's dream of creating an entirely medieval structure never materialized. It was the last project she worked on for Hearst, except for a minor remodeling of the first floor of Marion's Lexington Road house in 1946.[21] Thus, twenty-five years of correspondence and collaboration

THE 1945 DODGE firetruck that William Randolph Hearst bought for San Simeon after his triumphant return to the ranch and to the building project. It was housed in one of the fourteen garages east of the Roman Pool.

between William Randolph Hearst and Julia Morgan basically ended with two grand designs that never went beyond Morgan's pen.

A great loss to Morgan in the forties was the death of her chief designer, Thaddeus Joy, in 1942. There was still work to do on San Simeon, but Morgan's health did not permit her to return to supervise it.[22] Warren McClure took Morgan's place as supervising architect, and Maurice McClure, a hilltop employee since the early 1920s, took Loorz's place as construction superintendent, since Loorz's Stolte Construction Inc. required his presence all over the state to supervise large postwar industrial projects. Though she was not present

THE NORTH WING *facade has antique window frames set into modern concrete. Remodeling the North Wing on Hearst's postwar return to San Simeon was the major construction project in the final years.*

on the hilltop, Morgan's influence on the project continued. These two McClures—no relation to each other—had worked with her for decades, and her sensibilities pervaded their design decisions.

Hearst returned to the hilltop in September of 1945, bringing a large crew of workers to recommence construction.[23] At eighty-two, he had reason to feel triumphant. While the Hearst Corporation's holdings had been slashed by forty percent and the wire service and movie production company closed, sixteen daily newspapers and eight successful magazines had survived the cutbacks. Most importantly, the war had brought an increase in spending to the country, and the corresponding increase in advertising revenues consolidated the gains made by the earlier downsizing. Hearst was back in control of his businesses and back in control of San Simeon.[24] The crews rebuilt the airport and hangar, rewired all the buildings, and began an extension at the rear of the South Wing. Maurice McClure remembered

that lengthening the South Wing to make it more symmetrical with the previously expanded North Wing required moving another oak tree twenty-eight feet to the east.[25]

Their primary focus was the North Wing of Casa Grande.[26] These three floors of rooms above the Theater had already been partially completed on two separate occasions, for temporary use during Hearst's seventy-first birthday in 1934, and then in 1936–37, when the shutdown intervened. These rooms seem disconnected from the rest of the Main Building, in part because their only access to the Assembly Room and Refectory was from the first floor. The North Wing was among the last construction projects, and its rooms were therefore the least used. In its earlier stages it had often been used by upper-level staff: secretaries and housekeepers. In this final remodeling some of the former bedrooms were converted into sitting rooms, and the bathrooms were redone with marble walls and larger

RIGHT: LAMP. *American, 20th century. Glazed pottery and silk shade. Base: 19"; including shade: 34" (48.8 cm base; 87.3 cm with shade). Hearst Monument Collection, Casa Grande North Wing Fourth Floor, Room One.*

This fanciful globe of the world is further decorated with boats, fish, and a compass. The base is lit and the continents are formed in relief, raised slightly so that the light delineating them shines through from the inside. Hearst's records state that he officially bought this lamp, and many others, from Marion Davies in 1945. It was sent from Ocean House to San Simeon, after Hearst's economic problems necessitated that he sell the Santa Monica residence.

ABOVE: THE 1940S BATHROOMS *in the North Wing blend efficiency and glamour, as in this black-and-white marble example on the second floor, with gold fixtures and abundant mirrors.*

OPPOSITE: THE TOP FLOOR *of the North Wing, where a sixteenth-century domed Spanish ceiling was placed for maximum dramatic effect. Called* media naranja, *or half-orange, ceilings, such domes were used in Spain over stair halls in important buildings.*

windows and mirrors to make them as luxurious as any Hollywood abode of the 1940s. The two upper-story towers were expanded, and a sitting room was created between them, this fourth floor planned for Hearst himself to occupy.[27] The greater lightness and spaciousness of the North Wing is obvious when contrasted with the less well-lit, more crowded parts of Casa Grande constructed in the twenties. The marble-lined bathrooms and the plain white walls of the North Wing demonstrate more modern influence than any other portion of the building, but these were largely superficial changes. Though its exterior was never finished, drawings indicate that its ornament was to be as ornate as the rest of the Main Building's, even to extending the teak cornice along its upper floor.[28]

Hearst was eighty-two at his return, and he was no longer shuttling between his houses at Los Angeles, Wyntoon, and San Simeon. His personal secretary Joe Willicombe had finally retired during the war, his absence exerting a great impact on the Chief after their thirty years of working together. Hearst moved back to

RUG. *Tabriz, Persia. 1880. Silk. 12'5" x 9'5" (378.5 x 287 cm). Hearst Monument Collection, Casa Grande North Wing Fourth Floor, Room Three.*
This rug is divided into seven rows of cartouches, in which are inscribed calligraphic verses from Omar Khayyam.

WILLIAM RANDOLPH HEARST *looks earnestly at Marion Davies, dressed for a military ball in 1944.*

his earlier residence in House A, where his routine was to walk to the Refectory for meals and to stroll around the Esplanade after dinner.[29] While the legend that Hearst never wanted to hear the word *death* mentioned was completely untrue—it was a word he mentioned often himself, without difficulty—it is true that he was not particularly pleased to be reminded of his own mortality. His grandson John Jr., whom everyone called Bunky, lived at San Simeon in his early teens, from 1946 to 1947, and he remembered when his grandfather received a framed newspaper from the day of his birth, April 29, 1863, as a gift from his executives. "And it was the one time I've seen him kind of fighting inside himself because he accepted it very graciously, but he didn't

THE NORTH WING *is the only portion of the Main Building with long corridors. The Spanish furniture and tile floors emphasize the relative simplicity of this final construction project. America's taste for the Spanish style peaked in the 1920s. It was considered passé in the 1940s, though Hearst continued his allegiance.*

An Italian sixteenth-century *table serves as a desk in the Sitting Room of House A.*

Rabbit tiles *on the stair risers outside House A.*

HOUSE A was William Randolph Hearst's earliest and then final residence. He returned there at age eighty-two in 1945 and remained there until a worsening heart condition in the spring of 1947 required that he leave San Simeon and relocate to Beverly Hills.

THIS FLOOR TILE in House A carries on the marine theme appropriate to Casa del Mar.

HEARST'S FUNERAL in San Francisco's Grace Cathedral attracted thousands. Marion Davies was not among them. Douglas MacArthur was one of the honorary pallbearers.

particularly want to be reminded of the fact that he was born on the day that Lincoln is giving orders to the troops and . . . [it] reminded him of exactly how old he was."[30] Colleen Moore recalled asking Marion, who was only forty-nine at the time but having mobility problems, probably due to her long years of drinking, what she did to keep busy at the vast and somewhat empty estate. "A little sewing, and a little washing and ironing," Marion replied. Moore said, "Marion was no longer the little girl amusing the king. She was a woman in love with and looking after her man."[31]

One of the most interesting sidelights of the great contraction of Hearst's funds throughout the thirties was the necessity, after the reconsolidation in the forties, of accounting for Hearst's expenditures on San Simeon. Thus, there exists remarkable documentation

not previously available, since the prior records consist of Morgan's appeals for funds, Hearst's tardy responses and sporadic tallying of arrears, but little indication of the actual amounts spent.

In late 1944, Morgan began evaluating the expenditures at San Simeon. She was told by the corporation executives to create a document showing construction costing a total of 4 million dollars, an amount they later amended to $4,717,000.[32] Morgan went through several drafts before she could get the numbers to match this figure, which includes construction changes and payroll but excludes transportation, art objects, and the post–World War II remodeling, the last item alone totaling an additional 1.3 million dollars.[33] The final letter that exists in the historical record of thousands of letters between Hearst and Morgan and their staffs is a sum-mary of finances, written to Hearst at San Simeon in February of 1945. The dates listed for construction were from 1919 to 1942, and the total prewar cost of the three small houses and their terraces was five hundred fifty thousand dollars. The final cost of the Main Building and its landscaping features was listed at nearly 3 million dollars. The swimming pools were similar in cost, the Neptune Pool and landscaping at four hundred thirty thousand dollars and the Roman Pool, which was built only once, but which required the laying of the mosaic tile and the creation of the tennis courts, at four hundred thousand dollars. The animal shelters along the hillside cost forty thousand dollars and the cages in the concentrated zoo area of "Animal Hill," thirty-five thousand dollars. All the structures for staff and warehouse storage in the town of San Simeon came to one hundred ten thousand dollars. The only other large expense listed was nearly one hundred fifty thousand dollars for technical support, including septic tanks, reservoirs, and water and power lines.

These are not the only accountings that developed from Hearst's financial trials in the 1930s. The year 1937 saw the beginning of a huge object inventory, preparing for the vast disbursals of Hearst's art in the years to come. A master list of all the objects shipped to the West Coast included items that went to Wyntoon, Ocean House, and San Simeon. The total for all the art sent to the three vast estates—as nearly as Morgan's staff members and the warehouse crew could calculate from invoices, records, and estimates where no actual costs had been noted—comes to 5.4 million dollars.[34] It has been further estimated that the subtotal spent on the art that went to San Simeon was between 1.5 million and 2.5 million dollars for the moveable objects and another 1.2

million dollars for the built-in, stationary items such as window frames and ceilings, leading to a generous total of perhaps 3.5 million dollars for the entire San Simeon collection.[35] Therefore, the total expenditure for objects and construction, even including transportation costs, surely did not exceed 10 million dollars over nearly thirty years. This was far below the amount estimated by those who spread the exaggerated story that Hearst spent a million a year on his art collection alone, or 50 million dollars over fifty years.[36]

The years just after the war saw Hearst in good health. But in the spring of 1947, at eighty-four, he began having auricular fibrillations, an irregular heartbeat. He wanted to stay on the hilltop, and he even tried to persuade his own doctor, prominent southern California heart surgeon Myron Prinzmetal, to live in House C, which he proposed to have fitted with intercoms and alarms so that his requests from House A could be answered immediately. But the doctors would not permit a patient with a heart condition to live in such an isolated spot, and he was finally required to leave San Simeon and move to a home Marion bought in Los Angeles off Benedict Canyon.[37] Estelle Wahlberg, the wife of Hearst's valet, recorded in her diary that

HEARST'S DACHSHUND, Helena, waits in vain on her master's bed after his death on August 14, 1951. Beside the bed is a framed portrait of Marion Davies.

Hearst left San Simeon for Los Angeles on May 2, 1947.[38] Marion tried to console him, saying, "We'll come back, W. R. You'll see." But they never did. Hearst likely knew it was his last glimpse of his precious and still unfinished ranch, and the tears rolled down his face as they drove down the hill for the final time.[39]

Hearst's strength steadily deteriorated, though his mind was still clear. He continued to collect on a very small scale. He also donated many objects to the Los Angeles County Museum of Art. Its consulting director of art, William Valentiner, recalled that, although Hearst rarely left the house, "he was still amazingly active and shared a rare interest in what was going on in the art world." He purchased items outright for the Museum and also gave them pieces from his own collection. Valentiner continued, "we received regularly, every year, a selection from his vast collection, the value of which amounted during the last six years [of Hearst's life] to more than $2 million," yet another legacy from Hearst to his beloved California.[40]

and was hung over. Our plane to San Francisco didn't take off until about four o'clock, some six hours after my father passed away."[42]

Such a painful division among the people Hearst loved revealed the toll his ambiguous relationship with Marion had taken on everyone all along. There were more challenges to come. On August 26, 1951, Hollywood gossip columnist Hedda Hopper broke the news of an amended will. Hearst's first will left substantial trust funds to his sons and widow, and also created two large charitable trusts, the Hearst Foundation and the William Randolph Hearst Foundation. Marion had a lifetime income from another trust fund created in 1950, which gave her thirty thousand shares of corporation preferred stock. The amended will, in Marion's possession, now combined the voting power of Hearst's one hundred seventy thousand shares of common stock with her own thirty thousand shares, giving her control of the corporation.[43] Ten weeks after Hearst's death, on October 30, 1951, Marion voluntarily relinquished her

"Now [San Simeon] is in a future no

In Hearst's last years, Marion drank heavily, perhaps in response to seeing her influence among the family and corporation ebbing away as Hearst edged nearer to death, which finally came on the morning of August 14, 1951, in his eighty-eighth year. Both Marion's and Bill Jr.'s accounts agree that she was sedated and sleeping upstairs when Hearst died, but then they diverge. According to Marion, Hearst's body was spirited away without her knowledge. "I asked where he was and the nurse said he was dead. His body was gone, whoosh, like that. Old W. R. was gone, the boys were gone. I was alone. Do you realize what they did? They stole a possession of mine. He belonged to me. I loved him for 32 years and now he was gone. I couldn't even say good-bye."[41] According to Bill, they waited "an hour or more" to remove his father's body, during which time she could have been up if she had wanted to be: "If Marion had walked into any of the numerous rooms we were using, she would have heard everything. She didn't. That was clearly because she had been sedated, was exhausted,

new interest, retaining her thirty thousand shares of stock and the right to remain an adviser to the Hearst Corporation.[44] This arrangement, in effect, sealed a pact made long ago: Hearst wanted to take care of her, and she wanted to make it plain that their alliance was not about money. The very next day, Marion married former Hollywood stunt man Captain Horace Brown in Las Vegas on October 31, 1951. The woman who said, "I was always a bridesmaid, but never a bride," finally became one, though to the wrong groom.[45] Marion's friends despaired of Horace, who was tactless and witless at times, though there is no doubt that he felt protective toward her. Their ten years together were stormy ones, marred by Marion's attempts at divorce, which always ended in reconciliation.[46] In the late summer of 1961, when she was sixty-three, Marion died of cancer of the jaw, leaving an impressive number of charities behind her and a career that was nearly forgotten, overshadowed by the indelible portrait of Susan Alexander Kane.

Julia Morgan's years after the war were marred by ill health and forgetfulness. Her family had no doubt that she was aware of her worrisome lapses of memory. Morgan North remembered his aunt's final commission, a remodeling job in Berkeley: "She'd come over and check her measurements and when she'd go back to the office [in San Francisco] she had forgotten everything and was totally frustrated."[47] She closed her office in the Merchants Exchange Building in 1951, the year Hearst died, destroying many of her office records and taking to her Divisadero Street home both her personal papers and correspondence with Hearst.[48]

Then she traveled for as long as she could, though Morgan North recalled: "She didn't want to travel. She only traveled when she couldn't build."[49] There came the time when she could also no longer travel: she got confused in Spain and could not remember where she was or where her ship was.[50] Flora North said that Morgan hoped she would be lost at sea, adding that she had a horror of being a burden to anyone, having seen

THE HOPE ATHENA. *Italian. 2nd-century. School of Pheidias. Marble. 7'2" (21844 cm). Los Angeles County Museum of Art, William Randolph Hearst Collection.*

English collector Thomas Hope acquired this piece after its discovery in 1797. Hearst bought it in the 1930s and displayed it for a time in Casa Grande's Assembly Room. He donated it to the Los Angeles County Museum of Art in 1951, the year of his death.

one here can even guess as to." JULIA MORGAN

both her own parents go through a long decline before dying.[51] When her failing strength made it necessary, she hired a nurse and retreated to her own quarters. Family members and former staff spoke guiltily of being too busy to look in on her frequently, but it is likely that they would have been discouraged from being too attentive. "She delighted in having her family together two or three times a year, and the rest of the time she didn't want to be bothered," recalled Morgan North.[52]

When Julia Morgan died on February 2, 1957, at the age of eighty-six, she did not leave much money. She had not prepared sufficiently for the end of her earning days. Investments from an inheritance of her grandfather's fortune did not grow well, and this, coupled with the fact that she seldom made more than ten thousand dollars a year and had the habit of dividing up the dividends of a good year's business among the staff at Christmastime, all contributed to her shortage of funds.[53] Unfortunately, another problem was a fifteen-thousand-dollar bill she submitted to Hearst for the

work she had done on the Santa Maria de Ovila monastery project. By the time she billed him in the late 1940s, his health was fragile, and he never paid. This was perhaps a characteristic ending to a relationship that had disregarded money from the beginning: but she did not pursue it against him or his estate, and neither did her heirs. "It was one of those things," Morgan North recalled. "With pressure put on him, something undoubtedly would have happened, but what she wouldn't do in life we certainly wouldn't want to do in death. I would have had to face her in my conscience and it wouldn't work."[54] Julia Morgan's unassuming departure from the world was characteristic of a person who always deplored fuss. The family held no funeral for her. "Please give me a quick tuck-in," she had said, "with my own."[55]

The fate of La Cuesta Encantada after 1951 was uncertain. Bill Jr. recalled, "No member of the family or the corporation was in a position to maintain it. My father had told me several times that he had expected this. He hoped that the University of California would accept the house and gardens as a gift. However, the university declined."[56] The staff sank to eight at one point after Hearst's death.[57] But the Castle was not allowed to decay. Indeed, the family and the corporation honored the close relationship between these buildings and their contents, and they assiduously sought a role for San Simeon that would prevent the art collection from being sold and removed from the buildings. On January 30, 1958, La Cuesta Encantada was presented to the State of California, under the auspices of what was then known as the Division of Beaches and Parks, later renamed the Department of Parks and Recreation. The buildings, fixed objects, and 137 acres of land were all donated that day, and by 1972 the majority of the art collection, which never left the hill, was also deeded. The estate will never be completed, allowing millions of visitors to better understand the immediacy of Hearst and Morgan's spirited dialogue. The space for a planned bowling alley in the basement, the fountain intended for the north entrance, the basin slated for the additional Neptune Pool sculptures, the gymnasium planned at the back of the Roman Pool, and even the bare concrete exposed on the Main Building's facade all remain as they were when construction ceased. The Castle's vitality is expressed in its unfinished state, which displays the sense of boundless possibility embodied by both its creators.

LA CUESTA ENCANTADA from the air resembles a Mediterranean hill town: the cathedral at the peak of the hill, surrounded by the little houses. The Roman Pool to the east, topped by the tennis courts, and the Neptune Pool to the north, play the role of the abandoned Roman ruins that are often found at the outskirts of such towns.

CHAPTER TWELVE

A Twentieth-

On June 2, 1958, the private story of La Cuesta Encantada ended and the public one began. When the Castle opened as a State Monument, California's park administration was initially unprepared for the outpouring of interest that began on that first day and has continued unabated. The fantasy aspect of the buildings, the spectacular hilltop setting, the wide-ranging art collection, and the voyeuristic appeal of seeing firsthand such a legendary home and hearing about the love story that took place within it have always been a hit with the public.

Critical response, however, has been far less favorable. Throughout his lifetime Hearst attracted controversy—particularly in his last fifteen years—and the art and architecture critics' hostile responses to the house, such an obvious extension of the man, continued after his death.

Born in 1863, the year of Abraham Lincoln's Emancipation Proclamation, Hearst died in 1951, at the twentieth century's midpoint. At the time of his death, Hearst's anachronistic pro-American editorials and sensational, lowbrow newspaper stories seemed hopelessly primitive journalism. It was perhaps convenient at the time to forget that America in the 1950s had reached the very super-power status that Hearst had advocated all along, militarily, politically, and culturally, due in some measure to the worldwide influence of American newspapers, magazines, and movies, in whose development he had played such a large part.

The impulse to buy European art and improve on it by mixing it in eclectic settings, as Stanford White had advocated, also seemed antiquated and unsophisticated. To further complicate matters, modern architecture had

Century House

evolved from a minor presence before World War II to an overwhelming force after it. By the 1950s the Castle's period references appeared ridiculously excessive. Even more offensive to some was the broad range of Hearst's art collection. The wild abandon of his tastes outraged critics and collectors alike. By refusing to play the role of the decorous connoisseur, he seemed to cast aspersions on the process of acquisition itself. Aline Saarinen wrote in *The Proud Possessors* in 1958 that Hearst "acquired hundreds of thousands of objects by the carload," crowding many of them into "that phantasmagoria San Simeon . . . colossal, even wanton in its castle-ness," where the awful and the awesome cohabited.[1] W. G. Constable wrote in the same vein in 1964: "Without question, if this vast conglomeration had been sorted out by capable hands and eyes, and the junk disposed of, an impressive collection could have emerged, certainly of historic interest, if not of the highest quality. As it is, Hearst must go down in history not as a collector, but as a gigantic and voracious magpie."[2]

Neither Saarinen nor Constable was willing so soon after Hearst's death to acknowledge that Hearst's buying was inclusive, not exclusive. It was often not important to him that objects be the best, but was enough that they simply be: locks and keys from the Middle Ages, ox yokes, and antique shoes were welcome, along with superb examples of medieval and Renaissance tapestries, English silver, pottery, Renaissance furniture, and architectural fragments. In recent decades, however, antique objects from ordinary life have become sought-after by collectors, and a similar discovery of the history of technology and of architectural elements has shown Hearst to be a prescient collector.

San Simeon's location, so far from the traditional American country-house sites of the East Coast, further reinforced the perception of Hearst's provincialism. California was an upstart, as was William Randolph Hearst. To set this mansion on the wrong edge of the continent, and to fill it with all the wrong people, rankled easterners. Nathaniel Burt felt he must defend San Simeon in 1977 as "far from being the mere kitsch that most easterners have been led to believe it is. Though undoubtedly fantastic and flamboyant, its gardens and mansion . . . are full of real beauties and treasures. The interior is a museum of choir stalls, tapestries, Gothic statues and carvings, Renaissance furniture (and Tiffany lamps) and even a few paintings. The whole ensemble is worthy of its incomparable mountaintop and seaview site."[3] Robert A. M. Stern also praised the value of the setting and the skill with which the pieces were combined when he wrote in 1986:

LOOKING EAST *across the rooftops of Casa Grande toward the green hills beyond. From such vantages, often glimpsed out of Casa Grande's windows, the Mediterranean hill-town inspiration is particularly clear.*

Incorporating a large portion of Hearst's vast and varied collection into the design for the mansion, Morgan bril-

A SIXTEENTH-CENTURY limestone bas-relief depicting St. Paul, mounted on the entrance facade of Casa Grande.

liantly combined the ancient and the contemporary, the found and the commissioned, the genuine and the ersatz into a seamless, coherent compositional whole glued together in poured concrete. San Simeon was like a museum of architecture, its treasures subsumed by the Spanish and Spanish Colonial architecture—a not inappropriate choice of style, given the castle's location along the coast between important missions at San Luis Obispo and Carmel.[4]

This appropriateness of setting and style were both lost on Witold Rybczynski, who wrote of San Simeon a few years after Stern: "What is this Italian villa doing in the California Coastal Range? . . . this indiscriminate assortment of architectural fragments makes sense only as a costly piece of theatrical decor, a make-believe setting for the make-believe heroes and heroines of Hollywood whom he entertained. . . . A building that ignores its context . . . lacks a crucial ingredient—meaning."[5] Rybczynski failed to recognize San Simeon as a natural expression of the Spanish Colonial Revival architectural style—a conscious mixture of Spanish and Italian imagery—which predominated in California through the 1920s. Where Hearst and Morgan differed from other proponents of the style is that they based their selections on specific structures—fifteenth-century Italian and sixteenth-century Spanish—and incorporated antique elements into the building's fabric.

Umberto Eco admitted that mixing the past and present at San Simeon had ample historic precedent, noting, "this was how the great lords of the past amassed rare objects, and the same continuum of styles can be found in many Romanesque churches where the nave is now baroque and perhaps the campanile is eighteenth century, but . . . what offends is the voracity of the selection, and what distresses is the fear of being caught up by this jungle of venerable beauties, which unquestionably has its own wild flavor, its own pathetic sadness, barbarian grandeur, and sensual perversity."[6]

The sense of overwhelming abundance about San Simeon cannot be denied, but the rooms are not crowded with objects. Indeed, even now, the largest spaces regularly hold groups of fifty people without seeming overly full. It is the amazing range of objects that stupefies. Thomas Hoving ranked Hearst at only number eighty in his 1983 list of America's top art collectors, but conceded even as he did so that he was probably underestimating him: "Hearst is being reevaluated.

GERDAGO. HARLEQUIN LAMP. Austrian, early 20th century. Bronze, enamel, ivory, onyx. 23 ½ x 16" (58.7 x 40.6 cm). Hearst Monument Collection, House C Left Back Bedroom.
The boldly sweeping bronze figure of this dancer provides a contrasting setting for the delicately carved ivory face. The addition of the onyx base and an electrical armature transformed this sculpture into a table lamp. It is one of the few Art Deco pieces found in San Simeon's predominantly Renaissance collection.

TAPESTRY OF A HUNTING SCENE. *French, 15th century. Dyed wool.*
10'5" x 14'8" (317.5 x 447.1 cm). Hearst Monument Collection, Casa Grande Billiard Room.
In this scene of a stag hunt, the figures wear costumes of the late fifteenth century. Mille fleurs,
or "thousand flowers," tapestries such as this one featured a ground covered with
colorful patterns of flowers and foliage. They were woven from the end of the
fifteenth century through the early years of the sixteenth century.

He may have been much more of a collector than was thought at the time of his death. But he is still a prime example of the species Grand Accumulator."[7]

It seems just and fitting, however, that a leading proponent of mass culture should have had such all-embracing interests. Hearst's newspapers, while sensational, always aimed at breaking down cultural barriers. They were full of bold headlines, half-tone photographs, and visuals that could appeal to readers who were not all that familiar with the English language. Hearst also employed popular illustrators, such as Maxfield Parrish, Willy Pogany, and Henry Clive, for his *American Weekly* and *Hearst's Magazine* covers. He printed *The Katzenjammer Kids* by Randolph Dirks in 1897, which pioneered the use of talking balloons and featured characters based on the German comics that Hearst had first seen on his young travels abroad. Jimmy

Swinnerton, the first cartoonist to create a continuously presented graphic, worked for the Hearst newspapers from 1904 through 1958 and was a frequent guest at San Simeon. And it was only Hearst's fondness for the strip that kept George Herriman's then unpopular *Krazy Kat*—now one of the most highly regarded comics—in his newspapers from 1913 to 1944.[8] Hearst's lifelong fascination with both high art and low, finally considered an acceptable taste by the 1960s, was innovative in the twenties and thirties. He knew the value of images, whether lurid news photos, satirical drawings, mustard and ketchup bottles on his own antique Italian dining tables, or Gothic tapestries on the walls of the Refectory.

Clive Aslet gave San Simeon a lukewarm response in his comprehensive survey on the American country house in 1990. No fan of William Randolph Hearst's, he

OX YOKE. *Northern Italian, 17th century. Wood. 41" (104.1 cm). Hearst Monument Collection, Billiard Room Wing, Third Bedroom.*
Its relatively small size and detailed carving may indicate that this ox yoke was created for ceremonial rather than daily use. Its decorations are associated with the harvest: a cart and plow, agricultural implements, and a woman baking bread from the harvested grain. Hearst owned several antique ox yokes, pieces which represented the technological triumph of the harnessing of non-human power. Ox yokes have been in use since 4,000 B.C.

"far from being the mere kitsch that most easterners have been led to believe it is, . . .

once harshly described his purchase and remodeling of St. Donat's Castle in Wales: "St. Donat's never became a Xanadu, or even a San Simeon; but nowhere else does the romance with old materials for their own sake reach such a pitch of naked obsession. Romance, in fact, gave way to rape."[9] Aslet was more favorably disposed to San Simeon, a modern house built from the ground up, but he discounted its architectural effect.

> The texture of the architecture at San Simeon, often from poured concrete, is far less sympathetic than that of the Mission buildings he deplored. Even Julia

Morgan seemed to recognize that the house was best seen from a distance and that its strongest point was its color. But as a backdrop for the Hollywood folk who went there, it was in every sense ideal. It was not built around a patio: there was no need, for the place extended itself through several separate buildings grouped around highly architectural courtyards. . . . It was the apotheosis of the indoor-outdoor life.[10]

Aslet grasped the informality of San Simeon's social structure and the importance of Hearst's association with San Simeon's landscape and a life led in the outdoors. But he did not acknowledge the importance or

its gardens and mansion . . . are full of real beauties and treasures." Nathaniel Burt

OPPOSITE: CABINET ORNAMENTED WITH ENAMEL MEDALLIONS BY JEAN DE COURT. *French, 1562. Wood, enamel plaques, and bronze paw feet. 25 ½ x 28 x 14 ¾"* (64.8 x 71.1 x 37.5 cm). Hearst Monument Collection, Casa Grande Billiard Room.

As an enameller Jean de Court is known for his complex compositions and lively ornamentation, particularly in the hues of his colored enamels. Among the scenes depicted here are Jupiter seated with another god in a chariot and the abduction of Deianeira by the centaur Nessus.

THE CENTER MEDALLION *of Venus, Adonis, and Cupid, with Jean de Court's signature beside Cupid's bow and the date 1562. Most scholars agree that Jean de Court was court painter to Charles Bourbon in 1553, then to Mary, Queen of Scots from 1562 to 1567, and finally to Charles IX. He is thought to have been active until 1585.*

TWO BALCONY SCREENS *on the sides of House C were made from fifteenth-century Spanish wood balconies, altered to resemble* mushrabiyehs, *or Moslem screens. Thus, two simple Spanish window frames and balconies were turned into more complex and exotic features. Morgan wrote to Hearst in 1924: "We are working on the 'harem' bays for the towers. There is a great deal of work on these bays in spite of the elements you sent. They promise well."*

effectiveness of Hearst's collection of objects, or the skill with which Morgan integrated them into the building's interior and exterior fabric. For him, San Simeon remained little more than an empty shell.

As the 1990s proceeded, critics began to view the Castle more favorably, focusing both on the unique architectural collaboration between Hearst and Morgan and on the quality of the eclectic art collection itself. Allan Temko understood that the Castle's hedonistic spaces provided Morgan with an outlet for her creative passions:

> [T]he castle in the end was the key to the Morgan mystery. The swimming pools, in puritan terms, were sorcery. So were the guest suites, so sensitively designed for lovers, with carefully designed views over the countryside from the enormous beds. . . . It was a supreme

work of surrealist art. Half palace, half cathedral, the castle emanated from the deepest realms of [Hearst and Morgan's] beings. . . . Miss Morgan—it was always "Miss Morgan" and "Mr. Hearst"—turned dreams into buildings for her imperial client-patron-collaborator. Neither could have done it alone.[11]

The hilltop setting of La Cuesta Encantada has always inspired critical admiration, but in recent years that admiration has also addressed the skillful way in which the architecture complements the surroundings. Architect Charles Moore celebrated the stunning imagery of the Neptune Pool and its mixture of old and new objects on a matchless site.

> In a sense *to contemplate* means to look both back to the past and toward the future. Mythic proportions and classically heroic aspirations inflate the two swimming pools at San Simeon—William Randolph Hearst's palatial mountaintop retreat. . . . The outdoor pool was designed as a tribute to Neptune, god of the oceans. . . . In this grand liquid ballroom, Hollywood Olympians lucky enough to be granted coveted weekend invitations . . . swam high above the mortal realm fanning out below. With its antique trappings, the pool recalls the past while the views out toward the infinite skies inspire imaginative visions into the unknown. Its still water, like Giverny's, at one time contained something more than itself. Looking out over the terrace, however, one realizes that this pool, propped up with its Olympian costumes, defers to the ocean waters stretching toward the horizon.[12]

Mark Alan Hewitt, in his comprehensive historical survey *The Architect and the American Country House*, defends the innovation that Morgan displayed in creating a setting for Hearst's collection.

> It is tempting to view the . . . approach . . . of pastiche or assemblage of architectural fragments from actual buildings, as a method requiring no skill or originality whatsoever. Julia Morgan . . . would not have seen it that way, however. Though much of the material in that vast historical pile was salvaged or removed from European buildings, Morgan was required to act as artist, scholar, scene designer, and decorator in her synthesis of architectural elements. The building she designed had no precedent in architecture, yet evoked the historical auras of the various fragments Hearst had

THE SOUTH ALCOVE *of the Library, an elegant and harmonious room. It has a quiet graciousness.*
But Harpo Marx recalled that he and Marion Davies found it a spacious spot for practicing somersaults.

collected. Like many eclectic designers, she was equally willing to work with fragments or from scratch. Working within the restrictions imposed by the preexisting elements created an artistic challenge.[13]

It is left to John Julius Norwich to phrase a critical response which, while acknowledging the low opinion of the Castle the intelligentsia has held in the past, clearly lays out new criteria under which it will be far more favorably evaluated in the future.

> Hearst Castle [is] a palace in every sense of the word, though unique . . . in being the creation, not of a king or an emperor, but of a private citizen. Remembering that William Randolph Hearst was the model for Orson Welles's *Citizen Kane,* we would expect his vast mansion to be dark, gloomy, and not a little vulgar; but we would be wrong. My own recollection of Hearst Castle . . . is one of wonder and delight. The house is undeniably a hotch-potch, in which French tapestries rub shoulders with Dutch pictures, English furniture, Spanish tilework and heaven knows what else; but the quality of everything is so superb, the blending with the surrounding architecture so confident and assured, that one cannot find it in one's heart to criticize. I went prepared to mock; I remained to marvel.[14]

We can be certain that Julia Morgan would look with disfavor on this decades-long critical debate. She was angry with Walter Steilberg when he published a photographic survey of her buildings in a 1918 issue of *The Architect and Engineer of California.* "She was displeased with it," Steilberg recalled. "I think her only comment was, 'The building should speak for itself.'"[15] Nonetheless, she did have aspirations that she confessed to Steilberg and to her family: she was building a museum at San Simeon, rather than a residence. "She said, 'Of course, this is just temporary for his use. The country needs architectural museums, not just places where you hang paintings and sculpture.'"[16]

Marion knew that Hearst had a long-range plan for La Cuesta Encantada. "He took great pride in San Simeon, watching over it and inspecting it," she recalled. "He wanted it to be a museum. He didn't like anyone calling it a castle; it was always the ranch."[17] Hearst obliquely expressed his wishes for the estate when he hosted a reporter from *Newsweek* on the hilltop in the spring of 1946. At eighty-three, he had won and lost innumerable battles, and was now treated more like a lovable old relic than like a current newsmaker. When asked, "Have the large sums you have spent on art treasures been repaid by your enjoyment of them?" Hearst replied: "The enjoyment I have obtained is not so important as the enjoyment other people might obtain from [my collection]. I think it is important to have art objects . . . brought to this country. They find their way to museums eventually, and not everybody can go abroad."[18]

La Cuesta Encantada's grand exuberance speaks eloquently for the lives of William Randolph Hearst, Marion Davies, and Julia Morgan, all of whom created it through their spirit and dedication. Lived in for only one generation, over a mere three decades, it displays the same layered complexity of objects and styles developed in English country houses only by the collective efforts of generations of family and centuries of acquisition. Presided over by a movie star, its informality reflects both the eroding class barriers and the growing primacy of celebrity in America's social hierarchy. Designed by a woman architect, its lighthearted assemblage architecture blends accommodation with grand gesture, skillfully expressing William Randolph Hearst's romantic and theatrical taste. The parklands that surround the estate are not an elaborate set piece of pastoral beauty, as in many country houses, but a preservation of the rugged and unspoiled California landscape, so much of which has disappeared elsewhere throughout the state. It has even been immortalized—however unjustly—in America's greatest art form of our time, the cinema, and it lives on in the cultural imagination. It is the quintessential twentieth-century American country house.

THE VIEW *of San Simeon Bay from the lower loggia of House A. The trees visible on the coastal point were all planted by Hearst.*

Notes

Prologue

1. Mrs. Fremont Older, *William Randolph Hearst, American* (New York: Appleton-Century, 1936), 514. Hearst delivered this speech in Oakland, California, on 18 October 1930. He was concluding a cross-country lecture tour speaking on his recent expulsion from France because of his political views and the anti-French rhetoric in his newspapers.

2. George Hearst, *The Way It Was* (n.p.: Hearst Corporation, 1972), 39.

3. Ben Procter, *William Randolph Hearst: The Early Years, 1863–1910* (New York: Oxford University Press, 1998), 4.

4. George Hearst, *The Way It Was*, 10–11; Ralph Gregory, "George Hearst in Missouri," *The Bulletin* (Missouri Historical Society) 21, no. 2 (January 1965): 77.

5. Procter, *Hearst: The Early Years*, 7–10; Gregory, "George Hearst in Missouri," 83–85; Judith Robinson, *The Hearsts: An American Dynasty* (New York: Avon, 1991), 27, 49–50.

6. George Hearst, *The Way It Was*, 38.

7. Phoebe Hearst to Eliza Pike, 9 December 1866. Phoebe Apperson Hearst Correspondence Papers, c. 1864–1918. 72/204c. The Bancroft Library. Unless otherwise noted, all correspondence is by letter. Grammatical errors that do not affect meaning have been silently corrected throughout.

8. Procter, *Hearst: The Early Years*, 15.

9. Frank W. Lamb and Gertrude Lamb, *San Simeon: A Brief History* (Fullerton, Calif.: Sultana Press, 1971), 5; Geneva Hamilton, *Where the Highway Ends: Cambria, San Simeon, and the Ranchos* (San Luis Obispo, Calif.: Padre Productions, 1974), 134–36.

10. Hamilton, *Where the Highway Ends*, 134–39; Lamb and Lamb, *San Simeon*, 5–9.

11. Hamilton, *Where the Highway Ends*, 111, 205.

12. James van Ness to George Hearst, 17 October 1865; James van Ness to George Hearst, 28 November 1865; McDowell R. Venable to George Hearst, 7 June 1870. Bancroft Library.

13. Lamb and Lamb, *San Simeon*, 9; Hamilton, *Where the Highway Ends*, 123–27.

14. Campbell Grant, *The Rock Paintings of the Chumash: A Study of a California Indian Culture* (Berkeley: University of California Press, 1966), 30; Campbell Grant, "Chumash: Introduction," in *California*, ed. Robert F. Heizer, vol. 8 of *Handbook of North American Indians*, ed. William C. Sturtevant (Washington, D.C.: Smithsonian Institution, 1978), 505.

15. Grant, "Chumash: Introduction," in *California*, ed. Heizer, 505; Daniel E. Krieger, *San Luis Obispo County: Looking Backward into the Middle Kingdom* (Northridge, Calif.: Windsor Publications, 1988), 31.

16. James West and Ronald P. Sekkel, "An Archaeological Site Survey of the Hearst Ranch (Rancho Piedras Blancas), San Simeon, San Luis Obispo County, California," *Archaeological Survey Annual Report, 1968*, Department of Anthropology (Los Angeles: University of California, 1968), 268; Philip Hines, "The Prehistory of San Simeon Creek: 5800 B. P. to Missionization," ed. Betty Rivers (Sacramento: Department of Parks and Recreation, 1986), 37, 69.

17. David H. Chipping, "The Geology of San Luis Obispo County: A Brief Description and Field Guide" (San Luis Obispo, Calif.: California Polytechnic State University, 1987); Terry L. Jones and Georgie Waugh, *Central California Coastal Prehistory: A View from Little Pico Creek*, Perspectives in California Archaeology, vol. 3, Institute of Archaeology (Los Angeles: University of California, 1995), 5–6.

18. David Rogers, "The Santa Lucia Mountains: Diversity, Endemism, and Austere Beauty," *Fremontia* 19, no. 4 (October 1991): 5.

19. Bruce M. Pavlik, et al., *Oaks of California* (Los Olivos, Calif.: Cachuma Press and the California Oak Foundation, 1991), 25–27.

20. J. Smeaton Chase, *California Coast Trails: A Horseback Ride from Mexico to Oregon* (Boston: Houghton Mifflin, 1913), 162.

21. Older, *William Randolph Hearst*, 528.

22. George Hearst, *The Way It Was*, 35.

23. William Randolph Hearst to Phoebe Apperson Hearst, c. 1884. William Randolph Hearst Papers, 82/68c. Bancroft Library.

24. William Randolph Hearst Jr., *The Hearsts: Father and Son* (Niwot, Colo.: Roberts Rinehart, 1991), 90.

25. Procter, *Hearst: The Early Years*, 32–33.

26. David Nasaw, *The Chief: The Life of William Randolph Hearst* (Boston: Houghton Mifflin, 2000), 39–41, 44.

27. George Hearst, *The Way It Was*, 34.

28. Ibid., 35.

29. Gray Brechin, *Imperial San Francisco: Urban Power, Earthly Ruin* (Berkeley: University of California Press, 1999), 210–11.

30. Robinson, *American Dynasty*, 238.

31. Ibid., 250.

32. In "The Meaning of the *Maine*: Causation and the Historiography of the Spanish-American War" (*Pacific Historical Review* 58, no. 3, [August 1989]: 293–322), Louis A. Perez Jr. argues that the ubiquitous view that the destruction of the *Maine* triggered the Spanish-American War has prevented a thorough historiographical examination of the circumstances of the war itself. See also the study the National Geographic Society commissioned from Advanced Marine Enterprises, which concludes that a fire in a coal bunker of the *Maine* could have resulted in sufficient heat to touch off an explosion in the adjacent ammunition magazine, though the cause can never be completely ascertained. Thomas B. Allen, "Remember the *Maine*?" *National Geographic* 193, no. 2 (February 1998): 92–111.

33. Edwin Emery and Michael Emery, *The Press and America: An Interpretive History of the Mass Media*, 4th ed. (Englewood Cliffs, N.J.: Prentice-Hall, 1978), 247–49.

34. William Randolph Hearst to Phoebe Apperson Hearst, c. 1913. William Randolph Hearst Letters, 87/232c. Bancroft Library.

35. William Randolph Hearst to Phoebe Apperson Hearst, 30 August 1917. 87/232c. Bancroft Library.

36. Mrs. William Randolph Hearst Jr., *The Horses of San Simeon* (San Simeon, Calif.: San Simeon Press, 1985), 216–17.

37. William Randolph Hearst to Phoebe Apperson Hearst, c. 1917. 87/232c. Bancroft Library.

Chapter One: Early Visions

1. "The Work of Walter Steilberg and Julia Morgan," vol. 1 of *The Julia Morgan Architectural History Project*, ed. Suzanne B. Riess, Regional Oral History Office, The Bancroft Library (Berkeley: University of California, 1976), 56–57.

2. David Gebhard and Robert Winter, *Architecture in Los Angeles: A Compleat Guide* (Salt Lake City: Gibbs M. Smith, 1985), 16, 480.

3. "The Work of Steilberg and Morgan," Bancroft Library, 57.

4. W. A. Swanberg, *Citizen Hearst: A Biography of William Randolph Hearst* (New York: Bantam, 1963), 302–3. For a more detailed account, see Christopher Gray, "Hearst's Opulent Quintuplex," *New York Times*, 1 May 1994, sec. 10, 7.

5. Richard Longstreth, *On the Edge of the World: Four Architects in San Francisco at the Turn of the Century* (New York: Architectural History Foundation, 1983), 279–86; Robinson, *American Dynasty*, 248; W. R. Fairfield to Edward Hardy Clark, 28 May 1900. 82/68c. Bancroft Library. Hearst sold the Pleasanton Hacienda in 1925, after which it became a country club. Disposing of the property indicated San Simeon's increasing importance in his life.

6. Sara Holmes Boutelle, *Julia Morgan, Architect*, rev. ed. (New York: Abbeville, 1995), 172.

7. Ibid., 51–52.

8. Ibid., 51.

9. "The Work of Steilberg and Morgan," Bancroft Library, 241.

10. Morgan to Hearst, 13 September 1919; Morgan to Hearst, 12 February 1923; Morgan to Hearst, 13 May 1923; Morgan to Hearst, 27 May 1932. The Julia Morgan Collection, Special Collections, Robert E. Kennedy Library, California State Polytechnic University, San Luis Obispo, Calif.

11. "The Work of Steilberg and Morgan," Bancroft Library, 46.

12. Ibid., 53.

13. Ibid., 63.

14. Ibid., 68.

15. Morgan to Arthur Byne, 27 July 1922. Kennedy Library.

16. Jane Sarber, "A Cabbie in a Golden Era, Featuring Cabbie's Original Log of Guests Transported to Hearst Castle" (n.p., n.d.), 4–5.

17. Hearst to Morgan, 25 October, 1919. Kennedy Library. The formal Spanish names for the three cottages seldom appear in the letters between Morgan and Hearst, or in the reminiscences of former guests. Instead the "House A" (used by Hearst and Morgan) or occasionally "A House" nomenclature

seems to have been almost universal. The formal Spanish names first make their appearance on Hearst's letterhead stationery for La Cuesta Encantada, which sports photographs of each individual house. Hearst began using this stationery c. 11 January 1925. Hearst may have been disappointed that the Spanish names for the three houses were not generally used. In a letter to Morgan on 19 August 1933, concerning the Wyntoon houses, he wrote: "If we do not name the houses something that is obviously appropriate and easily remembered, they will unquestionably be called the A, B, and C cottages like the cottages on the ranch." (Kennedy Library.)

18. Hearst to Morgan, 25 October 1919. Kennedy Library.

19. Hearst to Morgan, 11 August 1919, telegram; Morgan to Hearst, 13 September 1919. Kennedy Library.

20. Hearst to Morgan, c. 12 September 1919. Kennedy Library.

21. Morgan to Hearst, 25 September 1919. Kennedy Library.

22. Hearst to Morgan, 25 October 1919. Kennedy Library.

23. Hearst to Morgan, 10 December 1919. Kennedy Library.

24. Hearst to Morgan, 27 December 1919. Kennedy Library. Though Casa Grande's exterior employs ecclesiastical motifs, its interiors are nearly all secular in their decor, with the exception of the Refectory.

25. "The Work of Steilberg and Morgan," 142; "Julia Morgan, Her Office, and a House," vol. 2 of *The Julia Morgan Architectural History Project*, ed. Suzanne B. Riess, Regional Oral History Office, The Bancroft Library (Berkeley: University of California, 1976), 72–73.

26. Mark Alan Hewitt, *The Architect and the American Country House, 1890–1940* (New Haven: Yale University Press, 1990), 38.

27. Thomas R. Aidala, *Hearst Castle: San Simeon* (New York: Hudson Hills Press, 1981), 90.

28. Hearst to Morgan, 10 December 1919. Kennedy Library.

29. Ibid.

30. Hearst to Morgan, 27 December 1919. Kennedy Library.

31. Hearst to Morgan, 31 December 1919. Kennedy Library. Hearst apparently saw no incongruity in fomenting war with Spain through his newspapers in 1898 and in embracing a romantic Spanish style for his residence twenty years later. For a history of the Spanish Colonial Revival architectural style, see David Gebhard, "The Spanish Colonial Revival in Southern California (1895–1930)," *Journal of the Society of Architectural Historians* 26, no. 2 (May 1967): 131–47.

32. Morgan to Hearst, 8 January 1920. Kennedy Library. Hearst telegraphed Morgan on 14 July 1920: "Our definite decision in favor of the unissuance makes it unnecessary to go into San Diego Expo stuff at all." *Unissuance* was almost surely a miscommunication of the word *Renaissance*. Hearst here rejected the World's Fair precedents in favor of authentic historical models.

33. Gebhard and Winter, *Architecture in Los Angeles*, 243.

34. Ibid., 481.

35. Peck to Hearst, 10 December 1919, telegram draft. Kennedy Library. Phoebe Hearst met the two-year-old Orrin Peck and his parents when she and George made their wedding trip across the isthmus of Panama in 1862. Peck became a painter and a protégé of Phoebe, as well as a close friend of William Randolph Hearst. He would doubtless have contributed significantly to San Simeon's architectural and interior styles had he not died early in 1921. Only a few of Peck's letters containing suggestions about the cottages and grounds survive.

36. Hearst to Morgan, 21 December 1919. Kennedy Library.

37. Ibid.

38. Hearst to Morgan, 11 January 1921, telegram. Kennedy Library.

39. Hearst to Morgan, 14 January 1920; Hearst to Morgan, 9 February 1920; Hearst to Morgan, 23 May 1920; Hearst to Morgan, 5 February 1921, telegram; Morgan to Hearst, 6 February 1921, telegram draft; Hearst to Morgan, 7 February 1921. Kennedy Library.

40. "The Work of Steilberg and Morgan," Bancroft Library, 130.

41. Morgan to Hearst, 18 October 1919. Kennedy Library; Chipping, "The Geology of San Luis Obispo County," III 19, III 22–23; Camille Rossi to Walter L. Huber, 26 October 1922. Kennedy Library.

42. Morgan to Hearst, 6 April 1920. Kennedy Library.

43. Morgan to Hearst, 15 December 1920. Kennedy Library.

CHAPTER TWO: WIDENING INSPIRATIONS

1. Samuel G. White, *The Houses of McKim, Mead, and White* (New York: Rizzoli, 1998), 193, 16.

2. Lawrence Grant White, *Sketches and Designs by Stanford White* (New York: Architectural Book Publishing, 1920), 24–25.

3. Michael Conforti, "Stanford White at San Simeon" (paper presented at the Society of Architectural Historians Convention, Cincinnati, 26 April 1991), 10.

4. Ibid., 11.

5. Lawrence Grant White, *Sketches and Designs*, 24–25.

6. Paul R. Baker, *Stanny: The Gilded Life of Stanford White* (New York: Free Press, 1989), 234.

7. Ibid., 391–93.

8. Wesley Towner, *The Elegant Auctioneers* (New York: Hill and Wang, 1970), 181–83.

9. Baker, *Stanny*, 306.

10. Hearst to Morgan, 16 May 1922. Kennedy Library.

11. Hearst to Morgan, 10 December 1919. Kennedy Library.

12. Samuel White, *Houses of McKim, Mead, and White*, 230.

13. Hearst to Morgan, 30 December 1919. Kennedy Library.

14. Morgan to the Bynes, 18 November 1921. Kennedy Library.

15. Robinson, *American Dynasty*, 123.

16. Phoebe Apperson Hearst to Jeannie Peck, 15 April 1885. Huntington Library.

17. Phoebe Apperson Hearst to George Hearst, 3 December 1873. 72/204c. Bancroft Library.

18. William Randolph Hearst to Phoebe Apperson Hearst, c. January 1889. 82/68c. Bancroft Library. Although there is no record of its purchase, Leopoldo Ansiglioni's *Galatea on a Dolphin* is indeed displayed in a pool on the Central Plaza of Casa Grande. About his dismissal from Harvard, Hearst's letter to *Time*, 11 January 1932, stated: "I was in the class of '86 at Harvard. I was not expelled in '87 nor any other year. I never did anything very bad at Harvard nor anything very good either. I was rusticated [sent away to continue studies at home] in '86 for an excess of political enthusiasm and a certain deficiency in intellectual attainments. I did not return to be graduated. There did not seem to be either reason or hope. I think the less said about my college career the better. Perhaps that is so with the rest of my career. However, exercise your own judgment, only please print the facts, or perhaps I should say, please don't."

19. Edward Hussey recalled the procedure for taking photographs of Hearst's objects, which involved setting up the piece with a scale next to it and indicating its dimensions. "So, we had an extensive book of photographs and information about all these various items that he had. Then she could look through that and actually use those things in the construction and the design of the building. There'd be a door and she'd have the actual dimensions of it and a picture of it, and she'd say, 'We'll use that in such and such a place.'" ("Julia Morgan, Her Office, and a House," Bancroft Library, 70.)

20. Walter Steilberg, Address to the Historical Guide Association of California, August 1966, transcribed by Morris Cecil, 29 March 1968 (San Simeon: Hearst San Simeon State Historical Monument), 6.

21. James T. Maher, *The Twilight of Splendor: Chronicles of the Age of American Palaces* (Boston: Little, Brown, 1975), 198–99. It is uncertain whether Hearst visited Vizcaya, though he surely was aware of its opulence and its architectural and interior scheme. According to Hearst biographer David Nasaw (*The Chief*, 266), Marion Davies was a guest there in February 1918, just when Hearst was vacationing in Palm Beach with Millicent. Hearst and Davies were seeing one another clandestinely at this time.

22. Clive Aslet, *The American Country House* (New Haven: Yale University Press, 1990), 273.

23. "The Work of Steilberg and Morgan," Bancroft Library, 133.

24. Morgan to Hearst, 19 May 1926. Kennedy Library.

25. Of these periodicals, probably the most influential was *Country Life*, inaugurated on 1 January 1897, a fortuitous time because after death duties were introduced in England in 1894, country estates—which were advertised in the magazine—began to be put up for sale with increasing frequency. *Country Life* focused on the great houses that were an incomparable part of Britain's landscape, and also on developments in garden design and in the collecting of antiques,

particularly furniture. For an account of the history of *Country Life*, see John Cornforth's *The Search for a Style: Country Life and Architecture 1897–1935* (London: Andre Deutsch, 1988), 12–85.

26. "Julia Morgan, Her Office, and a House," Bancroft Library, 161.

27. Boutelle, *Julia Morgan, Architect*, 23.

28. Ibid., 23–27; Paul R. Baker, *Richard Morris Hunt* (Cambridge, Mass.: MIT Press, 1986), 30.

29. Boutelle, *Julia Morgan, Architect*, 24, 29–30.

30. Richard Chafee, "The Teaching of Architecture at the Ecole des Beaux-Arts," in *The Architecture of the Ecole des Beaux-Arts*, ed. Arthur Drexler (New York: Museum of Modern Art, 1977), 82–95.

31. Boutelle, *Julia Morgan, Architect*, 30.

32. Morgan to Pierre and Lucy LeBrun, 14 November 1898. Kennedy Library.

33. Chafee, "The Teaching of Architecture at the Ecole," 83.

34. Boutelle, *Julia Morgan, Architect*, 39.

35. David Van Zanten, "Architectural Composition at the Ecole des Beaux-Arts From Charles Percier to Charles Garnier," in *The Architecture of the Ecole des Beaux-Arts*, ed. Arthur Drexler (New York: Museum of Modern Art, 1977), 118.

36. Hewitt, *The Architect and the American Country House*, 32.

37. "The Work of Steilberg and Morgan," Bancroft Library, 45.

38. Ibid., 90.

39. "Julia Morgan, Her Office, and a House," Bancroft Library, 104.

40. Ibid., 121.

41. "The Work of Steilberg and Morgan," Bancroft Library, 143.

42. Royal Cortissoz, introduction to *Monograph of the Work of Charles A. Platt* (New York: Architectural Book Publishing, 1913), iv; Keith N. Morgan, *Charles A. Platt: The Artist as Architect* (New York: Architectural History Foundation, 1985), 16.

43. The subject of Italian villas was treated a decade after Platt's 1894 work in Edith Wharton's influential *Italian Villas and Their Gardens*, published in 1904 with illustrations by Maxfield Parrish. This classic was in Hearst's library, and doubtless also in Morgan's, though no inventory of her library remains. Wharton's coverage of eighty Italian villa gardens focused on site planning, the use of water, and the beauty of the formal garden, eclipsed since the eighteenth century by the picturesque garden tradition.

44. Hewitt, *The Architect and the American Country House*, 61–65.

45. John Taylor Boyd, "Colonial Homes of Great Dignity" (part 16 of "The Home as the American Architect Sees It"), *Arts and Decorations* 35, no. 6 (October 1931): 24.

46. Morgan to Hearst, 9 July 1926. Kennedy Library. Bernard Maybeck asked Morgan to ask Hearst for permission to bring the president of the University of St. Louis to San Simeon so that Maybeck could show him "how irregular ground formation can be made an asset to a scheme."

CHAPTER THREE: THE BUILDINGS TAKE SHAPE

1. Morgan to Hearst, 1 January 1922. Kennedy Library.

2. Hearst to Morgan, 27 March 1922. Kennedy Library.

3. Hearst to Morgan, 11 February 1922, telegram. Kennedy Library.

4. Hearst to Morgan, 5 January 1922. Kennedy Library.

5. Morgan to Hearst, 19 January 1922; Hearst to Morgan, 15 March 1922. Kennedy Library.

6. Hearst to Morgan, 28 April 1922, telegram. Kennedy Library.

7. Hearst to Morgan, 12 February 1922. Kennedy Library.

8. Morgan to Hearst, 6 April 1922. Kennedy Library.

9. Morgan to Hearst, 15 April 1922; Morgan to Hearst, 29 April 1922, telegram draft. Kennedy Library.

10. Morgan to Hearst, 3 August 1922; Morgan to Hearst, 14 June 1922. Kennedy Library.

11. Morgan to Hearst, 9 May 1922, telegram draft; Morgan to Hearst, 12 May 1922. Kennedy Library.

12. Hearst to Morgan, 22 May 1922. Kennedy Library.

13. Hearst to Morgan, 5 January 1922; Hearst to Morgan, 9 September 1927, telegram; Hearst to Morgan, 17 October 1927, telegram; Morgan to Hearst, 9 January 1930. Kennedy Library.

14. Aidala, *Hearst Castle*, 78.

15. Longstreth, *Four Architects*, 283.

16. Hearst to Camille Rossi, 17 February 1927; Hearst to Morgan, 19 February 1927. Kennedy Library.

17. Aidala, *Hearst Castle*, 76.

18. Hearst to Morgan, 13 July 1923, telegram. Kennedy Library.

19. Morgan to Hearst, 12 December 1922. Kennedy Library.

20. Morgan to Hearst, 19 July 1922. Kennedy Library.

21. Morgan to Hearst, 3 August 1922; Morgan to Hearst, 2 September 1922. Kennedy Library.

22. Hearst to Morgan, 4 December, 1922, telegram. Kennedy Library.

23. Morgan to Hearst, 16 May 1923. Kennedy Library.

24. Hearst to Morgan, 5 February 1922, telegram; Morgan to Hearst, 4 May 1921, telegram draft; Hearst to Morgan, 9 October 1922; Hearst to Morgan, 10 July 1923; Morgan to Hearst, 11 September 1923. Kennedy Library.

25. Morgan to Hearst, 10 July 1923. Kennedy Library. This letter obliquely indicates that the Hearsts have at last moved into House A. Morgan refers him to some photographs of art objects "in the large grey covered books in your House A study."

26. Morgan to Hearst, 1 December 1923; Morgan to Hearst, 20 March 1924. Kennedy Library.

27. Thaddeus Joy to Morgan, 11 March 1923; Joy to Morgan, 15 March 1923. Kennedy Library.

28. *Arte y Decoración en España*, vol. 2 (New York: Architectural Book Publishing, 1918), plate 39, plate 40.

29. Morgan to Mildred Stapley Byne, 3 September 1921. Kennedy Library.

30. Interview with Sandra J. Heinemann, Hearst Castle researcher, 20 May 1999.

31. Morgan to Hearst, 20 May 1923, telegram draft; Morgan to Hearst, 21 May 1923. Kennedy Library.

32. Morgan to Hearst, 24 April 1923. Kennedy Library.

33. Hearst to Morgan, 20 September 1922; Morgan to Hearst, 13 September 1923; Morgan to Hearst, 30 October 1923. Kennedy Library.

34. Morgan to Hearst, 30 March 1924. Kennedy Library.

35. Hearst to Morgan, 21 December 1923. Kennedy Library.

36. Hearst to Morgan, 31 March 1924. Kennedy Library. The fruit was left on the citrus trees along the Esplanade to provide both color and a Mediterranean character.

37. Morgan to Hearst, 17 June 1924. Kennedy Library.

38. Hearst to Morgan, 27 March 1922; Hearst to Morgan, 5 January 1922; Hearst to Morgan, 9 February 1923; Morgan to Hearst, 19 May 1924. Kennedy Library.

39. Joseph Willicombe to Morgan, 24 July 1922; Hearst to Morgan, c. 2 February 1923. Kennedy Library.

40. Hearst to Morgan, 31 March 1924. Kennedy Library.

41. Morgan to Hearst, 20 March 1924; Hearst to Morgan, 31 March 1924; Hearst to Morgan, 11 May 1924, telegram; Morgan to Hearst, 17 June 1924; Hearst to Morgan, 23 June 1924, telegram. Kennedy Library.

42. Morgan to Hearst, 23 July 1924. Kennedy Library.

43. Morgan to Hearst, 22 June 1922. Kennedy Library.

CHAPTER FOUR: ARCHITECT/CLIENT

1. Harry Crocker, "William Randolph Hearst," unpublished reminiscences, Academy of Motion Picture Arts and Sciences, 52; John R. Hearst Jr., "Life With Grandfather," *Reader's Digest* 76, no. 457 (May 1960): 155.

2. "Julia Morgan, Her Office, and a House," Bancroft Library, 108. In the same interview, Coblentz said of Morgan, "She was a delightful person, if you weren't being scolded" (117).

3. Frances Marion, "Screenwriter for Hearst," interview by Gerald Reynolds, ed. Nancy E. Loe, *Oral History Project* (San Simeon, Calif.: Hearst San Simeon State Historical Monument, 1 September 1972), 2–3.

4. William Randolph Hearst Jr., *Father and Son*, 63–64.

5. Ibid., 64.

6. "Julia Morgan, Her Office, and a House," Bancroft Library, 115.

7. Ibid., 67.

8. Morgan to Huber, 14 July 1930. Kennedy Library.

9. Sara Holmes Boutelle, "Julia Morgan," in *Toward a Simpler Way of Life: The Arts and Crafts Architects of California*, ed. Robert Winter (Berkeley: University of California Press, 1997), 63–66.

10. "Julia Morgan, Her Office, and a House," Bancroft Library, 119.

11. Hearst to Morgan, c. 10 August 1928.

Kennedy Library.

12. Arthur Brisbane to Morgan, 21 May 1934; Hearst to Morgan, 26 October 1934. Kennedy Library.

13. Boutelle, *Julia Morgan, Architect*, 217–18. Julia Morgan built the Hearst Globe Wireless Station in San Mateo, California, in the 1930s and also remodeled the interior of the Hearst Building on Market Street in San Francisco during this decade. She additionally designed an unbuilt Hopi House in Pueblo Revival style on Hearst property (later National Park property) on the south rim of the Grand Canyon in 1936. In southern California, she worked on Marion Davies's two residences, on Benedict Canyon Drive, Santa Monica, and on Lexington Road, Beverly Hills, and also remodeled Marion's relocated bungalow dressing room, formerly on the MGM lot in Culver City. See "Buildings by Julia Morgan," an appendix to the revised edition of Boutelle's *Julia Morgan, Architect*, 1995.

14. Warren McClure to George Loorz, 29 June 1935. George Loorz Collection. San Luis Obispo County Historical Society Archives. San Luis Obispo, Calif.

15. "Julia Morgan, Her Office, and a House," Bancroft Library, 180.

16. Dorothy Wormser Coblentz Crow to James T. Maher, 10 February 1978. Hearst San Simeon State Historical Monument Archives.

17. Morgan to Hearst, 4 May 1927. Kennedy Library.

18. Robinson, *American Dynasty*, 166–72, 259, 263, 292, 302.

19. Boutelle, *Julia Morgan, Architect*, 170.

20. Morgan to Phoebe Apperson Hearst, 16 February 1899. 72/204c. Bancroft Library.

21. Boutelle, *Julia Morgan, Architect*, 41–42, 51 59, 69 73, 78–79, 88–95.

22. Marjorie M. Dobkin, "A Twenty-Five-Million-Dollar Mirage," in *The Anthropology of World's Fairs: San Francisco's Panama Pacific International Exposition of 1915*, ed. Burton Benedict (Berkeley: Lowie Museum of Anthropology, 1983), 79.

23. Robinson, *American Dynasty*, 355–56.

24. Boutelle, *Julia Morgan, Architect*, 100–4.

25. Hearst to Morgan, 4 April 1925. Kennedy Library. Hearst did not give up on acquiring the Panama Pacific International Exposition statues for San Simeon, even though his efforts were unsuccessful in the 1920s. In *The Builders Behind the Castles* (San Luis Obispo, Calif.: San Luis Obispo County Historical Society, 1990, 100–1), Taylor Coffman indicates that the plaster models of the fair statues were purchased by Hearst in 1935, transported to the San Simeon warehouses, but never used on the hilltop. They were dispersed from the warehouses after Hearst's death in 1951. See R. F. Grady to George Loorz, 1 March 1935, and George Loorz to R. F. Grady, 5 March 1935. San Luis Obispo County Historical Society Archives.

26. Robert C. Pavlik, " 'Something a Little Different': La Cuesta Encantada's Architectural Precedents and Cultural Prototypes," *California History* 71, no. 4 (Winter 1992/1993): 467.

27. *The Legacy of the Exposition: Interpretation of the Intellectual and Moral Heritage Left to Mankind by the World Celebration of San Francisco in 1915* (San Francisco: Panama-Pacific International Exposition Company, 1916), 76.

28. Morgan to Phoebe Apperson Hearst, 26 March 1919. 72/204c. Bancroft Library.

29. William Randolph Hearst Jr., *Father and Son*, 72. One continuing source of disagreement between Hearst and Morgan was the amount of lighting in the rooms. Morgan generally provided fewer fixtures than Hearst desired, leading him to write to George Loorz in 1936: "I want more light in the new rooms than Miss Morgan gives us. . . . This is a mania with me. I like a room that you can see your way around in." San Luis Obispo County Historical Society Archives.

30. Ibid., 72.

31. Morgan to Hearst, 2 October 1922. Kennedy Library. Here Morgan asks Hearst if he isn't afraid that expanding the bathrooms of House B would hurt the scale of the house. She also proposes changing the motor entrance to a foot entrance at the back of the house. Both are examples of how she quietly framed her concerns in the form of questions. On occasion she would plead ignorance (real or assumed) to Hearst's wishes. In her letter to Hearst of 22 April 1926, she apologized for not realizing the red brocade Hearst sent was for the Doge's Suite Sitting Room (a color that would have clashed with the soft-toned pastels in the adjoining bedrooms): she had assumed that he wanted the blue material instead. She apologized profusely and would have been happy to countermand her orders, though she added, helpfully, that "the hangings are almost ready to send us—and are very pretty." She carried the point.

32. "Julia Morgan, Her Office, and a House," Bancroft Library, 219.

33. Morgan to Hearst, 25 February 1927. Kennedy Library.

34. Morgan to Walter Steilberg, 7 October 1928, reproduced in "The Work of Steilberg and Morgan," Bancroft Library, 61c–61f.

35. "The Work of Steilberg and Morgan," Bancroft Library, 57, 90–91, 142. Walter Steilberg's ambivalence about the success of what he called San Simeon's "facade architecture" can be noted in his comment on p. 72 of the interview: "I think that in general it's true that San Simeon is better at a distance than it is close up." See also Edward Hussey, "Julia Morgan, Her Office, and a House," Bancroft Library, 67, and Boutelle, *Julia Morgan, Architect*, 14–15.

36. Morgan North, "Julia Morgan, Her Office, and a House," Bancroft Library, 202.

37. "The Work of Steilberg and Morgan," Bancroft Library, 135a. Morgan and Hearst occasionally invoked their own form of providence, in this case a figure in relief on Casa Grande's west facade whom they adopted as their patron saint, San Simeon. She wrote Hearst on 5 September 1933, about his recent purchase of armor intended for the Great Hall, "I am delighted to hear that San Simeon produced those horse armors!" Kennedy Library.

38. Hearst to Morgan, 26 August 1920, telegram; Hearst to Morgan, undated letter written between 7 March and 24 April 1927. Kennedy Library. Hearst jubilantly signed a letter to Morgan "your assistant architect" (26 April 1932). He had just conceived of turning the east wing, long planned for Casa Grande's rear courtyard, into a Great Hall displaying armor and tapestries. It was never built. Kennedy Library.

39. Morgan to Hearst, 22 April 1920. Kennedy Library.

40. Morgan to Hearst, 6 January 1925. Kennedy Library.

41. Morgan to Hearst, 15 September 1923; Morgan to Hearst, 19 May 1924. Kennedy Library.

42. "Julia Morgan, Her Office, and a House," Bancroft Library, 165.

43. Ibid., 147.

44. Morgan to Hearst, 19 May 1924. Kennedy Library.

45. Morgan to Hearst, 26 May 1921; Hearst to Morgan, 2 June 1921, telegram. Kennedy Library.

46. Morgan to Hearst, 18 March 1922. Kennedy Library.

47. Rossi to Hearst, 18 January 1932. Kennedy Library.

48. Hearst's hand-written notes to Morgan in the margin of Rossi's letter to Hearst, 18 January 1932. Kennedy Library.

49. Morgan to Hearst, 20 January 1932. Kennedy Library. Morgan described Camille Rossi's personality problems to Hearst in a letter dated 27 November 1927: ". . . Mr. Rossi has first been over friendly and confidential, realizes he has been so, and tries to get rid of his imagined 'enemy' by the small methods you know of. But it keeps him constantly plotting and building up these 'revenges' in his mind and is bad for him and the conduct of the work, and is certainly growing beyond just 'inexactitudes.'"

50. Rossi to Morgan, 18 January 1932. Kennedy Library.

51. Morgan to Hearst, 20 January 1932. Kennedy Library.

CHAPTER FIVE: A CALIFORNIA COUNTRY HOUSE

1. Hearst to Mr. Hadley, 18 September 1921; Hearst to Morgan, 26 March 1926. Kennedy Library.

2. Hearst to Morgan, 8 January 1925, telegram. Kennedy Library.

3. Morgan to Hearst, 7 May 1920; Morgan to Hearst, 19 April 1924. Kennedy Library.

4. Morgan to Hearst, 7 June 1925. Kennedy Library.

5. Hearst to Rossi, c. 7 February 1927. Kennedy Library.

6. Hearst to Rossi, 16 February 1927. Kennedy Library. February storms continued to provide more severe weather than the estate could withstand, even many years later, long after weatherproofing steps had been taken. Hearst wrote to George Loorz on 10 February 1938: "The windows in the houses all leak. Even the double windows leak—and leak in rivers. . . . We will have to completely reconstruct the window protection and on an entirely different basis. . . . Furthermore every year before winter, the

windows—and doors where exposed—must be tested by having the fire hose played on them. This is the only way. There is no use trying to live in lath houses—or bath houses . . . the houses must be made livable in *winter*—especially as we spend the summer in Wyntoon and San Simeon is a *winter* residence."

7. Hearst to Morgan, c. 15 February 1927. Kennedy Library.

8. Morgan to Hearst, 17 February 1927. Kennedy Library.

9. Hearst to Morgan, c. 15 September 1923. Kennedy Library.

10. Hearst to Morgan, 21 December 1923; Morgan to Hearst, 20 March 1924. Kennedy Library.

11. Morgan to Hearst, c. 31 December 1922. Kennedy Library.

12. Report from Bruce Porter, January 1923. Sara Holmes Boutelle collection.

13. Morgan to Hearst, 12 February 1923; Morgan to Hearst, 26 March 1925; Hearst to Morgan, 10 May 1925, telegram; Morgan to Hearst, 22 April 1925. Kennedy Library.

14. Hearst to Morgan, c. 11 January 1925. Kennedy Library.

15. Hearst to Morgan, c. 9 June 1922. Kennedy Library.

16. Morgan to Hearst, 23 April 1923; Hearst to Morgan, 19 May 1925, telegram; Morgan to Hearst, 25 May 1925, telegram. Kennedy Library. Construction of the second version of the Neptune Pool continued on and off through 1926–27, coinciding with the construction of another classically-inspired swimming pool, Julia Morgan's and Bernard Maybeck's pool for the University of California Women's Gymnasium, a gift to the Berkeley campus from William Randolph Hearst.

17. Hearst to Morgan, 14 August 1926. Kennedy Library.

18. Hearst to Joy, 6 January 1928, memorandum; Morgan to Hearst, 30 April 1928, telegram draft. Kennedy Library.

19. Hearst to Morgan, 12 February 1921; Morgan to Hearst, 7 March 1921. Kennedy Library.

20. Hearst to Morgan, 9 December 1925; Joy to Hearst, 30 October 1926. Kennedy Library.

21. Morgan to Hearst, 30 April 1928, telegram; Morgan to Hearst, 6 June 1928. Kennedy Library.

22. Morgan to Hearst, 3 December 1929, telegram draft. Kennedy Library.

23. Hearst to Morgan, 14 November 1923, telegram; Hearst to Morgan, c. 15 September 1923. Kennedy Library.

24. Hearst to Morgan, 11 January 1925. Kennedy Library. Another romantic idea Hearst proposed was a "labyrinth or maze. They are lots of fun and can be made very pretty also," he wrote to Morgan on 27 August 1925. Mazes were important garden features in sixteenth- and seventeenth-century European gardens, particularly at Windsor Castle and Villa d'Este, two of Hearst's favorite spots. He considered the possibility of making his proposed maze of roses "because it is impossible to break through the trellises and thus cheat" in a letter to Morgan c. 27 August 1925, but conceived a grander scheme yet in a letter to Morgan on 12 August 1926: "How about a maze in con-

nection with the zoo. I think getting lost in a maze and coming unexpectedly upon lions, tigers, pumas, panthers, wild cats, monkeys, mackaws [sic] and cockatoos, etc. etc. would be a thrill even for the most blase . . . we could have a great maze with all these 'animiles' [sic] and birds and with a pretty pool in the middle, with cranes and flamingos, etc., and a fountain and EVERYTHING." Sadly this feature was never built.

25. Morgan to Hearst, 22 April 1925. Kennedy Library.

26. Morgan to Hearst, 27 July 1927. Kennedy Library.

27. Brayton Laird, "Working in the Orchards of the Hearst Ranch," interview by Bruce Brown, ed. Robert C. Pavlik, *Oral History Project* (San Simeon, Calif.: Hearst San Simeon State Historical Monument, 19 December 1986), 4. While the grazing animals remained on the estate into the mid-1940s, the carnivores began to be removed and placed in zoos in the later 1930s when Hearst experienced financial troubles.

28. Hearst to Morgan, 11 January 1925. Kennedy Library.

29. Marion Davies, *The Times We Had: Life with William Randolph Hearst* (Indianapolis, Ind.: Bobbs-Merrill, 1975), 14.

30. Maurice McClure, "From Laborer to Construction Superintendent," interview by Metta Hake, ed. Bernice Joan Falls and Robert C. Pavlik, *Oral History Project* (San Simeon, Calif.: Hearst San Simeon State Historical Monument, 13 September 1981), 25.

31. King Vidor, "Work and Play with Hearst and Davies," interview by Rosie Wittig, ed. Nancy E. Loe, *Oral History Project* (San Simeon, Calif.: Hearst San Simeon State Historical Monument, 1975), 5–6, 13–14.

32. Alice M. Head, *It Could Never Have Happened* (London: Heinemann, 1939), 97.

33. Hearst to Morgan, 2 June 1926. Kennedy Library. Hearst never did allow San Simeon to be used as a Hollywood movie set, but c. 1920 he and Millicent and their family and guests used it for the elaborate home movie "The Lighthouse Keeper's Daughters." Hearst played the hero, John Jenkins, Millicent the kidnapped heroine. Even Julia Morgan made a brief, smiling appearance. Hearst's dialogue panels were corny and romantic: "Then through the shade/The cavalcade/Winds up the hill to where/John Jenkins is/Constructing his/Cloud castles in the air." While the exact date when Marion began to play the open role of hostess at San Simeon is unknown, the visit of June 1926 seems a likely candidate. Hearst began sending letters to Morgan using the Ambassador Hotel in Los Angeles as his return address in June 1925. He returned briefly to New York that November, came back to California in December, returned to New York in March 1926, and from May 1926 made Southern California his most frequent residence, presumably in response to his marital separation. Both Morgan and Hearst spoke about the Hollywood guests in such excited terms that it is unlikely great numbers of them had visited previously.

34. Morgan to Hearst, 3 June 1926. Kennedy Library.

35. Morgan to Arthur Byne, 14 March 1925. Kennedy Library. A further indication of the expansive construction plans of this period was Hearst's intention to build two more small houses, D and E, which he wanted to make "rather more luxurious than A, B and C." He mapped out his intentions in a handwritten, undated letter to Morgan c. August 1926. These houses were to be picturesque and commodious—particularly their bathrooms, unlike the cramped ones in the other three houses. Neither house was built. Only a staircase leading from the North Terrace to the Esplanade remains to show that House D (also called "Casa del Canyon") was planned for the north side of the hill. House E was planned for the south side. Kennedy Library.

36. Arthur Byne to Morgan, 16 June 1925; Morgan to Hearst, 27 July 1925; Morgan to Arthur Byne, 25 August 1925. Kennedy Library.

37. Roy Denning, ed., *The Story of St. Donat's Castle and Atlantic College* (Cowbridge, South Wales: D. Brown and Sons, 1983), 71; Head, *It Could Never Have Happened*, 68.

38. Fred Lawrence Guiles, *Marion Davies* (New York: McGraw-Hill, 1972), 176; Anne Edwards, "Marion Davies' Ocean House: The Santa Monica Palace Ruled by Hearst's Mistress," *Architectural Digest* 51, no. 4 (April 1994): 174; Hearst to Morgan, 22 June 1926; Hearst to Morgan, 23 June 1926. Kennedy Library.

39. Robert B. MacKay, Anthony K. Baker, and Carol A. Traynor, eds., *Long Island Country Houses and Their Architects, 1860–1940* (New York: W. W. Norton, in association with the Society for the Preservation of Long Island Antiquities, 1997), 231; Nasaw, *The Chief*, 365–66.

40. Hearst to Morgan, 19 February 1927. Kennedy Library.

41. Mildred Stapley Byne to Morgan, 22 October 1921. Kennedy Library.

42. Towner, *Elegant Auctioneers*, 419–20.

43. "The Seer of San Simeon," *Newsweek* 27, no. 18 (6 May 1946): 62–64.

44. Hearst to Morgan, 19 February 1927. Kennedy Library. On one ill-fated public occasion in July 1932, a class of landscaping students from California Polytechnic College in San Luis Obispo toured the estate. As they inspected the Roman Pool under construction, too many of them stood on the temporary wooden floor and it broke beneath them. Several dozen people fell ten feet down into the unfinished concrete pool below and there were many injuries—particularly to legs. The medical bills were paid by Hearst's insurance company.

45. William Randolph Hearst to Phoebe Apperson Hearst, January 1889. 82/68c. Bancroft Library.

46. Morgan to Hearst, 7 June 1926; Hearst to Morgan, 17 June 1926, telegram; Hearst to Morgan, 23 June 1926, telegram; Hearst to Morgan, 4 February 1927, telegram; Morgan to Hearst, 11 November 1926. Kennedy Library. A distinction must be made between "usable" and "finished." Hearst used both the Refectory and the Assembly Room, sometimes alternately, while they were still incomplete.

47. Morgan to Hearst, 24 June 1924. Kennedy Library.

48. Morgan to Arthur Byne, 14 March 1925. Kennedy Library. The choir stall wainscoting was installed in the Assembly Room in 1926. Four pairs of panels on the east wall were modified so that they could be used as doors. Two pairs lead to the Refectory and two open into stairwells, one of which contains the elevator. Popular legend has it that Hearst appeared from behind a hidden panel, when in fact he merely came down from the Gothic Suite by elevator. Casa Grande contains no secret passages.

49. Joy to Morgan, 14 March 1923, annotations added in the margin in Hearst's hand. Kennedy Library.

50. Frank R. Humrich to Hearst, 19 December 1925. Kennedy Library.

51. Morgan to Hearst, 26 April 1926; Hearst to Morgan, 26 April 1926, telegram. Kennedy Library. Hearst wrote to Morgan on 7 February 1926: "It seems a shame not to put genuine [antique] ceilings everywhere in this big house" when he was still committed to using the modern beams painted to resemble the ceiling decorations of Palazzo Chiaramonte in Palermo. Because they abandoned the modern scheme, all the main rooms of Casa Grande do indeed showcase antique ceilings.

52. Morgan to Hearst, 7 June 1926. Kennedy Library.

53. Letter from an unidentified guest at San Simeon to her grandchildren, 31 March 1936. Hearst Monument Staff Library.

54. Randolph S. Churchill, *Twenty-one Years* (Boston: Houghton Mifflin, 1965), 86–87.

55. John Spencer Churchill, *A Churchill Canvas* (Boston: Little, Brown, 1962), 88.

56. Winston S. Churchill to Clementine Churchill, 19 September 1929, *Winston S. Churchill*, vol. V, Companion part 2, Documents, *The Wilderness Years, 1929–1935*, ed. Martin Gilbert (Boston: Houghton Mifflin, 1981), 87.

57. Winston S. Churchill to Clementine Churchill, 29 September 1929, *Winston S. Churchill*, vol. V, Companion part 2, 96–97.

58. Hearst to Morgan, 11 March 1928; Morgan to Hearst, 17 July 1930. Kennedy Library.

CHAPTER SIX: MARION DAVIES INVITES HOLLYWOOD

1. Robinson, *American Dynasty*, 240.

2. Davies, *The Times We Had*, 207.

3. Anita Loos, *The Talmadge Girls: A Memoir* (New York: Viking, 1978), 65.

4. William Randolph Hearst to Phoebe Apperson Hearst, 1887. 82/68c. Bancroft Library.

5. Swanberg, *Citizen Hearst*, 206.

6. Robinson, *American Dynasty*, 245–46, 257.

7. William Randolph Hearst Jr., *Father and Son*, 13; Nasaw, *The Chief*, 82.

8. Guiles, *Marion Davies*, 19, 22, 30–36, 41.

9. Davies, *The Times We Had*, 10.

10. William Randolph Hearst Jr., *Father and Son*, 176.

11. Ibid., 239.

12. Ibid., 238, 242. Telegrams from Hearst to Morgan, 13 December 1928, one from Morgan to Hearst, 27 December 1928; and a telegram from Hearst to Morgan, 28 December 1928, all imply that Millicent Hearst was at San Simeon at this time. Though there is no documentation confirming that she spent Christmas day itself there, it seems a reasonable supposition. Kennedy Library.

13. Nasaw, *The Chief*, 337–39, 353.

14. Davies, *The Times We Had*, 53.

15. William Randolph Hearst Jr., "Memories of San Simeon and the Hearst Family," interview by Tom Scott, ed. Robert C. Pavlik, *Oral History Project* (San Simeon, Calif.: Hearst San Simeon State Historical Monument, August 1977), 42. In "Silent Movie Actress and Frequent Guest" (interview by Metta Hake, ed. Robert C. Pavlik, *Oral History Project* [San Simeon, Calif.: Hearst San Simeon State Historical Monument, 18 October 1981], 6), Aileen Pringle says that she was a guest on the occasion when Bill Jr. and Marion first met, and Bill was reticent to enter the room and meet Marion. Marion herself tells substantially the same story, but says it was George she met. Davies, *The Times We Had*, 44.

16. Davies, *The Times We Had*, 44.

17. Ibid., 51.

18. Neal Gabler, *Winchell: Gossip, Power and the Culture of Celebrity* (New York: Knopf, 1994), 183–86.

19. Adela Rogers St. Johns, "Hearst as a Host," interview by Gerald Reynolds, ed. Robert C. Pavlik, *Oral History Project* (San Simeon, Calif.: Hearst San Simeon State Historical Monument, April 1971), 7.

20. Davies, *The Times We Had*, 34.

21. Cecil Beaton, *The Wandering Years: Diaries: 1922–1939* (Boston: Little, Brown, 1961), 208.

22. Pringle, "Silent Movie Actress," *Oral History Project*, 4.

23. Davies, *The Times We Had*, 45. Steve Zegar, not "Pete," owned the cars.

24. Davies, *The Times We Had*, 234.

25. Ibid., 43.

26. Gretchen Swinnerton, "Jimmy Swinnerton: Hearst Cartoonist and Artist," interview by Thelma Anderson, ed. Rayena Martin, *Oral History Project* (San Simeon, Calif.: Hearst San Simeon State Historical Monument, 1978), 21. For descriptions of Marion's personality, see interviews with some of her family and friends: Arthur and Patricia Lake, her grandniece Marion Rose Lake Canessa, journalist Adela Rogers St. Johns, actresses Eleanor Boardman and Colleen Moore.

27. P. G. Wodehouse, *Author! Author!* (New York: Simon and Schuster, 1962), 80–81.

28. Patience Abbé, Richard Abbé, and Johnny Abbé, *Of All Places!* (New York: Stokes, 1937), 224.

29. Louise Brooks, *Lulu in Hollywood* (New York: Knopf, 1983), 40.

30. Charles Chaplin, *My Autobiography* (New York: Simon and Schuster, 1964), 312–13.

31. Colleen Moore, "The Jazz Age's Movie Flapper at San Simeon," interview by Gerald Reynolds and Metta Hake, ed. Nancy E. Loe, *Oral History Project* (San Simeon, Calif.: Hearst San Simeon State Historical Monument, 25 January 1977), 8.

32. Irene Castle, *Castles in the Air* (New York: Da Capo, 1980), 218.

33. Arthur Lake and Pat Lake, "Dagwood Bumstead and Marion Davies' Niece," interview by Metta Hake, ed. Rayena Martin, *Oral History Project* (San Simeon, Calif.: Hearst San Simeon State Historical Monument, 4 April 1984), 29–30.

34. Ilka Chase, *Past Imperfect* (Garden City, N.Y.: Blue Ribbon Books, 1945), 110. Joel McCrea recalled staying on in the Theater one night after a Norma Shearer picture when Constance Bennett, who was also a guest, ran through some screen tests for the male lead in her 1931 film, *Born to Love*. He watched his take and also those of several other stars. Hearst and Marion both complimented Joel on his acting, and the next morning when he was coming into Casa Grande, he ran into Louella Parsons, who told him he'd been picked to play the part. He was sure without the praises of W. R. and Marion, he never would have been selected. ("Hearst, Hollywood and San Simeon," interview by Metta Hake, ed. Nancy E. Loe, *Oral History Project* [San Simeon, Calif.: Hearst San Simeon State Historical Monument, 5 December 1982], 34–35.)

35. Moore, "Movie Flapper at San Simeon," *Oral History Project*, 8. Moore spoke of the costume parties in general. Three that were certainly held at San Simeon were the Hawaiian Party in 1931, the Pioneer Covered Wagon Party in 1933, and the Civil War Party in 1934. Many of the other parties often quoted in memoirs as having been held at San Simeon, including the Circus Party and the Little Kid Party, were actually hosted at Marion's Ocean House in Santa Monica.

36. Davies, *The Times We Had*, 143.

37. Marion, "Screenwriter for Hearst," *Oral History Project*, 2, 3–4.

38. Nancy Nelson, *Evenings with Cary Grant. Recollections in His Own Words and by Those Who Knew Him Best* (New York: Warner, 1993), 77–78. Cary Grant was a frequent guest at San Simeon for many years and was generally respectful of his hosts: "Grant was irritated by people who accepted Mr. Hearst's hospitality and then talked behind his back about his parsimony. They ignored his generosity and commented on the fact that he turned out the lights as he left a room." (Nelson, *Evenings with Cary Grant*, 77.) When Grant toured the Castle with his wife Barbara on 3 June 1983, he recounted the flour-bombing story as well as expressed his continued grateful feelings toward Hearst and Marion to his guide, Sally Scott.

39. Beaton, *The Wandering Years*, 204–12. Hearst wrote to Morgan on 30 March 1931 about a basement humidifier advertised in *House Beautiful* (one of his own magazines), which he thought they could use as a substitute for their placing water-filled vessels upstairs in the rooms. Humidifying a piece of furniture with a pan of water, as Beaton describes, is consistent with the steps they were already taking to add moisture to the rooms themselves.

40. Cary Grant interviewed by Robert G. Latson, 3 June 1983; Nelson, *Evenings with Cary Grant*, 76. Grant confirmed these alcohol intrigues to Sally Scott, 3 June 1983.

41. William Randolph Hearst Jr., *Father and Son*, 179.
42. St. Johns, "Hearst as a Host," *Oral History Project*, 8.
43. David Niven, *Bring on the Empty Horses* (New York: G. P. Putnam's Sons, 1975), 270.
44. Marion, "Screenwriter for Hearst," *Oral History Project*, 2.
45. Davies, *The Times We Had*, 23.
46. Ibid., 194.
47. Ibid., 257.
48. Ibid., 261.

CHAPTER SEVEN: CASA GRANDE UNDER EXPANSION

1. Morgan to Hearst, 9 October 1928. Kennedy Library.
2. Morgan to Arthur Byne, 31 October 1927. Kennedy Library.
3. Morgan to Hearst, 8 June 1927. Kennedy Library. The idea of using a genuine stone facing for the Main Building was first proposed in 1923. Hearst was initially unenthusiastic, worried, as Thaddeus Joy reported to Morgan, that "it would greatly increase the cost." (15 March 1923. Kennedy Library.) They first determined that they would apply stone to the lower part of the building only, but when they began the facing in 1927, they carried it all the way to the towers and were very pleased with the effect. The side and rear portions of the Main Building were never faced, leaving blunt reminders of Casa Grande's unfinished state.
4. Morgan to Hearst, 24 June 1924, telegram; Morgan to Hearst, 9 July 1924, telegram draft; Morgan to Hearst, 4 June 1927. Kennedy Library.
5. Charles Gates, "Serving Hearst and Davies as a Waiter and Butler," interview by Thelma Anderson, ed. Bernice Joan Falls and Robert C. Pavlik, *Oral History Project* (San Simeon, Calif.: Hearst San Simeon State Historical Monument, 4 October 1978), 7.
6. Morgan to Hearst, 17 December 1927. Kennedy Library; Gates, "Serving Hearst and Davies," *Oral History Project*, 3–4, 15; Fred Redelsperger, "Waiting Table at the Hearst Estates," interview by Metta Hake, ed. Laurel Stewart, *Oral History Project* (San Simeon, Calif.: Hearst San Simeon State Historical Monument, 15 October 1985), 13; Wilfred Lyons, "Working Various Jobs at San Simeon," interview by Ted Moreno, ed. Robert C. Pavlik, *Oral History Project* (San Simeon, Calif.: Hearst San Simeon State Historical Monument, 12 July 1987), 21–22. The construction crew's quarters were less private and less comfortable. In the early years the workers lived in tents that blew over in the heavy storms. In the later years they shared barracks, had a small commissary for buying necessities, and paid $1.00 a day out of their salaries for meals. The construction crew put in long hours when Hearst's arrival was imminent, and the Castle household staff worked long hours when he was in residence.
7. Morgan to Hearst, 13 May 1926; Hearst to Morgan, 4 July 1926. Kennedy Library; Lyons, "Working Various Jobs at San Simeon," *Oral History Project*, 5;

Redelsperger, "Waiting Table at the Hearst Estates," *Oral History Project*, 8.
8. Gates, "Serving Hearst and Davies," *Oral History Project*, 8.
9. Lyons, "Working Various Jobs at San Simeon," *Oral History Project*, 30.
10. Swinnerton, "Hearst Cartoonist and Artist," *Oral History Project*, 18.
11. Hearst, "In the News," Wednesday, 15 April 1942.
12. St. Johns, "Hearst as a Host," *Oral History Project*, 10.
13. Adela Rogers St. Johns, *The Honeycomb* (Garden City, N.Y.: Doubleday, 1969), 129.
14. Moore, "Movie Flapper at San Simeon," *Oral History Project*, 23.
15. Morgan to Hearst, 27 August 1931. Kennedy Library.
16. Hearst to Morgan, c. 15 February 1927. Kennedy Library.
17. A. Edward Newton, *Derby Day and Other Adventures* (Freeport, N.Y.: Books for Libraries Press, 1969), 217–18. At the end of the twenties, the media began profiling the estate, and its country-life traditions and architectural decoration became known to the public at large. On 21 July 1929 the *New York Times* published "A Renaissance Palace In Our West," which minutely described a site "which might have been the Apennines villa of some Renaissance grand ducal seigneur." *Fortune* in May 1931 wrote copiously about the lifestyle at San Simeon in its article on Hearst's companies, codifying in the public's mind the mythology of "the ranch." It read: "Observe also the ping-pong board under the Gothic mantel, the billiard table which balances it across the Great Hall, the 'Hearst Camp' on the official stationery, the swimming and riding and game-playing." A more in-depth business profile, detailing life at Wyntoon, ran in the same magazine in October 1935.
18. Morgan to Hearst, 18 September 1931. Kennedy Library.
19. Davies, *The Times We Had*, 211.
20. Hearst to Morgan, 15 February 1927; Hearst to Morgan, c. 15 February 1927. Kennedy Library.
21. Hearst to Morgan, 3 June 1930. Kennedy Library.
22. Hearst to Morgan, 23 June 1926, telegram. Kennedy Library.
23. Hearst to Morgan, 12 November 1923, telegram. Kennedy Library.
24. Hearst to Rossi, 7 February 1927; Morgan to Hearst, 9 October 1928. Kennedy Library.
25. Morgan to Hearst, 3 October 1927. Kennedy Library.
26. Hearst to Morgan, 3 November 1927. Kennedy Library.
27. Morgan to Hearst, 19 November 1927, telegram. Kennedy Library.
28. John R. Hearst Jr., "Life With Grandfather," 162.
29. William Randolph Hearst, "The Active Life" in *Selections from the Writings and Speeches of William Randolph Hearst*, ed. E. F. Tompkins (San Francisco: *San Francisco Examiner*, 1948), 446–47.
30. Hearst to Morgan, 31 December 1919; Hearst to Morgan, 4 February 1927, telegram; Hearst to Morgan, 24 July 1929. Kennedy Library.

31. Hearst to Morgan, 14 August 1926; Rossi to Morgan, 7 February 1927. Kennedy Library.
32. Morgan to Hearst, 22 July 1931. Kennedy Library.
33. Ludwig Bemelmans, *To the One I Love the Best* (New York: Viking, 1955), 153.
34. Ibid., 153–54.
35. Morgan to Hearst, 27 May 1932. Kennedy Library.
36. Hearst to Morgan, 26 April 1932. Kennedy Library.
37. Hearst to Morgan, c. 20 March 1932. Kennedy Library.

CHAPTER EIGHT: HEARST AS GRANDEE

1. Hearst to Morgan, 31 December 1919. Kennedy Library.
2. William Randolph Hearst to Phoebe Apperson Hearst, undated postcard. Bancroft Library.
3. Hearst essay on the back of his *Los Angeles Examiner* stationery, first appearing 14 August 1926. Kennedy Library. State Highway 1, which runs the length of the California coast, opened in 1937, after 16 years of construction and an expenditure of $9 million. The highway greatly reduced the privacy of La Cuesta Encantada, bringing sightseers along the lower edge of Hearst's ranch as their automobiles traveled what is still one of the world's most scenic roads.
4. John R. Hearst Jr., "Life With Grandfather," 158–59.
5. Moore, "Movie Flapper at San Simeon," *Oral History Project*, 23–24.
6. Mrs. William Randolph Hearst Jr., *The Horses of San Simeon*, 65, 69.
7. William Randolph Hearst to Phoebe Apperson Hearst, 30 August 1917. 87/232c. Bancroft Library.
8. Hearst to Morgan, 28 October 1927, telegram; Hearst to Morgan, 14 August 1929; Morgan to Hearst, 27 February 1930. Kennedy Library.
9. Hearst to Morgan, 10 September 1920, telegram. Kennedy Library.
10. Hearst to Morgan, 15 September 1920. Kennedy Library.
11. Morgan to Hearst, 17 October 1932. Kennedy Library.
12. Stanley Heaton and Elmer Moorhouse, "Gardening and Road Construction," interview by Metta Hake, ed. William Payne and Robert C. Pavlik, *Oral History Project* (San Simeon, Calif.: Hearst San Simeon State Historical Monument, 27 March 1984), 34.
13. Moore, "Movie Flapper at San Simeon," *Oral History Project*, 9.
14. St. Johns, "Hearst as a Host," *Oral History Project*, 2; Ralph G. Martin, *Cissy* (New York: Simon and Schuster, 1979), 260–61.
15. Mrs. William Randolph Hearst Jr., *The Horses of San Simeon*, 106.
16. William Randolph Hearst to George Hearst, 28 June 1888, telegram. 72/204c. Bancroft Library.
17. Mrs. William Randolph Hearst Jr., *The Horses of San Simeon*, 147, 151, 159, 177–78, 183.
18. Ibid., 215, 217.
19. Davies, *The Times We Had*, 94, 136.
20. Eleanor Boardman d'Arrast, "Remembering

W. R. and Marion," interview by Rayena Martin and Guy Roop, ed. Robert C. Pavlik, *Oral History Project* (San Simeon, Calif.: Hearst San Simeon State Historical Monument, 3 November 1987), 4; Vidor, "Work and Play with Hearst and Davies," *Oral History Project*, 16; Moore, "Movie Flapper at San Simeon," *Oral History Project*, 9; Loorz to Mac McClure, 19 June 1933. San Luis Obispo County Historical Society Archives.

21. King Vidor, *A Tree is a Tree* (Hollywood: Samuel French, 1989), 163.

22. Morgan to Hearst, 13 September 1925, telegram. Kennedy Library.

23. Morgan to Hearst, 10 October 1929; Hearst to Morgan, 30 May 1930, telegram. Kennedy Library.

24. Older, *William Randolph Hearst*, 543.

25. Morgan to Hearst, 12 August 1930. Kennedy Library.

26. Hearst to Morgan, 31 December 1919. Kennedy Library.

27. Loorz to Millard Hendricks, 14 April 1936. San Luis Obispo County Historical Society Archives.

28. Hearst to Morgan, 9 November 1931. Kennedy Library.

29. Cope Rand Means Co., Engineers, "Proposed Development of Piedra Blanca and Santa Rosa Ranches, San Luis Obispo County, California," 5 January 1921: 19–20, 31. Hearst San Simeon State Historical Monument Archives.

30. Hearst to Morgan, 24 September 1922; Hearst to Morgan, 16 May 1924; Hearst to Morgan, 7 July 1925, telegram; Morgan to Hearst, 2 September 1925; Hearst to Morgan, 29 December 1925, telegram; Hearst to Morgan, 26 March 1926, telegram; Morgan to Hearst, 11 October 1926; Hearst to Morgan, 12 April 1928, telegram; Hearst to Morgan, c. 7 August 1928; Hearst to Morgan, 3 April 1930. Kennedy Library.

31. Hearst to Loorz, 20 May 1937. San Luis Obispo County Historical Society Archives.

32. Hearst to Morgan, 1 August 1930, telegram; Hearst to Morgan, 3 August 1930, telegram; Morgan to Hearst, 4 August 1930. Kennedy Library.

33. Hearst to Morgan, 22 February 1930. Kennedy Library.

34. Nasaw, *The Chief*, 389.

35. Bernard Shaw, *Collected Letters, 1926–1950*, ed. Dan H. Laurence (New York: Viking, 1988), 109.

36. Bennett Cerf, *At Random: The Reminiscences of Bennett Cerf* (New York: Random House, 1977), 114.

37. Basil Woon, *Incredible Land: A Jaunty Baedeker to Hollywood and the Great Southwest* (New York: Liveright, 1933), 189.

CHAPTER NINE: FINANCIAL HAVOC

1. Hearst to Loorz, 8 March 1933. San Luis Obispo County Historical Society Archives.

2. Warren McClure Papers. Hearst San Simeon State Historical Monument Staff Library, 15.

3. Ibid., 10–11. The "little shack office" McClure referred to remains standing in the East Courtyard of Casa Grande.

4. Morgan to Pierre and Lucy LeBrun, 7 May 1899. Kennedy Library; Morgan North, "Julia Morgan, Her Office, and a House," Bancroft Library, 210.

5. Morgan to Hearst, 16 September 1932. Kennedy Library.

6. Hearst to Morgan, 21 September 1932, telegram. Kennedy Library.

7. Morgan to Hearst, 21 September 1932. Kennedy Library.

8. Morgan to Hearst, 1 October 1932. Kennedy Library.

9. Hearst to Morgan, 21 October 1932, telegram. Kennedy Library.

10. Morgan to Hearst, 7 December 1932. Kennedy Library.

11. Morgan North, "Julia Morgan, Her Office, and a House," Bancroft Library, 204, 225.

12. Loorz to Warren McClure, 9 October 1933. San Luis Obispo County Historical Society Archives.

13. Hearst to Morgan, 22 July 1929; Morgan to Hearst, 3 December 1929, telegram draft; Morgan to Hearst, 29 January 1930; Hearst to Morgan, 26 February 1930; Morgan to Hearst, 22 August 1930. Kennedy Library; Beaton, *The Wandering Years*, 212.

14. Hearst to Morgan, 12 November 1933. Kennedy Library.

15. Morgan to James LeFeaver, 26 April 1934, telegram. Kennedy Library; Loorz to Stolte, 3 May 1934. San Luis Obispo County Historical Society Archives.

16. Morgan to Mildred Stapley Byne, 1 November 1921. Kennedy Library; "Julia Morgan, Her Office, and a House," Bancroft Library, 167.

17. Hearst to Morgan, 26 October 1934. Kennedy Library.

18. Warren McClure to Loorz, 4 April 1935. San Luis Obispo County Historical Society Archives.

19. Louis Schallich to Loorz, 8 July 1935. San Luis Obispo County Historical Society Archives.

20. Willicombe to Morgan, 6 August 1936. Kennedy Library.

21. Hearst to Morgan, c. 21 August 1936. Kennedy Library.

22. Hearst to Morgan, 6 February 1920. Kennedy Library.

23. Hearst to Morgan, 9 February 1923; Hearst to Morgan, 31 March 1924. Kennedy Library.

24. Hearst to Morgan, 24 April 1927. Kennedy Library.

25. Morgan to Hearst, 15 March 1927; Morgan to Hearst, 3 June 1927. Kennedy Library.

26. Davies, *The Times We Had*, 113, 221; St. Johns, "Hearst As a Host," *Oral History Project*, 2. Davies recalled: "We'd have contests. One champion would take a lousy player, like me, and it was vice versa on the other side. The only thing you could do when you were on the side of a great tennis player was yell for a chair. . . . W. R. played in those tournaments. He didn't ask for a chair. He didn't have to. He had the most wonderful forehand drive. He usually played with Alice Marble, or he played singles. That was awfully hard, and I wouldn't say they were entirely kind to the host, but he did all right."

27. Morgan to Hearst, 11 December 1927, telegram draft; Hearst to Morgan, 13

December 1927, telegram. Kennedy Library.

28. Older, *William Randolph Hearst*, 541; Hearst to Morgan, 15 July 1928. Kennedy Library.

29. John Pellegrini, "The Roman Pool," interview by J. D. Allen et al., ed. Robert C. Pavlik, *Oral History Project* (San Simeon, Calif.: Hearst San Simeon State Historical Monument, 5 July 1973), 3.

30. Joseph Giarritta, "A Tilesetter Recalls His Days at San Simeon," ed. William Payne, *Oral History Project* (San Simeon, Calif.: Hearst San Simeon State Historical Monument, 1 August 1988), 5.

31. Hearst to Morgan, 21 September 1932. Kennedy Library.

32. Pellegrini, "The Roman Pool," *Oral History Project*, 9; Alex Rankin, "Plumbing the Castle," interview by Metta Hake, ed. Robert C. Pavlik, *Oral History Project* (San Simeon, Calif.: Hearst San Simeon State Historical Monument, 9 March 1986), 20 21.

33. Cassou to Morgan, 17 August 1936. Kennedy Library.

34. Hearst to Morgan, 11 November 1936. Kennedy Library.

35. "Will Close San Simeon Castle," *San Luis Obispo Daily Telegram*, 21 October 1935, 1. This residency maximum was changed from six months to nine months a few years later.

36. Hearst to Morgan, 21 May 1937. Kennedy Library.

37. Hearst to Morgan, 25 May 1937. Kennedy Library.

38. Loorz to Morgan, 2 July 1937. San Luis Obispo County Historical Society Archives.

39. Hearst to Morgan, 31 August 1938. Kennedy Library.

CHAPTER TEN: HEARST BESIEGED

1. Lindsay Chaney and Michael Cieply, *The Hearsts: Family and Empire—The Later Years* (New York: Simon and Schuster, 1981), 43; "Hearst Stock in Public Offering," *Fortune* 2, no. 2 (August 1930): 83.

2. Nasaw, *The Chief*, 531–32.

3. Swinnerton, "Hearst Cartoonist and Artist," *Oral History Project*, 19.

4. John Francis Neylan, "Politics, Law, and the University of California," interview by Corinne L. Gilb and Walton E. Bean, *Regional Cultural History Project* (Berkeley: University of California, 1961), 172–75.

5. Davies, *The Times We Had*, 249.

6. Ibid., 200–2.

7. Martin, *Cissy*, 377; William Randolph Hearst Jr., *Father and Son*, 59.

8. Nasaw, *The Chief*, 531.

9. Frank S. Nugent, "The Music Hall's 'Ever Since Eve' Has Been Old Hat Ever Since Adam," *New York Times*, 25 June 1937, 25.

10. Davies, *The Times We Had*, 195.

11. August Wahlberg, "Working for William Randolph Hearst as a Butler and Valet," interview by Metta Hake and Janet Horton-Payne, ed. Pendleton H. Harris and Laurel Stewart, *Oral History Project* (San Simeon, Calif.: Hearst San Simeon State Historical Monument, 18 August 1983), 45.

12. Guiles, *Marion Davies*, 300–1.

13. Davies, *The Times We Had*, 208–10.

14. Nasaw, *The Chief*, 530.

15. Germain Seligman, *Merchants of Art, 1880–1960: Eighty Years of Professional Collecting* (New York: Appleton-Century-Crofts, 1961), 87.

16. Armand Hammer, *Hammer* (New York: G. P. Putnam's Sons, 1987), 233.

17. "The English Buy Back Their Silver Cheap from Hearst," *Life* 3, no. 24 (13 December 1937): 76–77.

18. Nasaw, *The Chief*, 556.

19. Hammer, *Hammer*, 238; "Hearst Collection of Art to be Sold By 2 Stores Here," *New York Times*, 29 December 1940, Late City Edition, sec. 1, 1.

20. "Onward and Upward with the Arts: Monastery for Sale," *The New Yorker* 16, no. 51 (1 February 1941): 29–35.

21. Jack Alexander, "Cellini to Hearst to Klotz," *Saturday Evening Post* 214, no. 18 (1 November 1941): 16–17, 84, 86–89.

22. Hammer, *Hammer*, 245.

23. Loorz to Warren McClure, 4 August 1933. San Luis Obispo County Historical Society Archives.

24. Ferdinand Lundberg, *Imperial Hearst: A Social Biography* (New York: Equinox Cooperative Press, 1936), 381; Oliver Carlson and Ernest Sutherland Bates, *Hearst: Lord of San Simeon* (New York: Viking, 1936), xiii–xiv. William Randolph Hearst had been profiled in the early part of the century by Lincoln Steffens. The first full-length biography written about him was John K. Winkler's florid *W. R. Hearst: An American Phenomenon* (New York: Simon and Schuster, 1928), which grew out of a profile in *The New Yorker* a year previously. Winkler reissued his biography with an added subtitle, *A New Appraisal*, in 1955. The earlier biography concentrates on Hearst's career as a journalist, establishing through numerous anecdotes that he is a rare and original, but thoroughly American, type.

25. John Dos Passos, *The Big Money* (Boston: Houghton Mifflin, 1936), 546–52.

26. John Steinbeck, *The Grapes of Wrath* (New York: Viking, 1939), 281–82.

27. Aldous Huxley, *After Many a Summer Dies the Swan* (London: Chatto and Windus, 1939), 29.

28. Huxley to Harold Raymond, 20 August 1939, *Letters of Aldous Huxley*, ed. Grover Smith (London: Chatto and Windus, 1969), 446; Louella O. Parsons, "In Hollywood with Louella O. Parsons: Marion Davies," *Los Angeles Herald*, September 1946, reproduced in Davies, *The Times We Had*, 239.

29. Huxley to Harold Raymond, 19 February 1939, *Letters*, 440.

30. David King Dunaway, *Huxley in Hollywood* (New York: Harper and Row, 1989), 119–21.

31. William Randolph Hearst Jr., "Memories of San Simeon and the Hearst Family," *Oral History Project*, 26.

32. Robert L. Carringer, *The Making of "Citizen Kane"* (Berkeley: University of California Press, 1985), 111; Orson Welles and Peter Bogdanovich, *This Is Orson Welles*, ed. Jonathan Rosenbaum (New York: HarperCollins, 1992), 86. The images of a padlocked iron gate guarding a looming Xanadu and of Susan Alexander Kane at her jigsaw puzzle will have to be visualized for the purposes of this text. I was refused permission to reproduce these stills from *Citizen Kane*.

33. Simon Callow, *Orson Welles: The Road to Xanadu* (New York: Viking, 1995), 495.

34. David Thomson, *Rosebud: The Story of Orson Welles* (New York: Knopf, 1996), 145, 156; Robert Wise, "The Battle Over *Citizen Kane*," in transcript, *The American Experience*, WGBH Public Television, Boston, 9 December 1997, 24. Wise was Welles's film editor on *Citizen Kane*.

35. Davies, *The Times We Had*, 206.

36. Richard Norton Smith, *The Colonel: The Life and Legend of Robert R. McCormick, 1880–1955* (Boston: Houghton Mifflin, 1997), 396–97; Welles and Bogdanovich, *This Is Orson Welles*, 49. McCormick helped Marion Clair promote his WGN radio station. Other possible models for the millionaire subsidizing his opera-singing wife included Harold Fowler McCormick and his wife Ganna Walska, or Jules Brulatour, head of Kodak, and his wife, Hope Hampton. See Donald W. Rea, "A Critical-Historical Account of the Planning, Production, and Initial Release of *Citizen Kane*" (master's thesis, University of Southern California, 1966).

37. Orson Welles, foreword to Davies, *The Times We Had*.

38. Davies, *The Times We Had*, 265.

39. Welles, foreword to Davies, *The Times We Had*.

40. "Dusk at Santa Monica," *Time* 33, no. 11 (13 March 1939): 49–56.

41. Morgan to Warren McClure, 28 March 1939. Hearst San Simeon State Historical Monument Staff Library.

CHAPTER ELEVEN: HEARST'S FINAL RETURN

1. Hearst, "In the News," Tuesday, 25 November 1941.

2. Gebhard and Winter, *Architecture in Los Angeles*, 491.

3. "Julia Morgan, Her Office, and a House," Bancroft Library, 228.

4. Morgan to Van der Loo, 15 June 1940. Hearst San Simeon State Historical Monument Archives.

5. Suzanne Dewberry, "Perils at Sea: The Sinking of the SS *Montebello*," *Prologue: Quarterly of the National Archives*, 23, no. 3 (Fall 1991): 260–64.

6. Norman Rotanzi, "Fifty-Four Years at San Simeon," interview by Julie Payne, ed. Robert C. Pavlik, *Oral History Project* (San Simeon, Calif.: Hearst San Simeon State Historical Monument, 6 June 1988), 7.

7. Robinson, *American Dynasty*, 360; Hearst, "In the News," Wednesday, 5 March 1941.

8. Morgan to Hearst, 6 July 1943. Kennedy Library.

9. Hearst to Morgan, 9 July 1943. Kennedy Library.

10. "Julia Morgan, Her Office, and a House," Bancroft Library, 178.

11. Morgan to Hearst, 6 July 1943. Kennedy Library.

12. Hearst to Morgan, 2 April 1943; Hearst to Morgan, 1 November 1943. Kennedy Library.

13. Hearst to Morgan, 4 November 1943. Kennedy Library.

14. Ardoin to Morgan, 30 November 1943. Kennedy Library.

15. Hearst to Ardoin, 6 December 1943. Kennedy Library.

16. Morgan to Hearst, 15 March 1944. Kennedy Library.

17. Morgan to Hearst, 15 June 1944. Kennedy Library.

18. Robert M. Clements Jr., "William Randolph Hearst's Monastery," *American Heritage* 32, no. 3 (April–May 1981): 57.

19. "The Work of Steilberg and Morgan," Bancroft Library, 81.

20. Morgan to Steilberg, 5 February 1945. Kennedy Library.

21. "Plans Build to Reassemble Hearst Monastery," *San Luis Obispo County Telegram-Tribune*, 23 August 1995, sec. A, 3; Boutelle, *Julia Morgan, Architect*, rev. ed., 262.

22. Maurice McClure, "From Laborer to Construction Superintendent," *Oral History Project*, 13, 32.

23. Rotanzi, "Fifty-Four Years at San Simeon," *Oral History Project*, 7.

24. William Randolph Hearst Jr., *Father and Son*, 59–60; Nasaw, *The Chief*, 579–80.

25. Maurice McClure, "From Laborer to Construction Superintendent," *Oral History Project*, 28–29.

26. Byron Hanchett, *In and Around the Castle* (San Luis Obispo, Calif.: Blake, 1985), 8.

27. Ann Miller, "Housekeeper at the Castle," interview by Tom Scott, ed. Robert C. Pavlik, *Oral History Project* (San Simeon, Calif.: Hearst San Simeon State Historical Monument, 1977), 4.

28. Loorz, "Recapitulation of Architect's Interviews," 11 August 1936; 3 March 1937. San Luis Obispo County Historical Society Archives. Loorz kept detailed notes of his meetings with Morgan.

29. Roland M. Dragon, "Private Secretary to W. R. Hearst, 1946–47," interview by Michelle Hachigian, ed. Michelle Hachigian and John F. Horn, *Oral History Project* (San Simeon, Calif.: Hearst San Simeon State Historical Monument, 24 October 1997), 3, 16.

30. Hearst, "In the News," Friday, 3 May 1940; Hearst, "In the News," Wednesday, 25 March 1942; John Hearst Jr., "Life at San Simeon as a Young Man," interview by Wilmar Tognazzini, ed. Robert C. Pavlik, *Oral History Project* (San Simeon, Calif.: Hearst San Simeon State Historical Monument, 4 October 1978), 6.

31. Moore, "Movie Flapper at San Simeon," *Oral History Project*, 11, 25.

32. Morgan to William W. Murray, 9 November 1944; Morgan to Hearst, 20 February 1945; Murray to Morgan, 20 July 1945. Kennedy Library.

33. Morgan to Murray, 26 July 1945. Kennedy Library; Maurice McClure, "From Laborer to Construction Superintendent," *Oral History Project*, 7.

34. Morgan to Hearst, 20 February 1945; Morgan to Hearst, 30 August 1938. Kennedy Library.

35. Aidala, *Hearst Castle*, 236.

36. Morgan to Murray, 26 July 1945. Kennedy Library; Hammer, *Hammer*, 233; Oscar

Lewis, *Fabulous San Simeon: A History of Hearst Castle* (San Francisco: California Historical Society, 1958), 9. The data on Hearst's total art expenditures are still incomplete, but Morgan's $5.4-million figure, reported in a letter to Thomas J. White on 24 July 1937, and representing an accurate total of all Hearst's purchases for his three West Coast homes—Ocean House, San Simeon, and Wyntoon—demonstrates that outsiders' estimates of Hearst spending $50 million on his art collection are vastly exaggerated. Kennedy Library.

37. Miller, "Housekeeper at the Castle," *Oral History Project*, 2; Ann Miller, "San Simeon During its Time of Transition," interview by Eileen Hook, *Oral History Project* (San Simeon, Calif.: Hearst San Simeon State Historical Monument, 13 January 1982), 5–6.

38. Estelle Forsythe Wahlberg, 2 May 1947, diary. Hearst San Simeon State Historical Monument Archives. Estelle Wahlberg was the head housekeeper at San Simeon in the 1940s and married to August Wahlberg, Hearst's butler and valet.

39. Guiles, *Marion Davies*, 329.

40. Margaret Sterne, *The Passionate Eye: The Life of William R. Valentiner* (Detroit: Wayne State University Press, 1980), 315–16.

41. "W. R. Hearst, 1863–1951: Death Puts a Quiet End to Press Lord's Unquiet Career," *Life* 31, no. 9 (27 August 1951): 23–31. William Randolph Hearst died on 14 August 1951 and was buried at Cypress Lawn Cemetery in Colma, California, in the family crypt with his parents. Millicent Hearst died in December 1974 at age 92 and was buried at Woodlawn Cemetery in New York.

42. William Randolph Hearst Jr., *Father and Son*, 250.

43. Chaney and Cieply, *The Hearsts: Family and Empire*, 68; William Randolph Hearst Jr., *Father and Son*, 254–56; Guiles, *Marion Davies*, 335–37.

44. Chaney and Cieply, *The Hearsts: Family and Empire*, 92; Guiles, *Marion Davies*, 337; William Randolph Hearst Jr., *Father and Son*, 256.

45. Davies, *The Times We Had*, 53.

46. Guiles, *Marion Davies*, 341–51, 355–56. Marion Davies died on 22 September 1961 and was buried at the Hollywood Memorial Park Cemetery under her family name of Douras.

47. Morgan North, "Julia Morgan, Her Office, and a House," Bancroft Library, 212.

48. Boutelle, *Julia Morgan, Architect*, 241.

49. Morgan North, "Julia Morgan, Her Office, and a House," Bancroft Library, 185.

50. Ibid., 173.

51. Flora North and Morgan North, "Julia Morgan, Her Office, and a House," Bancroft Library, 174.

52. Ibid., 199, 214; Coblentz, "Julia Morgan, Her Office, and a House," Bancroft Library, 124.

53. Bjarne Dahl, "Julia Morgan, Her Office, and a House," Bancroft Library, 151.

54. Morgan North, "Julia Morgan, Her Office, and a House," Bancroft Library, 201.

55. North and North, "Julia Morgan, Her Office, and a House," Bancroft Library, 193.

56. William Randolph Hearst Jr., *Father and Son*, 5.

57. Rotanzi, "Fifty-Four Years at San Simeon," *Oral History Project*, 13.

CHAPTER TWELVE: A TWENTIETH-CENTURY HOUSE

1. Aline B. Saarinen, *The Proud Possessors: The Lives, Times and Tastes of Some Adventurous American Art Collectors* (New York: Random House, 1958), 74–75. Saarinen's book is composed of fifteen chapters, each devoted to a different collector or family of collectors. Hearst is not included.

2. W. G. Constable, *Art Collecting in the United States of America* (London: Thomas Nelson and Sons, 1964), 139–40.

3. Nathaniel Burt, *Palaces for the People: A Social History of the American Art Museum* (Boston: Little, Brown, 1977), 394.

4. Robert A. M. Stern, *Pride of Place: Building the American Dream* (Boston: Houghton Mifflin, 1986), 114.

5. Witold Rybczynski, *The Most Beautiful House in the World* (New York: Viking, 1989), 93.

6. Umberto Eco, *Travels in Hyperreality*, trans. William Weaver (New York: Harcourt Brace Jovanovich, 1986), 23.

7. Thomas Hoving, "America's 101 Top Collectors: Peter Widener, Pierpont Morgan—and After," *Connoisseur* (September 1983): 117.

8. *The Smithsonian Collection of Newspaper Comics*, ed. Bill Blackbeard and Martin Williams (New York: Smithsonian Institution Press and Harry N. Abrams, 1977), 330; Kirk Varnedoe and Adam Gopnik, *High and Low: Modern Art and Popular Culture* (New York: The Museum of Modern Art, 1990), 163–64.

9. Clive Aslet, *The Last Country Houses* (New Haven: Yale University Press, 1982), 201.

10. Ibid., 234.

11. Allan Temko, *No Way to Build a Ballpark: And Other Irreverent Essays on Architecture* (San Francisco: Chronicle, 1993), 263–64.

12. Charles W. Moore, *Water and Architecture* (New York: Harry N. Abrams, 1994), 129.

13. Hewitt, *The American Country House*, 40.

14. John Julius Norwich, foreword to *Great Residences: Illustrated Perspectives on Power, Wealth and Prestige* (London: Mitchell Beazley, 1993).

15. Steilberg, "The Work of Walter Steilberg and Julia Morgan," Bancroft Library, 52; Walter T. Steilberg, "Some Examples of the Work of Julia Morgan," *The Architect and Engineer of California* 55, no. 2 (November 1918): 39–107.

16. Steilberg, "The Work of Walter Steilberg and Julia Morgan," Bancroft Library, 62.

17. Davies, *The Times We Had*, 50.

18. "The Seer of San Simeon," *Newsweek* 27, no. 18 (6 May 1946): 62–64.

BIBLIOGRAPHY

MANUSCRIPT AND DOCUMENTARY SOURCES

Harry Crocker Collection. Margaret Herrick Library. Academy of Motion Picture Arts and Sciences. Beverly Hills, Calif.

Hearst Archives. California Historical Society. San Francisco, Calif.

Phoebe Apperson Hearst Papers. 72/204c. The Bancroft Library, University of California, Berkeley.

William Randolph Hearst Papers. 82/68c, 87/232c. The Bancroft Library, University of California, Berkeley.

George Loorz Collection. San Luis Obispo County Historical Society Archives. San Luis Obispo, Calif.

Hearst San Simeon State Historical Monument Archives. San Simeon, Calif.

Warren McClure Papers. Hearst San Simeon State Historical Monument Staff Library.

The Julia Morgan Collection. Special Collections, Robert E. Kennedy Library, California Polytechnic State University, San Luis Obispo, Calif.

Peck Family Papers. Huntington Library, San Marino, Calif.

The American Experience. "The Battle Over Citizen Kane," transcript. Public Broadcasting Service, 1997.

Canessa, Marion Rose Lake. "Remembering Aunt Marion." Interview by Wilmar N. Tognazzini, edited by Robert C. Pavlik. Oral History Project. San Simeon, Calif.: Hearst San Simeon State Historical Monument, 3 August 1977.

Chipping, David H. "The Geology of San Luis Obispo County: A Brief Description and Field Guide." San Luis Obispo, Calif.: California Polytechnic State University, 1987.

Conforti, Michael. "Stanford White at San Simeon." Paper presented at the Society of Architectural Historians Convention, Cincinnati, 26 April 1991.

Cope Rand Means Company, Engineers. "Proposed Development of Piedra Blanca and Santa Rosa Ranches, San Luis Obispo County, California." 5 January 1921. Hearst San Simeon State Historical Monument Archives.

d'Arrast, Eleanor Boardman. "Remembering W. R. and Marion." Interview by Rayena Martin and Guy Roop, edited by Robert C. Pavlik. Oral History Project. San Simeon, Calif.: Hearst San Simeon State Historical Monument, 3 November 1987.

Dragon, Roland. M. "Private Secretary to W. R. Hearst, 1946–47." Interview by Michelle Hachigian, edited by Michelle Hachigian and John F. Horn. Oral History Project. San Simeon, Calif.: Hearst San Simeon State Historical Monument, 24 October 1997.

Gates, Charles. "Serving Hearst and Davies as a Waiter and Butler." Interview by Thelma Anderson, edited by Bernice Joan Falls and Robert C. Pavlik. Oral History Project. San Simeon, Calif.: Hearst San Simeon State Historical Monument, 4 October 1978.

Giarritta, Joseph. "A Tilesetter Recalls His Days at San Simeon." Edited by William Payne. Oral History Project. San Simeon, Calif.: Hearst San Simeon State Historical Monument, 1 August 1988.

Hearst, John, Jr. "Life at San Simeon as a Young Man." Interview by Wilmar Tognazzini, edited by Robert C. Pavlik. Oral History Project. San Simeon, Calif.: Hearst San Simeon State Historical Monument, 4 October 1978.

Hearst, William Randolph Jr. "Memories of San Simeon and the Hearst Family." Interview by Tom Scott, edited by Robert C. Pavlik. Oral History Project. San Simeon, Calif.: Hearst San Simeon State Historical Monument, August 1977.

Heaton, Stanley, and Elmer Moorhouse. "Gardening and Road Construction." Interview by Metta Hake, edited by William Payne and Robert C. Pavlik. Oral History Project. San Simeon, Calif.: Hearst San Simeon State Historical Monument, 27 March 1984.

Hines, Philip. "The Prehistory of San Simeon Creek: 5800 B. P. to Missionization." Edited by Betty Rivers. Sacramento: Department of Parks and Recreation, 1986.

Jones, Terry L., and Georgie Waugh. Central California Coastal Prehistory: A View from Little Pico Creek. Perspectives in California Archaeology, vol. 3, Institute of Archaeology. Los Angeles: University of California, 1995.

The Julia Morgan Architectural History Project. Edited by Suzanne B. Riess. Regional Oral History Office. The Bancroft Library. Berkeley: University of California, 1976.

Laird, Brayton. "Working in the Orchards of the Hearst Ranch." Interview by Bruce Brown, edited by Robert C. Pavlik. Oral History Project. San Simeon, Calif.: Hearst San Simeon State Historical Monument, 19 December 1986.

Lake, Arthur, and Pat Lake. "Dagwood Bumstead and Marion Davies' Niece." Interview by Metta Hake, edited by Rayena Martin. Oral History Project. San Simeon, Calif.: Hearst San Simeon State Historical Monument, 4 April 1984.

Lyons, Wilfred. "Working Various Jobs at San Simeon." Interview by Ted Moreno, edited by Robert C. Pavlik. Oral History Project. San Simeon, Calif.: Hearst San Simeon State Historical Monument, 12 July 1987.

Marble, Alice. "Tennis at the Hilltop." Interview by Marie Nay, edited by Rayena Martin and Robert C. Pavlik. Oral History Project. San Simeon, Calif.: Hearst San Simeon State Historical Monument, 4 June 1977.

Marion, Frances. "Screenwriter for Hearst." Interview by Gerald Reynolds, edited by Nancy E. Loe. Oral History Project. San Simeon, Calif.: Hearst San Simeon State Historical Monument, 1 September 1972.

McClure, Maurice. "From Laborer to Construction Superintendent." Interview by Metta Hake, edited by Bernice Joan Falls and Robert C. Pavlik. Oral History Project. San Simeon, Calif.: Hearst San Simeon State Historical Monument, 13 September 1981.

McCrea, Joel. "Hearst, Hollywood and San Simeon." Interview by Metta Hake, edited by Nancy E. Loe. Oral History Project. San Simeon, Calif.: Hearst San Simeon State Historical Monument, 5 December 1982.

Miller, Ann. "Housekeeper at the Castle." Interview by Tom Scott, edited by Robert C. Pavlik. Oral History Project. San Simeon, Calif.: Hearst San Simeon State Historical Monument, 1977.

———. "San Simeon During its Time of Transition." Interview by Eileen Hook. Oral History Project. San Simeon, Calif.: Hearst San Simeon State Historical Monument, 13 January 1982.

Moore, Colleen. "The Jazz Age's Movie Flapper at San Simeon." Interview by Gerald Reynolds and Metta Hake, edited by Nancy E. Loe. Oral History Project. San Simeon, Calif.: Hearst San Simeon State Historical Monument, 25 January 1977.

Neylan, John Francis. "Politics, Law, and the University of California." Interview by Corinne L. Gilb and Walton E. Bean. Regional Cultural History Project. Berkeley: University of California, 1961.

Pellegrini, John. "The Roman Pool." Interview by J. D. Allen, Tony Knapp, Nate Ratner, and Ann Rotanzi, edited by Robert C. Pavlik. Oral History Project. San Simeon, Calif.: Hearst San Simeon State Historical Monument, 5 July 1975.

Pringle, Aileen. "Silent Movie Actress and Frequent Guest." Interview by Metta Hake, edited by Robert C. Pavlik. Oral History Project. San Simeon, Calif.: Hearst San Simeon State Historical Monument, 18 October 1981.

Rankin, Alex. "Plumbing the Castle." Interview by Metta Hake, edited by Robert C. Pavlik. Oral History Project. San Simeon, Calif.: Hearst San Simeon State Historical Monument, 9 March 1986.

Rea, Donald W. "A Critical-Historical Account of the Planning, Production, and Initial Release of Citizen Kane." Master's thesis, University of Southern California, 1966.

Redelsperger, Fred. "Waiting Table at the Hearst Estates." Interview by Metta Hake, edited by Laurel Stewart. Oral History Project. San Simeon, Calif.: Hearst San Simeon State Historical Monument, 15 October 1985.

Rotanzi, Norman. "Fifty-Four Years at San Simeon." Interview by Julie Payne, edited by Robert C. Pavlik. Oral History Project. San Simeon, Calif.: Hearst San Simeon State Historical Monument, 6 June 1988.

St. Johns, Adela Rogers. "Hearst as a Host." Interview by Gerald Reynolds, edited by Robert C. Pavlik. Oral History Project. San Simeon, Calif.: Hearst San Simeon State Historical Monument, April 1971.

Steilberg, Walter. Address to the Historical Guide Association of California, August 1966. Transcribed by Morris Cecil. San Simeon, Calif.: Hearst San Simeon State Historical Monument.

Swinnerton, Gretchen. "Jimmy Swinnerton: Hearst Cartoonist and Artist." Interview by Thelma Anderson, edited by Rayena Martin. Oral History Project. San Simeon, Calif.: Hearst San Simeon State Historical Monument, 1978.

Vidor, King. "Work and Play with Hearst and Davies." Interview by Rosie Wittig, edited by Nancy E. Loe. Oral History Project. San Simeon, Calif.: Hearst San Simeon State Historical Monument, 1975.

Wahlberg, August. "Working for William Randolph Hearst as a Butler and Valet." Interview by Metta Hake and Janet Horton-Payne, edited by Pendleton H. Harris and Laurel Stewart. Oral History Project. San Simeon, Calif.: Hearst San Simeon State

Historical Monument, 18 August 1983.

West, James, and Ronald P. Sekkel. "An Archeological Site Survey of the Hearst Ranch (Rancho Piedras Blancas), San Simeon, San Luis Obispo County, California." *Archaeological Survey Annual Report, 1968.* Department of Anthropology. Los Angeles: University of California, 1968.

BOOKS, PAMPHLETS, AND ARTICLES

Abbé, Patience, Richard Abbé, and Johnny Abbé. *Of All Places!* New York: Stokes, 1937.

Ackerman, Gerald M. *The Life and Work of Jean-Léon Gérôme, with a Catalogue Raisonné.* London: Sotheby's Publications, 1986.

Aidala, Thomas R. *Hearst Castle, San Simeon.* New York: Hudson Hills Press, 1981.

Aikman, Duncan. "A Renaissance Palace in Our West," *New York Times Magazine,* 21 July 1929, sec. v, 10–11.

Alexander, Jack. "Cellini to Hearst to Klotz." *Saturday Evening Post* 214, no. 18 (1 November 1941): 16–17, 84, 86–89.

Allen, Thomas B. "Remember the *Maine*?" *National Geographic* 193, no. 2 (February 1998): 92–111.

Art Objects and Furnishings from the William Randolph Hearst Collection. Presented by Saks Fifth Avenue in Cooperation with Gimbel Brothers. Under the Direction of Hammer Galleries. New York: Publishers Printing, William Bradford Press, 1941.

Arte y Decoración en España. Vol. 2. New York: Architectural Book Publishing, 1918.

Aslet, Clive. *The American Country House.* New Haven: Yale University Press, 1990.

————. *The Last Country Houses.* New Haven: Yale University Press, 1982.

Baker, Paul R. *Richard Morris Hunt.* Cambridge, Mass.: MIT Press, 1986.

————. *Stanny: The Gilded Life of Stanford White.* New York: Free Press, 1989.

Beaton, Cecil. *The Wandering Years: Diaries: 1922–1939.* Boston: Little, Brown, 1961.

Bemelmans, Ludwig. *To the One I Love the Best.* New York: Viking, 1955.

Bonfils, Winifred Black. *The Life and Personality of Phoebe Apperson Hearst.* 1928. Reprint, with a prefatory note by William Randolph Hearst Jr. and an introduction by Winton Frey. San Simeon, Calif.: Friends of Hearst Castle, 1991.

Boutelle, Sara Holmes. "Julia Morgan." In *Toward a Simpler Way of Life: The Arts and Crafts Architects of California,* edited by Robert Winter, 63–72. Berkeley: University of California Press, 1997.

————. *Julia Morgan, Architect.* Revised and enlarged edition. New York: Abbeville, 1995.

Boyd, John Taylor. "Colonial Homes of Great Dignity." Part 16 of "The Home as the American Architect Sees It." *Arts and Decorations* 35, no. 6 (October 1931): 21.

Brechin, Gray. *Imperial San Francisco: Urban Power, Earthly Ruin.* Berkeley: University of California Press, 1999.

Brooks, Louise. *Lulu in Hollywood.* New York: Knopf, 1983.

Burt, Nathaniel. *Palaces for the People: A Social History of the American Art Museum.* Boston: Little, Brown, 1977.

Callow, Simon. *Orson Welles: The Road to Xanadu.* New York: Viking, 1995.

Carlson, Oliver, and Ernest Sutherland Bates. *Hearst: Lord of San Simeon.* New York: Viking, 1936.

Caroselli, Susan L. *The Painted Enamels of Limoges: A Catalogue of the Collection of the Los Angeles County Museum of Art.* Los Angeles: Los Angeles County Museum of Art, 1993.

Carringer, Robert L. *The Making of "Citizen Kane."* Berkeley: University of California Press, 1985.

Castle, Irene. *Castles in the Air.* New York: Da Capo, 1980.

Cerf, Bennett. *At Random: The Reminiscences of Bennett Cerf.* New York: Random House, 1977.

Chafee, Richard. "The Teaching of Architecture at the Ecole des Beaux-Arts." In *The Architecture of the Ecole des Beaux-Arts,* edited by Arthur Drexler, 61–109. New York: Museum of Modern Art, 1977.

Chaney, Lindsay, and Michael Cieply. *The Hearsts: Family and Empire—The Later Years.* New York: Simon and Schuster, 1981.

Chaplin, Charles. *My Autobiography.* New York: Simon and Schuster, 1964.

Chase, Ilka. *Past Imperfect.* Garden City, N.Y.: Blue Ribbon Books, 1945.

Chase, J. Smeaton. *California Coast Trails: A Horseback Ride from Mexico to Oregon.* Boston: Houghton Mifflin, 1913.

Churchill, John Spencer. *A Churchill Canvas.* Boston: Little, Brown, 1962.

Churchill, Randolph S. *Twenty-one Years.* Boston: Houghton Mifflin, 1965.

Churchill, Winston S. *Winston S. Churchill.* Vol. V, Companion Part 2, Documents. *The Wilderness Years, 1929–1935.* Edited by Martin Gilbert. Boston: Houghton Mifflin, 1981.

Clements, Robert M., Jr. "William Randolph Hearst's Monastery." *American Heritage* 32, no. 3 (April–May 1981): 50–59.

Coffman, Taylor. *The Builders Behind the Castles: George Loorz and the F. C. Stolte Co.* San Luis Obispo, Calif.: San Luis Obispo County Historical Society, 1990.

Constable, W. G. *Art Collecting in the United States of America.* London: Thomas Nelson and Sons, 1964.

Cornforth, John. *The Search for a Style: Country Life and Architecture 1897–1935.* London: Andre Deutsch, 1988.

Cortissoz, Royal. Introduction to *Monograph of the Work of Charles A. Platt.* New York: Architectural Book Publishing, 1913.

Cummings, Hildegard. "Chasing a Bronze Bacchante." *Bulletin* (William Benton Museum of Art, University of Connecticut) no. 12 (1984): 3–19.

Davies, Marion. *The Times We Had: Life with William Randolph Hearst.* Indianapolis, Ind.: Bobbs-Merrill, 1975.

Denning, Roy, ed. *The Story of St. Donat's Castle and Atlantic College.* Cowbridge, South Wales: D. Brown and Sons, 1983.

Dewberry, Suzanne. "Perils at Sea: The Sinking of the SS *Montebello.*" *Prologue: Quarterly of the National Archives* 23, no. 3 (Fall 1991): 260–64.

Dobkin, Marjorie M. "A Twenty-Five-Million-Dollar Mirage." In *The Anthropology of World's Fairs: San Francisco's Panama Pacific International Exposition of 1915,* edited by Burton Benedict, 66–93. Berkeley: Lowie Museum of Anthropology, 1983.

Dos Passos, John. *The Big Money.* Boston: Houghton Mifflin, 1936.

Dunaway, David King. *Huxley in Hollywood.* New York: Harper and Row, 1989.

"Dusk at Santa Monica." *Time* 33, no. 11 (13 March 1939): 49–56.

Eco, Umberto. *Travels in Hyperreality.* Translated by William Weaver. New York: Harcourt Brace Jovanovich, 1986.

Edwards, Anne. "Marion Davies' Ocean House: The Santa Monica Palace Ruled by Hearst's Mistress." *Architectural Digest* 51, no. 4 (April 1994): 170–75, 277–78.

Emery, Edwin, and Michael Emery. *The Press and America: An Interpretative History of the Mass Media.* 4th ed. Englewood Cliffs, N.J.: Prentice-Hall, 1978.

"The English Buy Back Their Silver Cheap from Hearst." *Life* 3, no. 24 (13 December 1937): 76–77.

Fredericksen, Burton B. *Handbook of the Paintings in the Hearst San Simeon State Historical Monument.* N.p.: Delphinian Publications in cooperation with The California Department of Parks and Recreation, 1976.

Gabler, Neal. *Winchell: Gossip, Power and the Culture of Celebrity.* New York: Knopf, 1994.

Gebhard, David. "The Spanish Colonial Revival in Southern California (1895–1930)." *Journal of the Society of Architectural Historians* 26, no. 2 (May 1967): 131–47.

Gebhard, David, and Robert Winter. *Architecture in Los Angeles: A Compleat Guide.* Salt Lake City: Gibbs M. Smith, 1985.

Getty, J. Paul. *As I See It: The Autobiography of J. Paul Getty.* Englewood Cliffs, N.J.: Prentice-Hall, 1976.

Grant, Campbell. "Chumash: Introduction." In *California,* edited by Robert F. Heizer. Vol. 8 of *Handbook of North American Indians,* edited by William C. Sturtevant. Washington, D.C.: Smithsonian Institution, 1978.

————. *The Rock Paintings of the Chumash: A Study of a California Indian Culture.* Berkeley: University of California Press, 1966.

Gray, Christopher. "Hearst's Opulent Quintuplex." *New York Times,* 1 May 1994, sec. 10, 7.

Gregory, Ralph. "George Hearst in Missouri." *The Bulletin* (Missouri Historical Society) 21, no. 2 (January 1965): 75–86.

Guiles, Fred Lawrence. *Marion Davies.* New York: McGraw-Hill, 1972.

Hamilton, Geneva. *Where the Highway Ends: Cambria, San Simeon, and the Ranchos.* San Luis Obispo, Calif.: Padre Productions, 1974.

Hammer, Armand. *Hammer.* New York: G. P. Putnam's Sons, 1987.

Hanchett, Byron. *In and Around the Castle.* San Luis Obispo, Calif.: Blake, 1985.

Head, Alice M. *It Could Never Have Happened.* London: Heinemann, 1939.

Hearst, George. *The Way It Was.* N.p.: Hearst Corporation, 1972.

Hearst, John R., Jr. "Life With Grandfather." *Reader's Digest* 76, no. 457 (May 1960): 152–53, 155–59, 161–62.

Hearst, Mrs. William Randolph, Jr. *The Horses of San Simeon.* San Simeon, Calif.: San Simeon Press, 1985.

Hearst, William Randolph. "In the News," 10 March 1940–25 May 1942.

————. "Letters." *Time* 19, no. 2 (11 January 1932): 4.

————. *Selections from the Writings and Speeches of William Randolph Hearst.* Edited by E. F. Tompkins. San Francisco: San

Francisco Examiner, 1948.

Hearst, William Randolph, Jr. *The Hearsts: Father and Son*. Niwot, Colo.: Roberts Rinehart, 1991.

"Hearst." *Fortune* 12, no. 4 (October 1935): 42–55, 123–26, 128–30, 133–36, 139–40.

"Hearst at Home." *Fortune* 3, no. 5 (May 1931): 56–68, 130.

"Hearst Collection of Art to be Sold by 2 Stores Here." *New York Times*, 29 December 1940, late city edition, sec. 1, 1.

"Hearst Stock in Public Offering." *Fortune* 2, no. 2 (August 1930): 83.

Hewitt, Mark Alan. *The Architect and the American Country House 1890–1940*. New Haven: Yale University Press, 1990.

Honour, Hugh. "Canova's Statues of Venus." *Burlington Magazine* (1972): 658–70.

Hopper, Hedda. *From Under My Hat*. Garden City, N.Y.: Doubleday, 1952.

Hoving, Thomas. "America's 101 Top Collectors: Peter Widener, Pierpont Morgan—and After." *Connoisseur* (September 1983): 108–18.

Huth, Hans. *Lacquer of the West: The History of a Craft and an Industry, 1550–1950*. Chicago: University of Chicago Press, 1971.

———. "A Venetian Renaissance Casket." *Museum Monographs I*. St. Louis, Mo.: City Art Museum of St. Louis, 1968.

Huxley, Aldous. *After Many a Summer Dies the Swan*. London: Chatto and Windus, 1939.

———. *Letters of Aldous Huxley*. Edited by Grover Smith. London: Chatto and Windus, 1969.

Kimball, Fiske. "The American Country House." *The Architectural Record* 46, no. 4 (October 1919): 290–400.

Krieger, Daniel E. *San Luis Obispo County: Looking Backward into the Middle Kingdom*. Northridge, Calif.: Windsor Publications, 1988.

Lamb, Frank W., and Gertrude Lamb. *San Simeon: A Brief History*. Fullerton, Calif.: Sultana Press, 1971.

The Legacy of the Exposition: Interpretation of the Intellectual and Moral Heritage Left to Mankind by the World Celebration of San Francisco in 1915. San Francisco: Panama-Pacific International Exposition Company, 1916.

Lewis, Oscar. *Fabulous San Simeon: A History of Hearst Castle*. San Francisco: California Historical Society, 1958.

Longstreth, Richard. *On the Edge of the World: Four Architects in San Francisco at the Turn of the Century*. New York: Architectural History Foundation, 1983.

Loos, Anita. *The Talmadge Girls: A Memoir*. New York: Viking, 1978.

Lundberg, Ferdinand. *Imperial Hearst: A Social Biography*. New York: Equinox Cooperative Press, 1936.

MacKay, Robert B., Anthony K. Baker, and Carol A. Traynor, eds. *Long Island Country Houses and Their Architects, 1860–1940*. New York: W. W. Norton in association with the Society for the Preservation of Long Island Antiquities, 1997.

Maher, James T. *The Twilight of Splendor: Chronicles of the Age of American Palaces*. Boston: Little, Brown, 1975.

Marble, Alice. *Courting Danger*. New York: St. Martin's Press, 1991.

Martin, Ralph G. *Cissy*. New York: Simon and Schuster, 1979.

Moore, Charles W. *Water and Architecture*. New York: Harry N. Abrams, 1994.

Morgan, Keith N. *Charles A. Platt: The Artist as Architect*. New York: Architectural History Foundation, 1985.

Nasaw, David. *The Chief: The Life of William Randolph Hearst*. Boston: Houghton Mifflin, 2000.

Nelson, Nancy. *Evenings with Cary Grant: Recollections in His Own Words and by Those Who Knew Him Best*. New York: Warner, 1993.

Newton, A. Edward. *Derby Day and Other Adventures*. Freeport, N.Y.: Books for Libraries Press, 1969.

Niven, David. *Bring on the Empty Horses*. New York: G. P. Putnam's Sons, 1975.

Norwich, John Julius. Foreword to *Great Residences: Illustrated Perspectives on Power, Wealth and Prestige*. London: Mitchell Beazley, 1993.

Nugent, Frank S. "The Music Hall's 'Ever Since Eve' Has Been Old Hat Ever Since Adam." *New York Times*, 25 June 1937, 25.

Older, Mrs. Fremont. *William Randolph Hearst, American*. New York: Appleton-Century, 1936.

"Onward and Upward with the Arts: Monastery for Sale." *The New Yorker* 16, no. 51 (1 February 1941): 29–35.

Pavlik, Bruce M., Pamela C. Muick, Sharon G. Johnson, and Marjorie Popper. *Oaks of California*. Los Olivos, Calif.: Cachuma Press and the California Oak Foundation, 1991.

Pavlik, Robert C. " 'Something a Little Different': La Cuesta Encantada's Architectural Precedents and Cultural Prototypes." *California History* 71, no. 4 (Winter 1992/1993): 462–77, 548–49.

Perez, Louis A., Jr. "The Meaning of the *Maine*: Causation and the Historiography of the Spanish-American War." *Pacific Historical Review* 58, no. 3 (August 1989): 293–322.

"Plans Build to Reassemble Hearst Monastery." *San Luis Obispo County Telegram-Tribune*, 23 August 1995, sec. A, 3.

Platt, Charles A. *Italian Gardens*. Portland, Ore.: Sagapress, 1993.

Procter, Ben. *William Randolph Hearst: The Early Years, 1863–1910*. New York: Oxford University Press, 1998.

Robinson, Judith. *The Hearsts: An American Dynasty*. New York: Avon, 1991.

Rogers, David. "The Santa Lucia Mountains: Diversity, Endemism, and Austere Beauty." *Fremontia* 19, no. 4 (October 1991): 3–11.

Rybczynski, Witold. *The Most Beautiful House in the World*. New York: Viking, 1989.

Saarinen, Aline B. *The Proud Possessors: The Lives, Times and Tastes of Some Adventurous American Art Collectors*. New York: Random House, 1958.

Sarber, Jane. "A Cabbie in a Golden Era, Featuring Cabbie's Original Log of Guests Transported to Hearst Castle," N.p., n.d.

"The Seer of San Simeon." *Newsweek* 27, no. 18 (6 May 1946): 62–64.

Seligman, Germain. *Merchants of Art, 1880–1960: Eighty Years of Professional Collecting*. New York: Appleton-Century-Crofts, 1961.

Shaw, Bernard. *Collected Letters, 1926–1950*. Edited by Dan H. Laurence. New York: Viking, 1988.

Smart, Mary. *A Flight with Fame: The Life and Art of Frederick MacMonnies (1863–1937)*. With a catalogue raisonné of sculpture and a checklist of paintings by E. Adina Gordon. Madison, Conn.: Sound View Press, 1996.

Smith, Richard Norton. *The Colonel: The Life and Legend of Robert R. McCormick, 1880–1955*. Boston: Houghton Mifflin, 1997.

The Smithsonian Collection of Newspaper Comics. Edited by Bill Blackbeard and Martin Williams. New York: Smithsonian Institution Press and Harry N. Abrams, 1977.

St. Johns, Adela Rogers. *The Honeycomb*. Garden City, N.Y.: Doubleday, 1969.

Steffens, Lincoln. "Hearst, The Man of Mystery." *American Magazine* 63, no. 1 (November 1906): 2–22.

Steilberg, Walter T. "Some Examples of the Work of Julia Morgan." *The Architect and Engineer of California* 55, no. 2 (November 1918): 39–107.

Steinbeck, John. *The Grapes of Wrath*. New York: Viking, 1939.

Stern, Robert A. M. *Pride of Place: Building the American Dream*. Boston: Houghton Mifflin, 1986.

Sterne, Margaret. *The Passionate Eye: The Life of William R. Valentiner*. Detroit, Mich.: Wayne State University Press, 1980.

Swanberg, W. A. *Citizen Hearst: A Biography of William Randolph Hearst*. New York: Bantam, 1963.

Temko, Allan. *No Way to Build a Ballpark: And Other Irreverent Essays on Architecture*. San Francisco: Chronicle, 1993.

Thomson, David. *Rosebud: The Story of Orson Welles*. New York: Knopf, 1996.

Towner, Wesley. *The Elegant Auctioneers*. New York: Hill and Wang, 1970.

Van Zanten, David. "Architectural Composition at the Ecole des Beaux-Arts From Charles Percier to Charles Garnier." In *The Architecture of the Ecole des Beaux-Arts*, edited by Arthur Drexler, 111–323. New York: Museum of Modern Art, 1977.

Varnedoe, Kirk, and Adam Gopnik. *High and Low: Modern Art and Popular Culture*. New York: The Museum of Modern Art, 1990.

Vidor, King. *A Tree is a Tree*. Hollywood: Samuel French, 1989.

"W. R. Hearst, 1863–1951: Death Puts a Quiet End to Press Lord's Unquiet Career." *Life* 31, no. 9 (27 August 1951): 23–31.

Welles, Orson. Foreword to Marion Davies, *The Times We Had: Life with William Randolph Hearst*. Indianapolis, Ind.: Bobbs-Merrill, 1975.

Welles, Orson, and Peter Bogdanovich. *This Is Orson Welles*. Edited by Jonathan Rosenbaum. New York: HarperCollins, 1992.

Wharton, Edith. *Italian Villas and Their Gardens*. Illustrated with pictures by Maxfield Parrish. New York: Century, 1904.

White, Lawrence Grant. *Sketches and Designs by Stanford White*. New York: Architectural Book Publishing, 1920.

White, Samuel G. *The Houses of McKim, Mead, and White*. New York: Rizzoli, 1998.

"Will Close San Simeon Castle." *San Luis Obispo Daily Telegram*, 21 October 1935, 1.

Winkler, John K. *W. R. Hearst: An American Phenomenon*. New York: Simon and Schuster, 1928.

Wodehouse, P. G. *Author! Author!* New York: Simon and Schuster, 1962.

Woon, Basil. *Incredible Land: A Jaunty Baedeker to Hollywood and the Great Southwest*. New York: Liveright, 1933.

ACKNOWLEDGMENTS

Every book is a journey for its author. I am fortunate to have had many knowledgeable guides to lead me through mine. My special thanks go to Hoyt Fields, Chief Curator, Hearst San Simeon State Historical Monument, whose support for the project was both essential and unconditional—from first day to last. Kirk Sturm, Director-Superintendent of the Hearst Monument, brought his administrative talents to my aid many times. Both Rusty Areias, Director, California State Parks, and Stephen T. Hearst, Vice-President and General Manager, Sunical/S. F. Realties, assisted the book's progress. The non-profit group Friends of Hearst Castle, which raises money for Hearst Castle endeavors and will receive the royalties for this book, has also been helpful, particularly Executive Director David Gray, Chair Rhoda M. Ford, Development Director Sally Dunbar, and the Board of Directors. Martin Levin, literary attorney and publishing executive, encouraged me from the early days of the project. Paul Gottlieb, Publisher of Harry N. Abrams, Inc., has been a wonderful friend to me and to the Castle as well, showing an immediate and sophisticated understanding of the place and its purpose. My editor, Elisa Urbanelli, and the book's designer, Robert McKee, both worked with laudable skill and dedication. They spent many hours at the Castle and were able to take its essence home with them and transfer it onto the printed page.

I have benefited from many others' guidance. Art historians John Fleming and Hugh Honour were generous in sharing their impressions of the Castle's art collection. Nicholas Penny, Clore Curator of Renaissance Paintings at the National Gallery, London, and Burton B. Fredericksen, Director of the Getty Provenance Index, assisted me greatly in their evaluations of the Castle and its objects. Diana Keith Neal, Senior Director, Sotheby's London, was very helpful in her observations about the Castle's nineteenth-century sculpture. Art historian Jeannie Hobhouse and the Director of the American Museum in Britain, William McNaught, offered relevant reflections on art collecting and its display in country houses. At the Los Angeles County Museum of Art, Martin Chapman, Curator of Decorative Arts, and Mary Levkoff, Curator of European Paintings and Sculpture, were generous in their help to me personally and tireless in their dedication to the subject of Hearst the art collector and his benefactions to their museum. Hearst biographer David Nasaw graciously shared his excellent manuscript with me, and provided me with helpful comments on mine. Longtime Hearst Castle scholar James T. Maher also gave me his insights on the estate. I owe an additional and special thank you for their support to Randolph Apperson Hearst and Veronica Hearst, George Plimpton, and Austin and Kathryn P. Hearst.

Librarians and photo archivists were of considerable help to me in creating this illustrated book. Associate Dean Nancy E. Loe, Library Assistants Mike Line and Teresa Taylor, and Library Volunteers George P. Libby and Janet Crabaugh, all from Special Collections, Robert E. Kennedy Library, California Polytechnic State University, San Luis Obispo, rendered me great assistance during my fifteen months working with the Julia Morgan Collection. I transcribed over a thousand letters and surveyed several thousand architectural drawings, often with the tireless Mike Line at my side. (The majority of those drawings have since been relocated to the Hearst Monument's own archives.) Stacey Behlmer, Coordinator of Special Projects and Research Assistance at the Margaret Herrick Library, Academy of Motion Picture Arts and Sciences, Beverly Hills, shared her amazing fund of knowledge about the film colony, greatly enhancing my text and photographs. Lydia Cresswell-Jones, Specialist in the Art Nouveau and Art Deco Department of Sotheby's London, was generous in allowing me use of the Cecil Beaton Photographic Archive. Heidrun Klein pored over photographs at both her worksite, the Bildarchiv Preussicher Kulturbesitz, and another Berlin photo archive, the Berlinische Galerie, to ensure that I had images from the Erich Salomon collection. I would also like to thank Jack Von Euw, Photo Archivist, Susan Snyder, Head of Permissions, and Willa K. Baum, Division Head, Regional Oral History Office, at the Bancroft Library, University of California, Berkeley; larry Campbell, Deputy Director, and Emily Wolf, Photo Archivist, both at the California Historical Society, San Francisco; Nicole Wells, Coordinator, Rights and Reproductions, and Holly Hinman, Photo Archivist, both at The New-York Historical Society; Peter (Salomon) Hunter of The Hague; Laura Giammarco, Rights and Reproductions Coordinator at Time-Life Syndication; Stacey Sherman, Reproductions Coordinator, The Nelson-Atkins Museum of Art, Kansas City, Missouri; and Lynn Landwehr, Alison Nichols, Nancy Haworth Scott, and Catherine Trujillo, all at the San Luis Obispo County Historical Society and Museum. For permission to use their unpublished material I would like to thank Michael Conforti, Director, the Sterling & Francine Clark Art Institute; Virginia S. Hart, descendant of Harry Crocker; Barbara Grant Cohen, widow of Cary Grant; and Judy Bellis, who owns the John Van der Loo photographic archive. Princeton Professor Emeritus Robert Judson-Clark gave permission to photograph the Hearst Castle architectural model, on long-term loan to the San Luis Obispo County Historical Museum.

I relied on my many colleagues at Hearst Castle in countless ways. Photographer Victoria Garagliano provided me with outstanding photographs. Important help to both of us was rendered by Edward C. Redig, Maintenance Chief; Robert Conlen, Grounds Supervisor; Robert Soto, Restoration Supervisor; Frank Young, Museum Curator; and all of their staffs. Information Systems Technician Jack Raymond was my computer consultant, Landscape Architect Tom Craig provided the site and floor plans and, along with guide Muna Cristal, calculated the square footage of the buildings, and Guide Emeritus Gloria Freytag translated my German correspondence. The Guide staff, the members of the Historical Guides Association, and the rest of my colleagues at the Hearst Monument were also of great assistance. Muna Cristal, Dennis and Michele Judd, and Robert and Rayena Pavlik thoughtfully reviewed my manuscript. The Staff Librarians Michelle Hachigian and Denise Surber frequently came to my aid, and Head Staff Librarian Judy Anderson answered literally hundreds of my questions with grace, intelligence, and skill. Historian John Horn, Registrar Jeff Payne, Guide Supervisor Karen Beery, and Researcher Sandra J. Heinemann supplied me with technical information, insightful perceptions, and daily encouragement. It would be impossible to overstate the contributions of Curator Jana Seely and my research colleague James Allen: suffice to say that the strengths of this book come in large measure from their efforts.

I would especially like to thank my family for their wise counsel and cheerful support: Bruce Smith, Yoshiko Yamamoto, Kevin, Jason, and Timmy Kastner, and my husband George Kastner. Without George this book would not exist. His energy and insight enliven every page.

INDEX

Page numbers in *italics* refer to captions.

PHOTOGRAPH CREDITS

All photographs are by Victoria Garagliano, Hearst San Simeon State Historical Monument, except for the following:

Hearst San Simeon State Historical Monument Archives: 9, 22, 23 left, 26 right, 27, 32, 33 right, 34, 35, 36 right, 37 top right, 38, 39 bottom, 48 top, 58 top and middle, 60, 61 top, 63, 64, 66 top, 67 bottom, 73, 77 top, 81 top, 86, 87 top, 91 bottom, 92, 93 top and bottom left, 96, 101, 102, 103, 104 bottom, 105, 106 top, 107, 112 right, 118, 122, 123 top (Risvold Collection), 124, 127, 128, 137, 144 top and middle, 154 top, 157, 160, 161, 166, 167, 169 right, 172, 173 left, 182, 185 top, 187, 189 top, 206. Hearst San Simeon State Historical Monument: 41, 49, 184, 185 bottom left and bottom right, 214 bottom, 215, 216 bottom. Julia Morgan Collection, Special Collections, Robert E. Kennedy Library, California Polytechnic State University, San Luis Obispo, Calif.: 12, 16, 17, 18, 33 left, 44 top left, 45, 58 bottom, 61 bottom, 66 bottom, 67, 144 bottom, 147, 158 bottom, 159, 198 top. San Luis Obispo County Historical Society, San Luis Obispo, Calif.: 23 right, 78 bottom left, 82 bottom, 104 top, 132, 154 top, 155 top. Austin Whittlesey: 36 left, 37 top left and bottom left.

Courtesy of the Bancroft Library, University of California, Berkeley, Calif.: 39 top. Collection of the New-York Historical Society, New York, New York: 50 top and middle, 62 top, 112 left. John Swope/Time Inc.: 129 bottom. BISON ARCHIVES/Marc Wanamaker: 108, 156 left, 202 bottom. Erich Salomon Collection, Bildarchiv Preussicher Kulturbesitz and Berlinische Galerie, Berlin: 113 bottom, 120 top left, 121 top right, 125. Cecil Beaton Archive, Sotheby's London: 119, 120 top right, 121 top left and bottom, 129 left, 156 right. Courtesy of the Academy of Motion Picture Arts and Sciences, Beverly Hills, Calif.: 116 (detail), 120 bottom, 186 (116 Publicity Still of Marion Davies Courtesy of Turner Entertainment Co. A Time Warner Company. All rights reserved. 186 EVER SINCE EVE. 1937 Turner Entertainment Co. A Time Warner Co. All rights reserved). Nelson-Atkins Museum of Art, Kansas City, Missouri: 189 bottom. Allan Grant/Life Magazine (Time Inc.): 207. Los Angeles County Museum of Art, Los Angeles, Calif., William Randolph Hearst Collection: 209. Arte y Decoración en España, Vol II: 78 top left. Zdravko Barov: 138

Additional credits:

Illustrations: Hearst San Simeon State Historical Monument: 134, 135

Permission to publish William Randolph Hearst's "Poem to Pepi," courtesy of Austin Hearst and The Hearst Corporation